TALK OF LOVE

TALK

of

LOVE

HOW CULTURE MATTERS

Ann Swidler

THE UNIVERSITY OF CHICAGO PRESS
CHICAGO AND LONDON

Ann Swidler is professor of sociology at the University of California, Berkeley. She is author of *Organization Without Authority: Dilemmas of Social Control in Free Schools* and (with Robert Bellah, Richard Madsen, William Sullivan, and Steven Tipton) coauthor of *Habits of the Heart: Individualism and Commitment in American Life* and *The Good Society*. She is coauthor (with Claude Fischer, Michael Hout, Martín Sánchez Jankowski, Samuel Lucas, and Kim Voss) of *Inequality by Design: Cracking the Bell Curve Myth*.

The University of Chicago Press, Chicago 60637
The University of Chicago Press, Ltd., London
© 2001 by The University of Chicago
All rights reserved. Published 2001
Printed in the United States of America

00 09 08 07 06 05 04 03 02 01   1 2 3 4 5

ISBN: 0-226-78690-0 (cloth)

BF
575
.L8
S92
2001 — Apr. 02

Library of Congress Cataloging-in-Publication Data

Swidler, Ann, 1944–
    Talk of love: how culture matters / Ann Swidler.
        p.   cm.
    Includes bibliographical references and index.
    ISBN 0-226-78690-0 (hardcover : alk. paper)
        1. Love—United States—Public opinion.   2. Middle class—United States—Attitudes.   3. Interpersonal relations and culture—United States.   4. Public opinion—United States.   I. Title.

BF575.L8 S92 2001
306.7—dc21

                                                    00-060198

for Claude

Contents

Acknowledgments

Because I learned so much from the men and women whom I interviewed—things that first puzzled me, then intrigued me, and finally changed my thinking about culture—I am unusually indebted to their kindness in inviting me into their homes and into their lives. Although I sometimes refer to them as "ordinary people" to distinguish them both from the lifestyle experimentalists who populate my home turf of Berkeley, California, and from the cult members, political ideologues, and participants in exotic subcultures that sociologists often study, there was nothing ordinary about them. I thank them here for their extraordinary generosity.

I have been fortunate in my teachers, friends, colleagues, and students, and particularly fortunate that the boundaries among these have been so permeable. Neil Smelser encouraged my first efforts to think about love sociologically. Leo Lowenthal, Reinhard Bendix, and Robert Bellah taught me the importance of culture and offered powerful intellectual tools for its sociological study. Arlie Hochschild has been my friend, confidante, and intellectual sounding board. Bob Bellah, as teacher, collaborator, and friend, along with Dick Madsen, Bill Sullivan, and Steven Tipton, have offered a deep, selfless intellectual comradeship.

I depend on good conversation with stimulating friends to develop ideas and simply to feel fully human. For all those breakfasts, lunches, and dinners, and many cups of tea, thanks to Fred Block, Pat Bourne, Jane Collier, Ruth Collier, Carole Joffe, David Levine, Susanne Lowenthal, Mary Catherine Taylor, Kim Voss, and Joanna Weinberg. As I was finishing the final touches on this book, one of them asked, "So, after all this, do you like it?" The answer is, yes, I do, and I hope these friends to whom I owe so much will like it too.

I also am deeply indebted to friends and colleagues

who read the manuscript in various stages or who helped me work out the formulations here. To the incomparably generous Paul DiMaggio, a special thanks for close reading of the entire manuscript and an extraordinarily incisive set of suggestions (only some of which I was able to fully exploit). Thanks also to my hilarious, brilliant friend, Ron Jepperson, who, as Lévi-Strauss might say, is very good to think with. And for continuing stimulation, support, and shared engagement in thinking about how culture works, I would like to thank Wendy Griswold, Yasemin Soysal, Peter Stromberg, Steve Hart, and Jorge Arditi. Dick Scott, Buzz Zelditch, John Meyer, Vicki Bonnell, Lynn Hunt, and William Sewell Jr. offered valuable advice on early versions of all or part of the manuscript.

Doug Mitchell, my editor, deserves a paragraph of his own (a whole book, in fact, but he probably wouldn't want to wait). Paeans of praise to editors often seem excessive, but those who have had the good fortune to work with Doug—and it isn't work, but inspired intellectual play—know what an extraordinary person he is. His passion for ideas warms the soul.

Lesley Jenkins, Mary Garrett, and especially Rita Jalali conducted many of the interviews for this project. Orie Braun, Amy Schalet, and Elizabeth Armstrong provided valuable research assistance. Sue Thur and Judy Haier were willing, as always, to do far more than duty required. And Jennifer Moorhouse was an expert manuscript editor and a pleasure to work with.

I would also like to thank the institutions whose financial support made this project possible: the John Simon Guggenheim Memorial Foundation, the National Endowment for the Humanities, the Ford and Rockefeller Foundations, the Boy's Town Center of Stanford University, and the Committee on Research of the University of California, Berkeley. It is appropriate that I should have completed final work on this book in Paris, thanks to the French-American Foundation in New York and the kindness of my host, Professor Jean Heffer, of the Centre d'Études Nord-Américaines of the École des Hautes Études en Sciences Sociales.

My children, Leah and Avi Fischer, have provided constant, if sometimes distracting, entertainment during the course of work on this book. Life with them has taught me how the deepest meaning is often found in what one can least articulate. My beloved parents, Joseph and Gretchen Swidler, and my family, Cathy Fischer, Ralph and Rosette Fischer, and Mark and Wendi Swidler, have sustained me with their love.

And finally my husband, Claude Fischer, has been there for me and with me, really with me, throughout. I could hardly begin to list the thousands of ways, both intellectual and practical, in which he has helped. But all these laid end to end don't go halfway toward capturing what it has meant to love and be loved by him.

This is a book about love, about Americans, and about culture. It deals with each of these in a distinctive way, which requires some explanation.

This book is about the *culture* of love. It looks at middle-class Americans' views of such matters as what love is, how one knows when love is "real," what is required for a good relationship, whether love involves obligation or sacrifice, and where love fits into the larger scheme of life's meanings. It is less concerned with social, psychological, or biological explanations of who loves whom, why people marry the people they do, why some marriages last and others end in divorce, or why some lovers are happy and others miserable. Rather, it uses the ways one particular group of Americans think and talk about love to explore larger questions about culture and meaning—how culture actually works when people bring it to bear on a central arena of their daily experience and especially how culture is (or is not) linked to action. While most of the book rests on interviews about love, some of its arguments and evidence range much more widely, examining how culture is used in the political arena, in religious life, and in other cultural spheres.

LOVE

When I began this research, many academic colleagues greeted the topic with embarrassment or laughter—leave love to lovers; you can't study love. Sociologists investigate marriage and family life, but love has seemed too personal, too mysterious, and, I would argue, too sacred for serious sociological study. Now work on the psychology and sociology of emotions has made the study of love respectable, and we have increasingly rich historical, socio-logical, and cultural work on love. My own research has been informed by the important studies of Francesca Cancian (1987), Naomi Quinn (1987, 1996, Strauss and Quinn 1997), and most recently Eva Illouz (1997). There is also a large and growing popular and scholarly literature on the history of love (Rothman 1987; Sternberg 1998), on contemporary dating and marriage (Skolnick 1991; Scarf 1987; Lystra 1989; Kern 1992; Lindholm 1998), on passion and intimacy (Luhmann 1986; Giddens 1992), and on historical transformations of human sexuality (Laqueur 1990; Seidman 1991; Ullman 1997; Bailey 1999). But we still know very little about the most important aspect of love: what it actually means to people.

Students of culture usually study a society's core symbols—its reli-gious beliefs and practices; its art, literature, or music; its myths, folklore, and popular beliefs. Although love is a quintessentially personal, private experience, love is just as profoundly social and cultural.

Love is a central theme of our popular culture as well as our greatest art, from soap operas to Shakespeare. It is also one of the richest sources of the pervasive folk culture of gossip, commiseration, confession, and advice-giving. Indeed, love recommends itself to students of culture pre-cisely because, unlike many of the political and social attitudes sociolo-gists normally study, love really matters to most ordinary Americans. It is central, not peripheral, to their lives.

Love also provokes moral deliberation. For many Americans, in-deed, "morality" primarily involves conduct in the personal sphere of love and sexual intimacy (see Sabini and Silver 1982 and Taylor 1994 on gos-sip). People may take it for granted that murder or stealing is wrong, but they must stop to consider whether and when sleeping with someone is morally right; the ethics of divorce, fidelity, and adultery; and the obliga-tions of those who love each other. With the pervasive threat of divorce, men and women must continually consider and reconsider the ethical dilemmas of love and marriage.

Thus, from a sociologist's point of view, love is a perfect place to study culture in action. Here a rich and diverse cultural tradition permeates or-dinary lives. Whether people's beliefs about love sustain them or leave them disillusioned, whether people are confused or certain about love, whether they enjoy deep philosophizing or simply adopt convenient plat-itudes, for most people how they think and talk about love matters.

AMERICANS

To explore how people think about love, three research assistants and I interviewed eighty-eight middle-class men and women from suburban areas in and around San Jose, California. These were white, middle- and upper-middle-class representatives of the American mainstream, re-cruited through churches, neighbors, friends, coworkers, therapists, and a local community college.[1] (The methodological appendix provides a de-tailed description of the sample, the interview, and a copy of the interview guide.) These comfortable suburbanites were not so much "typical" as "prototypical" Americans. Their mainstream culture, with all its confu-sions and contradictions, provides the background against which most other Americans define their understandings of love. As I point out be-low, my interviewees had a complex, ambivalent relationship to the domi-nant culture. They were often critical of romance, disillusioned with prom-ises of happiness ever after, and even uncertain about the concept of love itself. But like other Americans, including those from other cultural tra-ditions or those whose relationships challenge mainstream expectations, they are continually aware of the discourses about love, commitment, self-discovery, and happiness the wider society makes available. Thus under-standing the lineaments of that culture matters far beyond the middle-class suburban milieu of the far-flung San Jose suburbs.

Because I was interested in when culture doesn't work as well as when it does, I wanted to talk with people who had had enough life expe-rience to test and perhaps alter what they once believed about love. I thus sought to interview adults in midlife (interviewees ranged from twenty to sixty years of age, with the great majority in their thirties and forties) who were or had been married. I included a substantial number who had been divorced, to find out how people reshape their understanding of love when it seems to fail them.

These interviews were in some ways very different from the standard social-scientific survey (see the methodological appendix). Lasting from ninety minutes to more than three hours, the interviews dealt with how people had grown up, what had led them to become who they were, what was important to them about work and family life. The interview dealt most centrally with love as a part of personal biography, asking people what they had learned about love, how their views had changed, and what they currently thought. I tried to explore not only general beliefs about love, marriage, and personal relationships but also more subtle matters, such as how people recognize signs and symptoms of love, what people find most confusing about love, and how people think about different kinds of love.

What was most distinctive about these interviews, however, was that they explored confusions and uncertainties as well as thought-out conclusions. I pushed at what people told me. If someone said "Communication is the most important thing in marriage," I tried to find out more about what she or he meant by that. Were there limits on what spouses could communicate? Did communication always work? What were concrete examples of communication that strengthened marriage? For interviewees who stressed personal growth, I asked whether personal growth made love precarious. For those who emphasized commitment in relationships, I asked whether commitment constrained personal growth. I probed for the ways people thought through issues in their own past or present relationships, and with some interviewees I also used structured stories about hypothetical couples to pose dilemmas about love (see the vignettes in the methodological appendix). With these stories I sought to explore the ways people put their ideas of love to use when they are trying to resolve problems (see Strauss and Quinn 1997).

I wanted to understand not only *what* my interviewees thought about love, but *how* they thought. I was interested in the varying views often held by the same people, and in the circumstances under which one understanding would give way to another. Inspired by Lawrence Kohlberg's studies of moral reasoning (1981, 1984), I was interested not just in the conclusions people drew but in the ways they brought together cultural images, feelings, experiences, and ideas to think about a problem. I wanted to know which views people would defend and which were only casual impressions, and what experiences, even of the sort that people normally do not articulate, grounded those views.

The effect of the interviews was to explore not only what people thought but what resources they had for thinking about love. Indeed, in the course of the interviews I began to realize that most people do not actually have a single, unified set of attitudes or beliefs and that searching for such unified beliefs was the wrong way to approach the study of culture. Instead of studying the views of particular individuals, I came to think of my object of analysis as the cultural resources themselves—the traditions, rituals, symbols, and pieces of popular culture—that people drew on in thinking about love. I wanted to know how much people stretched the limits of the cultural traditions they brought to bear on experience, and how they combined or reappropriated elements of different traditions.

In exploring cultural traditions, I also interviewed ideological specialists—ministers and therapists—whose province it is to articulate theories of love. I wanted to understand how the cultural conceptions promoted by these experts were actually adopted by those who tried to use them, and what alterations these lay users of therapy or religion made in the process. I also sought to trace the influence of novels and self-help books to see how the popular culture of love touched the lives of my respondents.[2]

CULTURE

This study's approach to culture is unusual in several ways. Rather than contrasting two or more groups with different cultural understandings of love, or describing an exotic culture unfamiliar to most readers, it explores the culture of love among a relatively homogeneous group of middle-class Americans. That is because it analyzes a different *dimension* of cultural life than most studies of culture do.

This book explores variations in the way culture is *used*. The middle-class Americans I interviewed draw from a common pool of cultural resources. What differentiates them is how they make use of the culture they have available.

Uses of culture vary. Some people (usually a small minority) try to live ideologically pure lives. For them, every aspect of daily life must be examined and made consistent with their beliefs. For others, most of life is unexamined, although a rich set of cultural traditions, from wedding anniversaries to bits of remembered advice from their mothers to the lyrics of popular songs, may seem to make life more meaningful. And still others are cynical about the culture most take for granted. This book explores such variations in the ways culture is appropriated, mobilized, and linked to experience.

Culture's influence can be understood only when we have new ways of thinking about how cultural materials are actually put to use. How do people who share similar cultural understandings integrate them differently into their lives? One man may invest his adolescent ideal of love with greater and greater meaning as he matures, feeling ever more deeply that his wife is his perfect sweetheart. Another may become disillusioned with his earlier views, adopting a cheerful cynicism about love. The middle-class suburbanites I interviewed draw largely on a common set of cultural motifs, but they differ in the style and intensity of their cultural practices and in the substantive meanings they derive from common cultural materials. It is this sort of variation I seek to understand.

Exploration of the varied ways culture is used can, I believe, reinvigorate the study of how culture affects social life. If we wish to explain individual action or wider social patterns in cultural terms, it will no longer do to say "Americans do it this way" or "the French do it that way" because of their culture. Cultures are complex and contradictory, and even a common culture can be used in very different ways. Thus, effective cultural explanation depends on understanding how culture is put to use.

In place of the traditional Weberian focus on "ideas" as the "switchmen" that direct human motives, or Parsonian analysis of culture as norms and values, contemporary analysts think of culture in semiotic terms, as discourse; in structural terms as "schemas"; in performative terms as "practices"; and in more embodied terms as "habitus." Contemporary culture theorists focus less on what particular individuals think or believe than on (1) how the larger semiotic structure—the discursive possibilities available in a given social world—constrains meaning (by constructing the categories through which people perceive themselves and others or simply by limiting what can be thought and said) and (2) the ways the material and social environment directly penetrates actors to shape their habits and skills (Bourdieu 1977; Swidler 1986), their tastes (Bourdieu 1984), their emotional vitality (Collins 1981), or their embodied sense of self and situation (Joas 1996). Other theorists have attempted to understand how cultural meanings construct "social structure" itself. With very different agendas, William Sewell Jr. (1992) and John Meyer (1983, 1987) have both tried to show how preexisting cultural schemas constitute such apparently structural realities as factories, organizations, and nation-states.

This book examines how culture works by analyzing what middle-class Americans say about their ideas and experiences of love. But it does not confine itself to such materials. It also addresses the grand sociological tradition of cultural analysis, asking what new insights come from considering variations in cultural intensity and coherence and such processes as the adoption, assimilation, and rejection of cultural materials.

OVERVIEW

The book proceeds in three broad steps. Part I, "Culture's Confusions," draws on interview materials to reexamine the standard ways sociologists and other social scientists have thought about how culture works in the lives of ordinary people. Chapter 1 considers how varied and sometimes contradictory people's ideas about love are and how difficult it is to say, for particular individuals or for a larger community, just what their culture consists in. Chapter 2 suggests that we think of cultures as "tool kits" or repertoires of meanings upon which people draw in constructing lines of action. Cultures inculcate diverse skills and capacities, shaping people as social actors, to be sure—by providing them tools for constructing lines of action, not by molding them to a uniform cultural type.

Part II, "Culture from the Inside Out," looks in greater detail at the ways people use culture to organize individual experience and action. Chapter 3 examines the different forms culture takes—ranging from platitudes, hypocrisy, and cynicism through faith, commitment, and ideological conviction. By looking at variations in how deeply or systematically people bring cultural understandings to bear on their experience, it raises questions about whether more deeply held or more coherent understandings affect experience and action more powerfully than superficial or incoherent ones. Chapter 4 proposes that the general approaches people develop for dealing with life, what I call "strategies of action," are the crucial nexus at which culture influences social action. The cultural repertoire a person has available constrains the strategies she or he can pursue, so that people tend to construct strategies of action around things they are already good at. Chapter 5 continues the examination of how culture structures action by comparing the way culture works in "settled" and "unsettled" lives.

Part III, "Culture from the Outside In," examines how three "external" constraints on culture—codes, contexts, and institutions—mediate culture's effects on action. Chapter 6 describes two contrasting ways interviewees think about love—in mythic terms like those of the movies and in prosaic-realistic terms stressing the messy complications of daily life. It asks why both modes of thinking persist in the same people, and why people sometimes use one mode and sometimes the other. Chapter 7 explores the consequences for middle-class Americans of thinking about love as a free, individual choice. It shows that people derive very different implications from the common vocabulary of American voluntarism, and that even the common language of "choice" (and the related rejection of sacrifice and obligation) can be made to support both commitment and self-actualization. Chapter 7 then asks what institutional experiences reproduce the discourse of voluntarism as the preferred way for Americans to talk about love and commitment. Chapter 8 examines how culture, which is often quite incoherent in the subjective experience of individuals, can nonetheless powerfully shape action. Well-publicized cultural codes redirect action by reframing its meaning; contexts such as polarized meetings or contested political arenas impose their own logic on ideas and action; and institutional demands continually renew the plausibility of cultural formulations people consciously reject.

The conclusion turns to a set of broad questions about contemporary empirical and theoretical work on culture. It lays out the larger questions that I believe the sociology of culture should address: whether and in what senses culture is coherent or incoherent; what we mean when we claim that something has, or is, a "cultural logic"; and whether some cultural elements anchor or organize others.

This is a book about how ordinary people talk about love, both when they have it and when they lose it. It is also, inevitably, a book about what it means to be one kind of American. And finally it is a book that will, I hope, force us to rethink our assumptions about the ways culture works in shaping individual experience and in structuring collective action.

PART I

Culture's Confusions:

Who Wrote the Book of Love?

CHAPTER 1

FINDING CULTURE

*T*he difficulty of studying culture begins with the problem of finding it. In studying Americans' culture of love, what, precisely, are we looking for?

At one level, the culture of love is everywhere, filling paperback racks, pouring from car radios, shimmering on the movie screen. In the immensely popular Harlequin romances, women resist dangerous seducers, pursue a spirited individualism, and are rewarded with love as were their sisters in the classic English romantic novels, from Richardson's *Pamela* to Jane Austen's *Pride and Prejudice* (see Watt 1957; Modleski 1984; Radway 1991). Such is the power of this mythic drama that its variants still dominate our literature, our popular entertainment, and our imaginations. In hit songs and pulp fiction, as in the conversations and commiserations of friends and lovers, love is described and dissected. These sources do not all agree on what love is, but from "Love means never having to say you're sorry" to "Love is not love which alters when it alteration finds," the culture of love is all around us.

The difficulty comes not in finding cultural stories and symbols, but in discovering how culture in this sense (art, entertainment, or the advice friends give one another) affects culture as lived, the meanings that shape people's day-to-day lives. And here we run into a host of problems. These are not just a matter of art versus life, but of the complex ways people use the diverse culture surrounding them.

Among sociologists and anthropologists, debate has raged for several academic generations about the proper definition of the term "culture." Since the seminal work of Clifford Geertz (1973a), the older definition of culture as the entire way of life of a people, including their technology and material artifacts, or that (associated with the name of Ward Goodenough) as everything one would need to know to become a functioning member of a society, has been gradually displaced in favor of defining culture as the publicly available symbolic forms through which people experience and express meaning (Keesing 1974; Wuthnow 1987). In Geertz's (1973b:89) now classic definition, culture is "an historically transmitted pattern of meanings embodied in symbols, a system of inherited conceptions expressed in symbolic forms by means of which men communicate, perpetuate, and develop their knowledge about and attitudes toward life." Seeing culture as meaning embodied in symbols focuses attention on such phenomena as beliefs, ritual practices, art forms, and ceremonies, and on informal cultural practices such as language, gossip, stories, and rituals of daily life. I would follow Ulf Hannerz's (1969:184) "minimal definition of culturalness, in line with . . . the essence of conventional usage . . . that there are social processes of sharing modes of behavior and outlook within [a] community." But I would add Geertz's emphasis on the role of particular symbolic vehicles (rituals, stories, sayings) in creating and sustaining those modes of behavior and outlook. Indeed, culture is specifically the set of symbolic vehicles through which such sharing and learning take place.

Whether they define culture as public symbols, entire ways of life, or individual knowledge, conventional views leave us very much at a loss when it comes to studying how culture is actually put to use by social actors. In the traditional Geertzian view, cultural materials were assumed to form a unified "cultural system," and the question of how particular pieces of culture actually become meaningful for people—when they are put to use and in what ways—could hardly be raised.[1] Contemporary theorists, on the other hand, take cultural disjunctures and contradictions largely for granted. From Foucault's "genealogical" approach to the multiple layers of overlapping practices that constitute the modern subject, to Levi-Strauss's emphasis on "bricolage," to Bourdieu's insistence on the fundamental contradictions (the "misrecognition") at the heart of any system of cultural hierarchy, many contemporary theorists have subverted or abandoned the notion of culture as a unified system. Yet the implications of such a stance for drawing links between culture and action have hardly been explored. The task cultural analysts set themselves is still most often describing the unifying principle of a cultural system (or, for Foucault

[1970, 1972] for example, the unifying principles of each level in an "archaeology" of overlaid cultural systems), leaving aside the question of how actors might navigate among multiple competing "systems" or how the polysemy and multivocality of cultural symbols might shape the ways people actually bring culture to bear on experience. Describing how one culture differs from another has been the central task of the cultural analyst. Questions about the diverse ways any particular culture is used by its possessors have seemed unnecessary or irrelevant. But understanding how cultures change, or indeed, understanding what difference it makes for someone to participate in a particular culture, will require that sociologists address the problems created by the diverse uses of common cultural materials.

DISTANCED CULTURE

To begin with the most obvious problem, people know much more of their culture than they use. One San Jose suburbanite, now a successful lawyer, recollects that as a child he "went to church every Sunday for over fifteen years without missing once. I was very into that." He was "very much into Boy Scouts, a real achiever type." "Very serious about what [he] was doing," he thought he might "get into [religion] in a bigger way," perhaps by becoming a minister. But as an adult, he is "almost uninvolved in community activities": "Now I divide my time between my work and my family at home, and that's where I get my satisfaction. I don't have much of a desire to be involved." So, we must ask, is his earlier religious enthusiasm, or indeed his Boy Scout ideals, now part of his culture? In what sense does cast-off faith maintain its influence?

Indeed, time often distances people from even their most intense cultural experiences. The same young lawyer, now married several years, recalls his first "terrible crush at age fifteen": "restless, excited, dizzy, you know all those trite things that people say about it, all the puppy love sort of thing. Boy, it hit me like a ton of bricks." When the relationship broke up, he was crushed.

> I can still remember playing that Kingston Trio record over and over
> again and feeling that my life had lost all meaning. Kingston Trio
> # 16. They all seemed to be sort of sad songs too. One of them was
> "Try to Remember" from The Fantastiks. . . . I still have the record.

But despite the intensity of the experience, it lacked staying power. "I was just so terribly overwhelmed, and then a month or two later it was all gone. It was almost as if it hadn't happened."

Like his religion, this lawyer's teenage love was eminently cultural. It is still available to him in memory, and yet is very little part of his life. How should we understand this? The Kingston Trio is culture, but perhaps no longer "his" culture? Or the Kingston Trio is still his culture, but put somehow on hold? Or perhaps romantic love and the Kingston Trio have already been assimilated into his experience, so that he no longer finds the specific symbols engaging. His current view that he has outgrown both adolescent infatuation and the Kingston Trio may itself be a cultural frame for distancing some experiences while embracing others.[2] But the sociology of culture as it currently exists has little to say about such variations in the meaning of cultural experience.

Changes in biography and cultural context, which can leave us more bemused than moved by our past enthusiasms, make it difficult to say what a person's culture actually is. Unless we assume that everything a person has known or experienced is in some sense still "current" (an assumption whose problematic implications I discuss below), we have a hard time describing the uses people make of culture they have outgrown. What we clearly need are more differentiated ways of describing not the content of culture, but the varying—what?—confidence, seriousness, engagement with which people hold it.

Even culture that is not distanced by the passage of time is often distant in other ways. We see a movie, but we find it stupid or unconvincing. We are aware of our culture's love mythology, but we know it isn't "true." Does that mean it does not affect us? Or does culture affect us in the same way whether we accept or reject it? Aside from the distinction between "current" and "past" cultural experience, we need some distinction between "vital" culture and culture that remains insulated from experience.

Skepticism—ranging from suspended judgment, to doubt, to outright rejection—is a usual, not exceptional, response to culture. For example, almost all my interviewees understand the term "love" and use it frequently in interpreting the world, yet their dominant reaction to the love culture surrounding them is rejection. They usually invoke the "Hollywood" image of love (associated especially with "the movies") only to condemn it. While few go so far as the therapist, herself divorced, who says, "My friends and myself, we are sort of lost as to what love means; it just does not have a whole lot of meaning," many agree with her disparagement of romantic ideals. The divorced women she counsels "have been disappointed by that Hollywood image they thought existed when they first got married. They thought there would be that magical love—dancing through the stage and stuff—and that in actuality it is not there."

Most men and women agree with the therapist's view that love "is mainly hard work and partnership and getting some gratification. Love grows, but infatuation love is a problem that we grew up with. It is not real." They blame a culture that, in their view, purveys a false image of love. An insurance executive, describing his failed first marriage, says, "It was all based on this superficial TV image of what it was. There was not any real discussion about how feelings were. . . ." His own view of love still includes romance, but he carefully brackets off this kind of love from what he considers "real": "Well, we're all born and raised in this concept of this movie-star love. A romantic ideal." He still enjoys "that flash of movie-star love," but "no one can keep up that intense one-sided appearance forever." Eventually "we got to get down to really what's there." A suburban homemaker distances the movie image with humor: "I think I had kind of a Doris Day image thing about marriage . . . I would keep the bod up and have my hair nice, wear high heels, scrub the toilet looking real pretty, and have those beautiful meals on the table when he came home." People thus use common cultural images as they formulate their own views; yet we must see that they frequently use culture by distancing themselves from it.[3]

Cultural skepticism is not limited to "playful" fictions (Huizinga 1956) such as those of "the movies." We always select among cultural competitors for our engagement, so that our cultural universe is much wider and more diverse than the culture we make fully our own. Thus we may know about punk rock without actually having heard any, or we may know what it sounds like but hate it, or we may even listen to it occasionally without any great involvement. For only a very few does punk become a way of life (Hebdige 1979; Frith 1981), but it becomes part of the culture even of many who prefer "101 strings."

When it comes to more serious cultural matters—religious beliefs or fundamental views of the world—skepticism plays an even more important role. We are always surrounded by diverse viewpoints, and we actively (though often unconsciously) select among them—rejecting most without a second thought. We could hardly function if we were open, ready to be persuaded, by any new cultural message that came along. Typical responses to new religious cults provide a striking, but not unusual, example. When entreated by a devotee of a new religion, most people brush aside even what sound like plausible appeals, assuming that sound reasons exist for dismissing its claims.

We enter the cultural fray armored with systematic doubt. We do not believe everything we read, or everything our friends say. Indeed, most of our active cultural involvement in everyday life is not joyful participation in shared ritual, but the demanding work of dismissing, criticizing, or filtering the culture with which we come in contact.

Thus much of our "traffic with symbols" (to use Clifford Geertz's [1973b:92] phrase) is of a rejecting rather than an accepting sort. The pervasiveness of indifference and skepticism in cultural life means, in turn, that we cannot study culture by studying the publicly available repertoire of expressive symbols if we do not know when and how these are used. Nor, alternatively, can we identify the culture of particular individuals or groups simply by asking in what they believe, since they are touched by a great deal of culture they ultimately reject.

It may be objected that skepticism is a peculiarly modern ailment, a symptom of our cultural malaise. Peter Berger and Thomas Luckmann (1967) have argued something like this, claiming that the cacophony of competing cultural claims in modern society has undermined confidence in any of them. But both anthropological and historical evidence suggests otherwise. Heresies have been a pervasive problem in Western religions since the golden calf. Medieval historians agree that Christianity never managed fully to eliminate its pagan rivals, and even within Christian Europe, skepticism could easily lead to heresy (Le Roy Ladurie 1978; Ginzburg 1980). As one fifteenth-century miller saw it, the soul could not be immortal because "when man dies he is like an animal, like a fly. . . . when man dies his soul and everything else about him dies" (Ginzburg 1980:69). And as Keith Thomas's *Religion and the Decline of Magic* (1971) shows, when a historian looks for subterranean traditions, they are there in abundance. Among the educated elite in England between 1500 and 1700, rational, scientific thinking coexisted happily with what we would now regard as the wildest magical and superstitious notions, including belief in witchcraft, use of amulets and potions, magical cures, and incantations. Indeed, both the "traditional" past in which there was a deeply shared cultural consensus and the culturally unified "primitive" tribe are in all probability illusions.

Anthropologists, who presumably study the most integrated, consensual societies, find widespread disagreement about the meaning of central cultural symbols (Fernandez 1965; Stromberg 1981; Bourdieu 1990). In all societies people make choices about what cultural meanings to accept and how to interpret them.[4]

If disagreement and skepticism are pervasive in cultural life, we cannot describe culture unless we have a way of dealing both with what people believe and with what they know and disbelieve. In the cases of punk rock and religious cults, the dividing line between the culture a person holds and the culture he or she rejects seems fairly clear. But the important cases are more ambiguous and difficult to interpret.

Frank and Emily Trumbell, now in their late thirties, several years ago faced a serious marital crisis. In desperation they turned to society's experts on marital troubles, a minister and a therapist. These specialists offered the prevailing wisdom about failing marriages, encouraging each member of the couple to do what was best for herself or himself as an individual. But Frank and Emily wanted advice that would help them stay married, not advice about how to become more autonomous individuals, which might or might not save their marriage. So they took what they could use—and discarded the rest.

> Emily: The minister I went to see kept encouraging me to be independent, and to live for myself, and not to think about Frank and our relationship, just to look out for Emily. Nothing about the commitment we had made to one another, and striving to get along, wanting to make changes so we could get along.
>
> Frank: To help yourself. I got the same advice. I was never told to get out of the relationship. I was told that what I have responsibility for is my own life, and I need to look at my own life and develop my own individuality and look out for myself.

This "therapeutic" view of love—in which a marriage should be evaluated by how well it meets the needs of the married partners as individuals—was not really what Frank and Emily wanted to hear, so at one level, they simply did not listen. On the other hand, they wanted to improve their marriage, so they followed some of the marriage counselor's advice. Frank "asserted" himself with Emily. "I was expressing my opinion and my views, and if I wasn't satisfied with what was going on I said so." They changed the "whole dynamics" of their relationship. But they embraced the therapeutic ethic only on their own terms. Emily describes how she held on to her own language for thinking about her marriage even while she learned new approaches to the relationship itself:

> At no time during the time I was going to see [the pastor] did he say do you love him, or any of those kinds of questions. But I knew I wanted to be married to Frank, and I knew that I wanted to make it work, and I knew that I loved him . . . and the last thing in the world I wanted was to live apart from him.

This middle-class couple, like most people most of the time, adopted a new cultural perspective selectively. They listened to the experts, but with reservations, appropriating only what they could use and leaving the rest.[5]

The discriminating use of culture goes beyond selective adoption. When people appropriate cultural materials, they adapt them to their own purposes. One of the most fascinating examples of this complex process of appropriation is the countercultural language of "self-actualization" and self-discovery used by the settled, middle-class couples I interviewed. For them, the belief that one must find oneself and learn to express one's feelings in order truly to love another is very widespread. Yet repeatedly, this commitment to self-development was seen as a way of sustaining rather than undermining stable, middle-class marriages. (For fuller treatment of these themes, see chapter 6.) Self-development, many couples argued, can come only from continually working things out with another person rather than "running away from yourself." Discovering your true feelings allows you to share yourself more fully with a partner.

The richest example of this adaptation of 1960s countercultural language to middle-class marriages of the 1980s is the church-sponsored Marriage Encounter movement (see Bosco 1972; Gallagher 1975; Demarest, Sexton, and Sexton 1977), which claims to have enrolled more than two million couples in its weekend "encounters" for married, and now engaged, couples. These couples are taught to explore, express, and share "feelings." Drawing on the imagery and the language of self-actualization, right down to the word "encounter"—which conjures up the encounter groups of the 1960s—Marriage Encounter teaches couples to describe the texture, taste, and color of their "feelings" and to believe that nothing anyone "feels" (as opposed to "thinks") can possibly be threatening to their spouse. But far from creating the painful confrontations, group sex, or quest for new life alternatives that one might associate with sixties-style encounter groups, Marriage Encounter promotes the view that sharing one's feelings with one's spouse is like writing a "love letter," and that commitment to one's marriage is "God's plan," as opposed to the "world's plan," which drives couples apart. The psychic self-discovery taught by Marriage Encounter fuses with Christian imagery about marriage to argue that through sharing the infinite mystery of personal feelings, couples can make their marriages the greatest adventure of a lifetime. Thus cultural materials are reappropriated in ways that continuously change their meanings as they are adapted to varied lives.[6]

Frank and Emily Trumbell were unusual in their clear sense of what they did not like about the new cultural framework the marriage counselors offered them. This comes in part from their involvement in the Marriage Encounter movement. The counselors they saw may well have advised them to put their individual interests ahead of commitment to their marriage. But Marriage Encounter, with its clear message that marriage should come first, helped them diagnose the inadequacies of therapeutic understandings. And here we can see the difficulty of identifying, in specific instances, what constitutes someone's culture. Frank and Emily, like most of us, could formulate a clear view of one cultural ideal only from the perspective of another.

Often our ability to describe a cultural perspective, or to see it at all, comes only from our skepticism about it. The culture we fully accept does not seem like culture; it is just real life. So for Emily, "love" and "marriage" are real, and "being more independent" is suspect; while for Laura Martin, the therapist, it is love that is "unreal" and individual needs that constitute reality. The difficulty of studying culture stems from this: that when culture fully takes, it so merges with life as to be nearly invisible (on this point see Biernacki 1995:12–37). And the culture that is visible, the world of conscious beliefs, rituals, and philosophies of life, can be seen in large part because it has not completely fused with experience.

Students of culture ordinarily describe the content of cultures, the experience of a typical participant in a particular culture. But such a procedure assumes precisely what should be the focus of our questions— how culture enters and shapes experience. As I have tried to show, most of the expressive culture with which people normally come in contact has an ambiguous relationship to experience. People make use of varied cultural resources, many of which they do not fully embrace. The analytic problem then is to describe the varied ways people use diverse cultural materials, appropriating some and using them to build a life, holding others in reserve, and keeping still others permanently at a distance.

Refocusing Studies of Culture

If the theoretical task is to describe how culture is used, the varied ways it enters and shapes experience, there is a related tactical question about where to focus cultural studies. The most influential contemporary approach to studying culture has been Clifford Geertz's (1973c) "thick description."[7] This method embodies important theoretical commitments, highlighting some questions, making others hard to ask, and pushing still others out of sight.

For Geertz, thick description is opposed to explanation—that is, to the attempt to use culture to explain social action. In the "semiotic approach,"

> culture is not a power, something to which social events, behaviors, institutions, or processes can be causally attributed; it is a context, something within which they can be intelligibly—that is, thickly— described. (1973c:14)

The method of thick description nonetheless embodies important causal assumptions. Geertz approaches a problem by choosing a "text" from the world of expressive symbols—a ritual, a story, or a performance. Thus the cultural object is always center stage in his account, with the rest of the social world ranged around it. Geertz then defines his task as interpreting the meaning of the piece of culture he has chosen to examine, by describing it in its ramified connections to other aspects of social and cultural life.[8] He may describe a Javanese shadow-puppet play (1973d) or a cockfight (1973e). Or he may recount a complex story, like that of the multifaceted dealings among the Jewish trader Cohen, the French Captain Dumari, and the Marmushan sheikh in Morocco in 1912, which forms the centerpiece of his essay on thick description (1973c:7–9).

Geertz prefers exploring ritual events that deeply engross their participants. But whatever piece of culture he chooses, his method is the same. He focuses on a cluster of symbols, moving out from that core to the social and symbolic experience within which it has meaning. Thus he "interprets" the Balinese cockfight (Geertz 1973e) by following the many strands of Balinese life that wrap themselves around this vivid public play: Balinese conceptions of animality in human nature, the symbolic sexual significance of cocks, the status rivalries played out in betting on cockfights, and the excitement added to the sport by Indonesian government attempts to outlaw it.

These meanings and many more are relevant to the potentially infinite task of thickly describing any particular piece of culture. And here lies both the seductive appeal and the analytic sleight of hand in Geertz's method. Since those natives who enjoy (or create) shadow-puppet plays, religious rituals, or Moroccan poetic competitions (Geertz 1976) bring to these distinctively cultural activities a background of other conceptions, interests, and experiences, anything that is part of their world is necessary to our understanding of what their culture means to them. This is equally true whatever the cultural occasion Geertz examines, and whatever the experiences of its celebrants.

By making the cultural event central in his account, Geertz makes it hard to ask how central it is in the lives of its participants. All culture is vividly lived, because he examines it only at its peak and for those most centrally involved in it. We learn about the "deep play" in a successful cockfight, but we know almost nothing about the use made of this cultural experience by those for whom it is "shallow play," entertaining but not compelling. For Geertz, social life is a context for expressive symbols, and there is no need to describe how the symbols are brought to bear on social life.

Geertz does ask how cultural symbols shape experience. His classic formulation, in "Religion as a Cultural System" (1973b), is that religion provides "models of" and "models for" reality. Systems of religious symbols describe what is in the world ("models of") and allow people to formulate attitudes and feelings appropriate to such a world ("models for"). Sacred symbols (ritual occasions are paradigmatic examples) "synthesize a people's ethos . . . and their world-view" (1973b:89)—that is, they make experientially convincing both the appropriateness of the ritual's characteristic mood in a world constituted as the religious vision describes it and the realism of the religious worldview given the mood the ritual has evoked. Successful rituals create this reciprocal validation of ethos and worldview experientially, as a lived reality.

This remains the most powerful formulation we have of what it is culture actually does for people. Cultural systems define the kind of world people face, so that they can act with some confidence within it. And cultural systems both teach and express general orientations to that world— what Geertz has called "moods and motivations" or "ethos." But that analysis does not take us very far in understanding the varying ways people appropriate and use cultural meanings.[9]

Geertz exercises an almost ascetic restraint in describing the effects culture might have on action and experience. This view is best exemplified in his essay "Art as a Cultural System" (1976), the companion piece to those on religion, ideology, and common sense. Art both depends upon and helps to sustain "the feeling a people has for life" (1976:1475). He rejects the "functionalist" view that "works of art are elaborate mechanisms for defining social relationships, sustaining social rules, and strengthening social values" in favor of a kind of muted aestheticism:

> Nothing very measurable would happen to Yoruba society if carvers
> no longer concerned themselves with the fineness of line, or, I dare-
> say, even with carving. Certainly, it would not fall apart. Just some
> things that were felt could not be said—and perhaps, after awhile,
> might no longer even be felt—and life would be the greyer for it.
> (p. 1478)

Yoruba line carving, Geertz says, "grows out of a distinctive sensibility the whole of life participates in forming—one in which the meanings of things are the scars that men leave on them" (1976:1478). But how would such a view help us in examining the diverse aspects of our own culture? Do cowboy movies "grow out of a distinctive sensibility the whole of life participates in forming"? And is that sensibility shared by impressionist painting, cool jazz, and romantic comedies, all of which cowboy-movie fans may also enjoy? While Geertz would not argue explicitly that cultures are unified wholes, in which a single sensibility pervades all of life,[10] his formulation makes sense only if we imagine cultures as unified around a shared sensibility. If cultures are more discordant than this, with competing perspectives and clashing sensibilities, he can say little about how these modes of understanding intersect, interact, or compete.

Geertz's method also directs attention away from the varied ways people use or hold culture. By focusing on the most engrossing moments of public ritual occasions, he keeps from view the more partial, ambivalent, incomplete uses of culture.[11] We, as outsiders, imagine ourselves at the head table at the cultural feast, experiencing fully the vivid events we see before us. But what of those who live mainly in the "pale, remembered reflection" (Geertz 1973b:120) of a variety of contrasting cultural meanings? What of those who live culturally sparse, relatively "grey" lives, little touched by vibrant ritual?

To address such issues requires turning Geertz's method, as well as his theory, inside out. Instead of describing a particular piece of culture's resonances with other aspects of life and the glow it casts over them, one would start with those who use culture, asking what they do with the different ways of framing meaning they have available. This is the approach I have taken here.

Such an approach addresses two related issues: cultural variety, including the diversity of cultural resources available to particular individuals and groups; and the variable ways people hold or use culture—ranging from intense ideological commitment to the casual or indifferent use of platitudes. The payoff of such an investigation is a better causal analysis of the relations between culture and social structure, especially of the ways culture affects social action and social organization, on the one hand, and the ways culture itself changes, on the other. Trying to understand how people selectively appropriate and use cultural meanings can lead to the ability to ask why in some situations cultural symbols lose their force or plausibility while in others they remain vibrant and persuasive; or why people sometimes invest beliefs, rituals, and symbols with ever increasing meaning, while at other times they live with great gaps between culture and experience. Answers to such questions in turn suggest reasons why cultural systems are vulnerable to drastic change at some periods and not others, and why individuals are receptive to new experiences and new ways of framing meaning at some times and not others.

Such questions about how culture is adopted or abandoned are crucial to effective analysis of culture's effects on social action and social organization. If people in some sense choose among diverse cultural resources and put them to use in different ways, culture's effects are mediated by such variability.

In my view we are also more likely to develop powerful analyses of how culture works if we accept the challenge of studying our own culture, where exoticism is not available to make us feel that we have accomplished much simply by making the strange familiar. When we deal with a culture that is all too familiar, as middle-class American culture is for most of us, then the challenge is to develop more powerful theoretical ways to interpret patterns of cultural appropriation and rejection, cultural continuity and change. There are not simply different cultures: there are different ways of mobilizing and using culture, different ways of linking culture to action. It is these differences in culture's uses that I investigate in the pages that follow.

CHAPTER 2

Repertoires

To describe how culture works, we need new metaphors. We must think of culture less as a great stream in which we are all immersed, and more as a bag of tricks or an oddly assorted tool kit (see Swidler 1986) containing implements of varying shapes that fit the hand more or less well, are not always easy to use, and only sometimes do the job.

The difficulty with images of tool kits and magicians' tricks is that they imply conscious choice or rational manipulation. After all, people are often "used by" their culture as much as they use it.[1] Indeed, most current understandings of culture assume that it constructs the very selves who act and the terms in which action, self, and world can be understood. We do not think of people as separate enough from their culture to "use" it.[2] I share this view of culture's constitutive role (see Sewell 1985, 1992; Meyer and Jepperson 2000), but I would insist that cultures constitute multiple selves, worlds, and modes of action. As I shall try to show below, people do use culture as a tool kit, even when one of the cultural tools they may pick up or put down is precisely the kind of self they inhabit.

Culture as Repertoire

Perhaps we do best to think of culture as a repertoire, like that of an actor, a musician, or a dancer. This image suggests that culture cultivates skills and habits in its users, so that one can be more or less good at the cultural repertoire one performs, and that such cultured capacities may exist both as discrete skills, habits, and orientations and, in larger assemblages, like the pieces a musician has mastered or the plays an actor has performed. It is in this sense that people have an array of cultural resources upon which they can draw. We can ask not only what pieces are in the repertoire but why some are performed at one time, some at another.

Adding a cultural style, mood, or justification of action to one's repertoire may not be easy. Indeed, one advantage of thinking of culture as repertoire is that it emphasizes the ways culture is like a set of skills, which one can learn more or less thoroughly, enact with more or less grace and conviction (Sudnow 1978). Thinking of culture as repertoire makes us aware that cultural symbols, rules, or rituals only sometimes "work" for people. Just as a musician may have easier, more assured mastery over some parts of her repertoire than others, so our mastery of culture varies. Some cultural orientations are so ingrained that they require neither effort nor self-consciousness. Others require laborious concentration. And still other parts of a repertoire are insecurely learned, so that one may act out a cultural attitude without being very good at it.

In this chapter I examine how people select among parts of a repertoire, picking up and putting aside cultural themes. Then I explore the circumstances under which people shift from one part of their repertoire to another, and what anchors or invokes the varied scripts they use.[3] Particularly important here is the way different parts of people's life organization—core situations or problems—provide contexts within which particular pieces of culture make sense. People run through different parts of their cultural repertoires, selecting those parts that correspond to the situation or exemplary problem (in something like Kuhn's [1970] sense of "exemplar") that currently holds their attention.

In the examples that follow, I try to illustrate both the fluidity and the logic with which persons mobilize different parts of their cultural repertoire. While I deal first with the conscious "ideas" about love and marriage people present in discussion, the analysis applies just as forcefully to the "moods and motivations" and the ritual experiences a culture generates.

DEBATING

The easiest way to see culture as a repertoire is to examine a situation in which people mobilize several parts of their repertoires simultaneously: when they have a position to defend and they are willing to call up any argument that seems plausible. Ideals of love—deeply held, yet always precarious—often generate precisely this superfluity of reasons.

Love is a peculiar notion, both in its literary rendition and in ordinary life. One of its oddest aspects is the uncertainty about whether love does, or should, have reasons.[4] In my interviews, for example, people had great difficulty explaining why they love the people they do. Asked why he married his wife, Donald Nelson, a Silicon Valley engineer, replied, "I wish I knew. It was funny, because I wasn't looking . . ." It is not that his reasons were too intensely personal to describe. In fact, he insisted on the mundane aspects of his choice: "We liked each other. We got along well." He simply could not give reasons for what now seems to him quite inevitable: "We got along. I don't know what it is. It just seemed like the one."

But love is not entirely without reasons. Indeed, despite his generally awkward style, Donald Nelson was able to offer a wealth of arguments about why one should stay married—arguments drawn from independent, and sometimes contradictory, traditions of thought.

In mainstream American culture, two contrasting vocabularies apply to the problem of love, and Americans operate in the gaps and overlaps between them (see Swidler 1980; Quinn 1996). One way to think of love is as a voluntary choice. Then the question is whom one loves and why, and what one gives and receives in a relationship. One chooses well; gets a good deal; is more or less contented, satisfied, happy, and so forth. The other way to think about love is as a commitment, a bond that is no longer purely voluntary, if it ever was. If love is a commitment then it is unique, irreplaceable, and not fully rationalizable into a set of benefits given and received. Sometimes the emotional punch of the word "love" comes from its power to signify a relationship beyond choice—one in which the normal expectation of reciprocity need not apply. At other times love signifies the ultimate choice, based on the unsurpassed virtues of the beloved.

Logically, love as choice and love as commitment may well be incompatible, since free choice implies that one could cease to prefer the person to whom one is already committed. But the quite logical engineer drew freely on both cultural images to justify enduring marriage. First, his marriage should last because it is especially "right" for him. How did he know she was the one he wanted? "Oh, I guess we wanted to see each other. There was no facade. We communicated." What is love? "I guess it's feeling right about someone." But if the idea of finding the right person implies "choosing," it becomes the wrong metaphor. Asked whether he worried when he married that there might be a more "perfect person out there somewhere," he burst out laughing: "You mean like shopping for a car or something? I don't know. I didn't even think about it." Choosing someone to love isn't like shopping, and shouldn't be.[5]

Another reason that people should stay married, however, is that they freely chose the marriage bond. "I guess it's because I believe there's no point in getting married unless you really think it should last a lifetime. If you don't want that kind of a relationship, you don't have to get married." So marriage rests on a voluntary choice, but one of a special kind—a contractual relationship to which one is bound because one agreed to it in the first place.

Enduring relationships are good, then, first because one has found the right person and second because one has freely chosen a relationship and should stick to it. But there are other reasons, which draw on other images of the nature of love. Here the imagery becomes more organic than contractual. Love "grows like a flower. If you make sure you care for it, it grows, but if you stomp on it, it certainly doesn't last."[6] Lasting relationships are good because "You're kind of a pair. You grow with each other. It's a life you share together."

Finally, even if the general rationales that justify staying married do not work for everyone, Donald Nelson argues that a lasting relationship is good for him, given his own character: "Like I say, I'm not that type of person. I never dated much, ran around much. I am basically very quiet."

Rightness, choice, commitment, growth, personal predilection—none of the reasons Donald Nelson adduces for marrying or staying married is unusual. Indeed, he is out of the ordinary only in his somewhat awkward sincerity. While there is a dominant theme to his concerns about love and marriage (the need for mutual respect and consideration—a topic to which we shall return), he in fact draws on a hodgepodge of images to describe what love is, what keeps it alive, and why it should be preserved.

The core of his thinking seems to be his own evident satisfaction with his marriage, but around that is arrayed a variety of reasons why it is good to do what he is doing. His decision to marry he sees, at least in retrospect, as primarily a matter of rapport, communication, understanding—"feelings" that are very important but hard to articulate. Staying together requires attention and consideration, like that of a gardener nurturing a flower, but it is also a kind of obligation based on a freely chosen contract. There are also satisfactions from staying with one person and being a couple. And then if all else fails, he just finds himself to be the kind of person who prefers stable, married life.

This repertoire of reasons is not a unified argument for the virtues of lifelong marriage, nor is it inconsistent in the sense of being flawed by some logical or practical contradiction. Rather, these rationales are organized around their common conclusion: this shy engineer's evident desire to stay married. Like many of us much of the time, he has little need of a coherent rationale for his day-to-day life, as long as his life seems to be working. Instead, he has a patchwork of cultural accounts on which he can draw, which handle most of the questions he poses to himself or which are posed for him by his environment. But for what kinds of people under what circumstances does life pose persistent questions for which they need an extensive repertoire of elaborate answers? Under what circumstances will fewer, simpler, less developed answers do?

Another suburban professional, this time a young, successful lawyer, talked about love in a very different style than did the sober engineer, but he justified lasting marriage in very similar terms. The lawyer, Ted Oster, fell madly in love with his wife—"really flipped," in his phrase. After ten years of marriage and two children, he still feels that she is "that right, special person." More articulate and more introspective than the engineer, Ted Oster nonetheless draws on very much the same repertoire of arguments about why one should stay married. First, of course, there is his satisfaction with his own marriage. "Mostly it's just you know this person is really good. It's worked so well before up until now, and it continues to do that because you expect it to, and it does by and large." For him, responsibility to a freely chosen contract is less important than responsibility to one's children ("I think it would be wrong for kids not to be able to grow up in a family"), but his desire to avoid "the sense of failure at making the relationship work" is certainly reminiscent of the engineer's view that if you choose to get married, you should stick to it. Like the engineer, he also falls back on the argument that lasting marriage is right for him because of his own character, his personal preferences: "[Having multiple relationships] is just not something that interests me. . . . I'd have to be probably a hell of a lot stronger than maybe I am now, and a lot more self-reliant, maybe falsely so, but I'd sure have to replace what I have now with something else."

The young lawyer develops a much richer version of the engineer's organic argument that it is good to be "a pair," to "grow together," and to have "a life you share together":

> I have seen us get from a good relationship in terms of sharing with
> each other and so on to one that's much, much deeper. . . . It's one
> that you can't develop over a brief period of time, and also I think
> probably harder to develop with somebody that you meet at this stage
> in your life. Your having grown through your twenties with someone
> is good. Having first children and doing all those things, you could
> never do it again with anybody else. For me I would rather—I think

intellectually that life's experiences will be best shared with somebody going through all those stages together.

I get satisfaction in growth with Debby in proceeding through all these stages of life together. O.K. That's what makes it all really fun. It makes it meaningful and gives me the opportunity to share with somebody, have an anchor, if you will, and understand where I am.

Here he expands Donald Nelson's ideal of growth and sharing into a more general claim about what makes for a good, satisfying, and meaningful life. "It means much more that way, so everything that we go through now takes on more meaning than it would if I were to even experience that with somebody in a casual relationship." A shared history gives life greater meaning and also creates a richer sense of self, providing "an anchor," to "understand where I am."

Despite his greater verbal facility, Ted Oster's justifications of lasting marriage were no more unified than those of Donald Nelson, and in fact he traveled almost exactly the same ground. What is striking is that both men, despite their different styles, drew on similar repertoires when they tried to justify lasting marriage. But they also elaborated those various justifications to different degrees. For the engineer, the fact that one freely chooses marriage explained why one is obligated to try to stay married; while for the lawyer, the desire not to feel like a failure at marriage was only one reason why it would be "wrong" to get divorced, and was not elaborated into a positive rationale for staying married. The sense of sharing that occurred to the engineer only as a kind of personal benefit of marriage provided the lawyer with a very general vision of how a meaningful life is to be lived.

Thus in looking at the more-or-less reasoned arguments people make, we see them drawing from their repertoires, trying various rationales, with little concern about coherence among them. We also note that some people elaborate their reasons more than others do, and that two people who have very similar repertoires may nonetheless differ greatly in the emphasis they accord particular views.[7] How some people enrich or elaborate parts of a standard repertoire, while letting other parts lie fallow, is central to the analysis of how culture is used. It is an issue to which we shall return in later chapters.

Even this simple example of the variety of arguments two men can develop to justify enduring marriage suggests new ways of thinking about how culture works. First, it seems evident that for these men, their cultural understandings of love are organized not around the logical coherence of a single image, metaphor, or theory of love but around a core situation or problem. Several models of what love is like (a choice, a commitment, a growing organism) are acceptable as long as they support the marriages these men wish to sustain. Indeed, the apparent incoherence of their medley of arguments might, from another point of view, be seen as an advantage. If what one wants to do is support and justify a given way of life, having a rich variety of rationales available should strengthen one's position. If one argument fails, there are plenty of others available (see Bourdieu 1990).

Such ready tacking back and forth between one argument and another may seem to smack of cynicism, or at least of self-delusion. But this view is based on our systematic misapprehension of the way culture works. While cultural meanings may indeed give human beings some analytic distance from their experience (see V. Turner 1969) and some leverage over problems of action, for most people most of the time culture is mobilized piecemeal, to tinker at the edges or to defend their existing patterns of life. Even when people actively mobilize ideas to solve problems rather than just to confirm their current life arrangements (Quinn 1996; Strauss and Quinn 1997), they still benefit from having multiple understandings to draw on. No conscious cynicism is required; only normal commitment to the embedded features of one's own life. And in the case of love, where many aspects of daily life are imbued with multiple layers of meaning, it would be a betrayal of the "reality" of that experience to try to encompass it in a single, consistent worldview.

Second, what makes a particular image, metaphor, or argument acceptable is its fit with a given mode of life. For Donald Nelson, choosing a spouse the way one chooses a car is laughable (though not utterly beyond his cultural imagination),[8] because it violates the spirit of his current commitment to his marriage. In this, and in other cases, we evaluate cultural images by the consequences we would draw from them in core life arenas. Thus, in some sense, cultural understandings are tied to concrete cases (R. Miller 1996). And our commitments in those concrete cases make given cultural principles more or less acceptable.

What then is the use of cultural imagery, if justifications are so fluid, incomplete, and incoherent? The question of culture's uses will, of course, occupy us throughout this book. But here I want to suggest that a cultural repertoire allows people to move among situations, finding terms in which to orient action within each situation. At the same time, cultural imagery is used somewhat the way bats use the walls of caves for echolocation. Bats know where they are by bouncing sounds off the objects around them. Similarly people orient themselves partly by bouncing their ideas off the cultural alternatives made apparent in their environments. A social or political novelty (stories of "open marriage" or the nomination of a woman for the presidency) will make us devour newspapers and solicit the opinions of our friends partly because we want to expand the repertoire of arguments and attitudes we have available for orienting ourselves to a new phenomenon. We locate our own views by their distance from as much as their agreement with opinions available in our environments. And we seek to maintain a repertoire of cultural attitudes, images, and arguments wide enough so that we can orient ourselves among them.

SHIFTING FRAMES

The image of a repertoire or tool kit makes sense when we consider how people use arguments in debate. But what about the more deeply held understandings that ground people's sense of life meaning? Even here, when people talk about their own core concerns, they continue to mobilize divergent, sometimes contradictory cultural frames. Their cultural repertoire turns out to include not simply varying images and arguments but multiple cases, stories, or examples that may each differently define the nature of a given situation. When people shift such stories midstream, we may say that they are shifting the cultural frame within which the situation is understood (Goffman 1974; Padgett and Ansell 1993).

Such shifts in cultural framing are different than the shotgun approach of a debater, throwing out arguments on the chance that one might hit the mark. Here, a person operating within one set of assumptions comes to a problem he cannot handle within his dominant scheme. Then, after floundering for a while trying to adapt his frame to unexpected difficulties, he may quite abruptly jump from one frame to another. This does not signal a loss of confidence in the first vessel, but simply a temporary abandonment of one craft while one navigates choppy waters in another.

Just such a leap—between frames, feelings, and underlying imaginative renderings—occurred during the interview with Donald Nelson, the contented, rationalist engineer. Awkward and hard to draw out on most issues concerning love and marriage, he turned out to have a well-elaborated theory of how partners in a relationship should treat each other. The basis of a good marriage, for him, is "respect." Partners should "understand" each other, each accepting and supporting the other. He portrayed each person tolerating the other person's interests; he supports his wife "in whatever she wants to do." Respect means mutual acceptance of differences—not trying, for example, to convert one's spouse to one's religious beliefs or interfere with the other person's activities. Donald indeed seemed proud of how different he and his wife are—different in what they enjoy, different in their religious values, and separate in most of their activities. "I respect her beliefs, and she respects mine." Respect requires emotional sympathy, "understanding what each other feels," but, even more important, allowing each other freedom of action. "She does the things she wants to do." The examples are homely: she takes a needlepoint class in the evenings; he is engrossed in building an elaborate home telescope; but the principle is intensely felt. The greatest virtue in marriage is giving the other person freedom to do what he or she wants, and the cardinal sin is denying that freedom. Asked what damages relationships, he said, "I guess trying to impose your will on another person, have no regard for the other's feelings. A total disregard for someone's feelings." Beyond this? "I don't know what else. I'm sure there's lots of other things, but I haven't thought too much about it."

For this serious engineer, respect is important because of what is at issue in relationships. The problem, as he sees it, is how two people can integrate autonomous lives, allowing each other room to enjoy their own pastimes, follow their own beliefs, and meet their own needs. As an example of respect in operation, Donald recounted a time early in his marriage when he had felt confined and bored in their small apartment, and his wife supported his buying a ham radio to amuse himself. He sees the same principle at work in his wife's willingness to tolerate his time-consuming hobbies, especially work on the telescope. When asked whether honesty is important in relationships, he saw its value for letting "the other person know that something is wrong" so that problems could be solved. The issue of honesty in relationships did not suggest problems of intimacy, trust, or self-exposure, as it does for many other interviewees; what mattered to him was mutual respect between autonomous partners.

In the midst of this well-worked-out picture of how two people should manage a relationship, Donald Nelson said something surprising. Asked what he would do if his wife should become ill and require constant care, he abandoned the language of autonomy and mutual respect in favor an image of absolute commitment, sacrifice, and selfless love: "If you love [someone] . . . it is just something you do for them. It's something you want to do." Even if it means giving up hobbies, interests, freedom?

Yeah. Nora is the most important thing in my life.

Q.   She's important as her and not just because she gives you support for the things you like to do?

Certainly that too, but she's important because she's—I love her.

Thus in an interview where for more than an hour Donald Nelson never spontaneously used the word love, and downplayed any hint of romance (Why did he marry Nora? "It just worked out. . . . We got along." How did he know she was the one? "Oh, I guess we wanted to see each other. There was no facade. We communicated." Was the idea of love important? "Not at first. It kind of grew. . . . We liked each other. We got along well."), he suddenly expressed a vision of love radically different in tone and substance from anything that had gone before.

This sudden shift in cultural vocabulary was provoked when Donald's attention shifted to a new scene, one that called up a different part of his cultural repertoire. His declaration that "Nora is the most important thing in my life" is potent testimony to a vision of "love" as selfless commitment, which organizes one sense Donald has of his life. Yet this dramatic image is not normally uppermost in his mind, and indeed it surfaced not when he was asked about love directly but when a particular scene or situation evoked it. The frame that worked very well to describe what he values most about his marriage—the mutual respect of two autonomous individuals—broke down, or perhaps we should say it fell silent, before the problem of desperate dependence. His language of "respect," with its image of spouses supporting each other's separate endeavors, was never meant to handle a situation of decisive choice. When the vocabulary of respect failed him, an entirely different moral vision was available in reserve. In this part of Donald's cultural repertoire, relationships embody ultimate choices, ultimate commitments, and "If you love someone" you know what you have to do.

I do not know how or whether this stolid engineer's beliefs would actually lead him to sacrifice himself for an invalid wife. But he provides a particularly dramatic example of a sudden shift in cultural frame when, working through a set of problems within one frame (how people who love each other should treat each other; how spouses can get along), he comes to its limits—that is, to the limits of the problems with which it can effectively deal. It is in this sense that Donald Nelson, like the other people I interviewed, relies on a repertoire of cultural meanings from which he can draw selectively in varying contexts. Indeed, while most transitions are not so dramatic, many of the shifts I described above as opportunistic strategies of debate can be understood just as well as a slight shifting of ground when one frame for understanding experience seems to fail before problems that do not quite fit its assumptions.

Donald Nelson's sudden shift from one frame to another also reflects more general dilemmas of American culture. As we shall see in chapter 7,

Americans frequently employ a utilitarian, individualist logic in thinking about personal relationships. They talk about getting a fair exchange for what they give, communicating clearly their expectations and demands of others, and preeminently, acting so as to maximize good outcomes for themselves, expecting others to do the same. (See Bellah et al. 1985.)

For people in intimate relationships, however, such a language is seldom sufficient. Like Donald Nelson, with his well-elaborated ideal of "respect" for individual differences, most of my interviewees talk quite naturally in individualist terms, about choice, about wanting to do things for one's partner, and about love that has to be spontaneous to be real. But in relationships they also find themselves interdependent in ways they have difficulty formulating in these terms. This tension between a dominant voluntarist vocabulary and experiences of unavoidable interdependence shows up in their frequent inarticulateness about why they "chose" to marry the people they did (since at one level "choosing" no longer has much to do with what is significant about their relationships) and their insistence that the people they married are somehow, ineffably "right" for them. It also emerges in the occasional, surprising moments when, working through a difficult problem in their usual, individualist vocabulary, they find themselves painted into a corner and then, like Donald Nelson, suddenly open a door we did not know was there. It is as if they break out of one vocabulary into other, deeper—if less thoroughly explored—passages.

SCENES

We have seen above that people switch cultural frames when they imaginatively engage new scenes or situations. But the tendency for cultural frameworks to be organized around imagined situations is more general. Indeed, a cultural repertoire remains diverse partly because it contains frameworks for making sense of many different scenes or situations of action, and each scene retains an autonomous logic, independent of other, potentially related, scenes.[9] The ways elements of interviewees' cultural repertoires are organized around scenes or stories becomes evident when we examine the ways they responded to a set of structured dramas of love.

In some interviews, we asked people not only about their own lives but about a set of hypothetical stories or vignettes. (See the methodological appendix for the full set of vignettes and details on how they were administered.) These were simplified problems that might arise in relationships, posing dilemmas that interviewees were asked to solve. The stories ranged from that of a married couple in which one spouse falls in love with someone else to that of an unmarried woman (or man, since we varied the gender of each vignette's protagonist) who cannot decide which of two people to marry.

The vignettes described dramatic situations, recognizable less from everyday life than from soap operas or the columns of "Dear Abby." Often these stories evoked culturally stereotyped responses—no surprise if we and our interviewees were on the same wavelength. On the other hand, we tried to create real dilemmas, so that our interviewees would have to think—mobilizing the cultural resources they think with. We attempted to balance the pros and cons of each hypothetical situation, hoping that interviewees would be unable to find pat answers for the problems our stories posed.

One of the least successful vignettes from this point of view turned out to be among the most revealing. The following story (read aloud, as were all the vignettes, by the interviewer) preceded a series of questions about who is right and why:

> Linda and George have a very close relationship. They have always preferred to do most things together and they have shared more of their thoughts and feelings with each other than with anyone else. Linda, however, is starting to feel that perhaps they should do more things with other people and develop some separate activities of their own. George says that this might lead them to grow apart and make their love for each other less deep. Linda says it might make their love deeper if they were more independent.

The vignette was unsuccessful because our attempts to balance two views of relationships failed. Opinions were lopsided in favor of Linda (or George when he is the one seeking autonomy). Indeed, in many cases interviewees took a vehement dislike to the more dependent partner, arguing, for example, that George was too dependent, lacked confidence in himself, was trying to live only through Linda, and so forth.

What was interesting, first, was how strongly interviewees could react to a contrived situation about which they had little information. Their ability to read much more into the vignette than we had put there was, I think, a sign that we were tapping into a culturally well-elaborated problem. Our interviewees conveyed the sense of having been through this argument, imaginatively or in person, many times before, and they recognized both the outlines of the conflict and the roles and attributes of the participants. They were angry at George for demanding such complete absorption from Linda.

A typical reaction was that of a health-care worker in her thirties, divorced for several years:

> He [George] feels threatened with her wanting to be more independent. He's clinging to that—the symbiotic nature of their relationship.
>
> [Linda's view of love] is inclusive rather than exclusive. The more love that you have . . . the more [you] can share. . . . It just keeps passing. It keeps transferring. It keeps growing.
>
> Each person ought to bring their own richness and independence to a relationship, and to be two separate parts to a whole. That's just really important. For this world to survive we need more of that. We need more people who are strong, independent, and self-sufficient emotionally, physically. To be able to take care of your own needs and not always rely on another person to do it . . .
>
> Q.   What is George's view of love?
>
> He feels pretty dependent. He feels pretty needy. For him to say—do it all, do all those things together, our love will deepen if we do everything together, that's suffocating.

Interviewees do not simply have attitudes, or values, or norms about relationships that they then apply to the case of George and Linda. Rather they have vivid scenarios about what a dependent person is like, about how relationships can go wrong, and about what it would mean to live out particular stories. These images provide one fundamental element organizing individuals' cultural understandings.[10]

Response to the vignettes, or indeed to any question about social attitudes, depends heavily on how the issue is framed, on what kind of scene is imaginatively invoked by the question.[11] "Attitudes" are usually understood as a kind of positive or negative evaluation of some object, and "values" are usually seen as the ranking of options in a hierarchy of preferences. But in responses to these vignettes we see instead that people orient themselves by following out the implications of a particular scenario. If they focus on a different detail of the story, or in some other way reconfigure the scenario, they can switch their attitude toward it entirely.

The vignette of George and Linda tends to evoke one image, but it can be interpreted in other ways. Interviewees easily attribute to George the moral failings of the overly dependent person, but they occasionally read in a different drama, seeing Linda, for example, as someone who puts her own interests ahead of the relationship. Differing opinions about George and Linda are grounded in different constructions of their story.

One unusual interviewee—Les Newman, a well-educated young

businessman and committed Baptist, experienced in articulating how his worldview differs from that dominant in his secular environment—illustrates beautifully the crucial role that scenes or stories play in anchoring social attitudes. He took a middle position in the conflict between George and Linda, but not by finding some midpoint on a single attitudinal continuum. Instead he alternately invoked two different stories, one favoring George and the other favoring Linda, demonstrating how the formulation of a single attitude draws on a repertoire of competing cultural images.

> I find myself playing the middle ground. I find her attitude very selfish [Linda is the dependent one in this version of the vignette] in the sense that—I'm assuming that we're talking about two married people, so I'll treat it that way—even though they are married they are still two different individuals and they do not exactly have the same interests. I don't think there is anything wrong with him having other activities. But at the same time, I find his attitude a little too open-ended when he says he wants to make sure it would be an independent life with independent activities. If he means to do these to the exclusion of activities with his wife, that's wrong. I don't see anything wrong with activities not done with the spouse as long as those activities don't take priority over the spouse. I think it's necessary that you do continue activities together to sort of maintain the bond, the closeness, the communication with each other to ensure that the marriage endures.

Here Les Newman defined his own position by navigating carefully between what he considered the Scylla of one dangerous way of life and the Charybdis of another. He played out each position in his imagination, fleshing out the drama that might unfold. This tendency to set up competing scenes or dramas as a way of locating his own position continued when he was asked why he considered Linda's view "selfish":

> Well, what I mean is that even if two people are married they're not going to find that their interests, abilities and individual gifts they've got are going to be identical. Let's say, for example, if he could sing, and she couldn't carry a tune in a bucket, for her to say, "Listen, I can't sing, so I don't want you to go anywhere and sing either." That's a very selfish attitude. But at the same time, if he says, "Look, I sing great, see you later, I'm going on the road for a year," that's carrying independent activities a bit far.

In response to one simple story, it is remarkable that this Christian businessman could quickly come up with a wide range of related stories and images, which he somehow had "on file" as parts of his own past musings, his repertoire of knowledge and experience, or his cultural imagination. It may be, indeed, that he had on file not specific stories but a culturally structured capacity for generating appropriate stories. Note again how easily he filled in additional lines, fleshing out the parts of the actors in the George-Linda drama:

> Q. What is Linda's view of love, as opposed to George's? What is his view of love?

> To me it seems like her definition of love is based on activities— "The more we do together, the more we love each other." His seems much more founded upon "We said the vows; we signed a piece of paper. It doesn't matter whether we do anything together or not. That ceremony years back has established the relationship." She defines it as activities, and I think he just defines it as saying that it exists is enough. "We said we love each other, so therefore we love each other, and we don't need to do anything together." I'm not sure how he thinks doing independent activities is going to strengthen their love. It's certainly maybe going to broaden his scope over the things he does and the good times he has. I think there are people who say "We're married, so we love each other," and don't feel there's any need to contribute any more than that.

Thus this businessman had available a wide range of images—of persons, situations, and stories—with which he fleshed out the vignette he was given. And he did not have just one take on the situation. As he talks, we can hear him running through one interpretation after another, looking for plausible ways of embodying—and indeed defining—his sense of the proper balance between independence and dependence in marriage. He focuses his own thinking only by mobilizing a wide range of images and stories. In this sense, to participate in a culture is not to share in some uni-fied worldview but to draw on a repertoire of scenes and scenarios. The point George Herbert Mead made about role-playing—that one can't ad-equately play a particular role, like that of "girl" or "second-baseman," without knowing as well how the complementary roles are played—applies just as strongly to other sorts of cultural learning. One incorpo-rates and uses a range of views to frame one's thinking about particular problems.

Les Newman seems to have drawn his interpretive repertoire from both standard cultural dramas and from his own experience, without feeling a need to separate the two. Both provide possible images of what might happen in varied circumstances. Excessive independence could threaten a relationship because "I have known people that have gotten so involved in their independent, individual activities that they haven't left anything for each other." But Linda's plan of spending all their time together might be a threat too "because I don't think two people can spend one-hundred percent of their time together without getting on each other's nerves. . . ." Rules of thumb and cautionary tales both work to the same effect, giving him a way of defining his own position by bouncing his sense of what is right off the varied scenarios he imagines could flow from either George's or Linda's "extreme" positions about togetherness in relationships.[12]

This thoughtful Christian was unusual in the elaborateness of his worldview and in his insistence on finding a balance between "extreme" positions. (Indeed, I have reported only a few of his many evocations of the problems of excessive individualism and excessive dependence in relationships.) But he nonetheless well illustrates two more general points about the way cultural repertoires operate. First, it is clear that he used a wide range of particular cases, images, and examples to think through a problem, finding out what he thought in part inductively, by figuring out which in his repertoire of dramas would have a good or bad ending in the sort of situation he was considering. His position was not so much a point on a unified continuum as a crossroads among a selection of stories. Second, even though he was perfectly able to think in terms of general rules (indeed, unusually so, as in his use of "the golden rule"), a great deal of his thinking was tied more specifically to concrete cases, images of the outcomes of typical situations, personalities, and acts. Thus he used a cultural repertoire full of stories (not information, strictly speaking, but rather projections of what persons and situations of this sort often lead to) to organize his own worldview and to respond to new situations.

Other theorists, such as the social ethicists Albert Jonsen and Stephen Toulmin (1988; Toulmin 1981), have noted that people in fact work out their moral intuitions through analogies to concrete cases for which they already know the "right" answers. But these interviews show just how many cases with potentially competing outcomes there are and how problematic "casuistry" really is. Any given situation, personal or imagined, might be assimilated to a variety of culturally available cases.

Without yet being able to say why it is so, by now we begin to see that some conception of culture as a repertoire or tool kit is useful in understanding how culture is actually brought to bear on experience.

In the interviews we have examined so far, persons show great complexity in the ways they mobilize culture for practical use. They do not simply express perspectives or values instilled in them by their culture. Instead, they draw from a multiform repertoire of meanings to frame and reframe experience in an open-ended way. In debate, they may be unselective, taking up any arguments that seem handy. In other situations, they take up one cultural frame (usually corresponding to an imagined case or situation) until they run up against an unsolvable problem. Undaunted, they usually simply escape the conundrum by jumping outside its boundaries, invoking another situation, another metaphor, another symbolic frame. This frequent shifting among multiple cultural realities is not some anomalous sleight of hand but the normal way in which ordinary mortals (as distinguished, perhaps, from trained philosophers) operate.[13] People know much more culture than they draw on in any one instance (DiMaggio 1997), and they slip frequently between one reality and another, switching the frames within which they understand experience. Geertz has written (1973b) of culture as the defense against meaninglessness, making potentially incoherent experiences cohere. Less attention has been paid to the capacity of culture for creating multiple possible meanings, for teaching the imaginative capacity to provide alternative, sometimes competing frames for experience (but see Victor Turner 1969 and Renato Rosaldo 1989:91–108).[14]

Finally, when people think through problems, they implicitly assume particular situations or cases in framing their own positions. As ethnomethodology has long pointed out, a person must supply some set of background assumptions in order to make any situation, event, or principle interpretable. To a greater extent than ethnomethodology has recognized, these frames or assumptions are matters of culture rather than personal construction. But cultures are also multiplex, offering varied ways of rendering any situation.

Such variability within cultures and the corresponding variety of the cultural repertoires available to individuals are neither unorganized nor unlimited. In the next chapter we will begin to ask how particular organizations of culture are linked to action, and whether some cultures allow more latitude than do others for movement between cultural frames.

PART II

How Culture Works: Love Stories

CHAPTER 3

Examined and
Unexamined Lives

*T*he rabbi of the synagogue I attend was asked why some worshipers
cover their heads with their prayer shawls while reciting
the "Shema," the prayer in which Jews affirm the one God.
He described a talmudic debate about whether simply
reciting the required prayers fulfills one's religious obligations in regard to daily worship, or whether one has to
mean them. The rabbis answered that reciting the prayers
was sufficient for all but the Shema: for this prayer, one
has to mean what is said. Some people cover their heads,
cover their eyes, or even pinch themselves to make themselves attend to its meaning, to be conscious of the words
as they recite them.

This chapter deals with something very like the
problem the rabbis faced: the variation in the ways people
"mean it" when they use their culture. Culture comes in
the form of platitudes and clichés as well as deeply held beliefs; cynicism and disillusionment can coexist with earnest adherence; and muddled meanings operate alongside coherent ones. In the last chapter, I argued that
culture is diverse in content—that people draw on dis-
parate ideas, images, and attitudes from a repertoire of
cultural meanings. In this chapter I look at how much of
this diverse repertoire people actually *use* and at the varied *ways* people use it. I ask how people connect themselves with the culture they do use: whether they take
their culture seriously, cynically, or lightheartedly; how
closely they link their culture to their lives; and how coherent this culture is.

People vary in the "stance" they take toward their culture—how seriously versus lightly they hold it. For example, Nina Eliasoph (1990, 1998:131–64) has described how many people distance themselves from their political opinions by being flippant, self-deprecating ("I don't know anything about politics, but . . . "), or indifferent. My interviews addressed more personal concerns in an interview situation that led interviewees to present themselves "seriously," laying claim to their ideas as their own. Nonetheless, they also had ways of distancing themselves from the interview—occasionally by saying "I don't know" or "I guess so" when a question struck a wrong note,[1] and more frequently by offering platitudes and generalities. Even when people spoke sincerely, they varied in how they individualized or invested with personal meanings the cultural formulas they used to describe their lives.[2]

To understand the diverse ways individuals use culture, we need to focus both on how people appropriate cultural meanings, making them their own, and on how they come to name their own experience in cultural terms.[3] These are of course two sides of the same process, the connection of culture to personal experience. Nonetheless, these processes may seem to operate separately. When Ted Oster, the philosophically inclined lawyer of chapter 2, says "I had always heard, and I wanted to believe, that when you find that special someone, you'll know she's right," he is appropriating and personalizing a cultural formula. When he says "If I were to have a different kind of marriage, I would just have to be a different kind of person, less dependent or whatever, than I am," he is using terms provided by the larger culture to name his own experience, but the culture has disappeared into the experience it names.

A number of recent works on "discourse" ask how ordinary people construct arguments (Billig 1987, 1992), analyze political issues (Gamson 1992), or recount narratives (Riessman 1990; Liebes and Katz 1990).[4] Among such scholars, no consensus has yet emerged on the critical features of ordinary discourse researchers want to measure. Gamson (1992) has focused on the features of group political discussions that can lead to action: whether groups develop a consensual way of framing an issue, whether they integrate examples from their own experience into their analysis of the issue, and whether they draw action implications from their analysis. Billig has described the fluid ways people use popular culture to engage in a range of commentary on their own society (1992) and the rhetorical strategies that make commonsense reasoning possible (1987). Riessman (1990:116–18) examines how people use narrative structures to explain their lives to themselves and others. She makes distinctions among narratives that present a concrete moment in the past, those that describe the past in general summary terms, and "hypothetical narratives" that contrast the past as it was with some alternative that might have been. Liebes and Katz (1990) examine the different ways audiences both accepted as real and distanced themselves from the lives portrayed in the television serial *Dallas*. Some cultural groups saw the world portrayed on *Dallas* as real but alien; others viewed it as familiar but fabricated; and still others stood outside it, critiquing the ideological motivations behind the series. Liebes and Katz also contrast the ways differing groups create narratives: around plots with coherent story lines versus around characters who are more deeply revealed by the cumulation of incidents over time. The very variety of these schemes for analyzing the properties of discourse shows how difficult it can be to conceptualize the central dimensions along which modes of cultural appropriation and use differ.

Since I am interested ultimately in how and why culture affects action, I explore the dimensions of culture's uses that should significantly affect its impact. In the powerful Weberian formulation, ideas influence action when they are coherent ("rationalized" in Weber's terminology) and when they are applied fully to daily life (as they were in ascetic Protestantism). In exploring such variation in the talk of ordinary people, I am trying to establish whether these dimensions of culture's use help account for when and why culture makes a difference. I argue here and in subsequent chapters that these variations, while real and important, do not provide the best tools for analyzing culture's effects on action and experience.

I focus first on how much of the available culture people use. Second, I examine how fully people integrate their culture with their experience (versus segregating their culture from experience). Finally, I focus on the coherence of those cultural resources people bring to bear on experience. The chapter proceeds by indirection—examining pairs of people who are similar socially yet differ in the style with which they use their culture, or occasionally those who differ in important respects yet seem to use their cultural resources in similar ways.[5]

I also offer a caveat here. Both the philosopher Jeffrey Stout (1986) and the sociologist Bennett Berger (1995) have questioned whether it is possible to use interview materials such as these to assess how people hold their ideas. Stout (pp. 33–38) argues that looking for articulate principles behind people's ways of life can miss the narrative coherence or the taken-for-granted situational realities that ground moral understandings. Berger (pp. 110–12) notes that how deeply someone believes something (that love equals passion, for example) may not correspond to the ardor with which she or he says it.[6] I agree in part with both these points, and I note in subsequent chapters how much of people's cultural understanding is anchored in situations and stories. Nonetheless, the very different ways people talk about their experience—the varying distance they maintain toward the culture they use and the differing ways they link culture and experience—capture important elements of the way culture is mobilized to frame and guide action. But the limitations of such analyses also suggest the need for alternatives to standard sociological images of why and how culture matters.

How Much Culture

People vary greatly in *how much* culture they apply to their own lives. Some people draw on a wide range of cultural precepts, psychological theories, personal incident, and anecdote, while others move within narrow confines, using one or two formulas or phrases again and again.

Nora Nelson is an occupational therapist, in her late thirties, married for nine years to Donald Nelson, the Silicon Valley engineer we met in chapter 2 (and who said, "Nora is the most important thing in my life"). While she does not lack for cultural resources—she is a practicing Catholic and she once attended a three-weekend *est* training—she frames her experience almost exclusively in a narrow range of commonsense terms.

Asked at the beginning of the interview whether anything particularly important was happening in her life right then, she replied, "There's not really anything on my mind. I'm happy." And from her point of view, if you are happy, you don't need to think much about things. She is a devout Roman Catholic and her husband an atheist: "We're quite a combination. He doesn't believe in God." She "would like him to believe in God, but each to their own." Their religious difference created no problem about marrying: "Well, I fell in love with him. He could have been anything. I knew his family before I married him. It has worked out well." Was there something especially wonderful about him? "I don't know. I guess I never really thought about it that much."

It is not that Nora is unenthusiastic or uncertain about her marriage. Indeed, just the opposite. She can't remember having worried about whether she was really in love, precisely because the relationship seemed so right: "In fact, I really wasn't planning on getting married. I always said I'd get married when I was forty-five or fifty. He really didn't want to get married either. He had never met anyone that he wanted to marry, and I don't think I ever had either until I met him."

What stands out for Nora is that she was, and is, "in love" with her husband. How did she know she was in love? "I don't think I would ever have thought of marrying him if I wasn't in love with him. I had been asked to marry a few times before." And what was different about this time? "I don't know. I was just more serious, I guess, about him." And what was it about him? "I don't know what it is. Chemistry or something. It was there. I don't know." Although her parents "probably didn't like the idea" of her marrying a non-Catholic, "they liked Donald, and they knew I really wanted to marry him. I was in love with him."

Nora Nelson's insistence that she loves her husband and that she is "happy" can be contrasted with the much richer way in which, for example, Ted Oster (the lawyer introduced in chapter 2) described his own happy marriage. First, he offered more varied and richer cultural formulations to describe how and why he married as he did. For him, his past life was filled with incident—the girl he almost married even though he wasn't sure she was the special, right person for him; the particular way he and his wife met, including the party at which he suddenly felt emotionally connected to her; the later deepening of their relationship as they shared children and the ups and downs of living together.

Ted Oster also more frequently generalizes, talking not just about his own experience but about the nature of good relationships in general—the importance of communication, the danger of taking each other for granted, whether each person must find that one special person who is right for him or her. Contrast this with the way Nora Nelson turns even general questions back to her sense of her own life as happy. Asked about "honesty" in relationships, she replies, "I think it's important. You should be able to trust someone. Yeah. I think it's important." Her lackluster support for the importance of honesty resembles her answers to many other questions. She seems to suggest that even if these ideas are widely believed to be important, they are not very important to her because her own life is not problematic:

> Q.   So if a wife found that her husband had been lying to her about something, let's say something financial or whatever?
>
> I don't think we have that many problems. I don't think there is anything to hide.
>
> Q.   I mean in general do you think that might be a problem, not in your relationship?
>
> Let's see. Lying about money? I don't know. I wouldn't like anybody lying about anything, I guess.
>
> Q.   Do you force yourself to be honest with him when there's something difficult to talk about?
>
> Yeah. I try. I haven't anything to hide, I guess.

Nora Nelson has clearly remained immune to the culture of psycho-babble, so that she does not give the standard responses to buzzwords like "honesty" and "communication." This unwillingness to use currently fashionable language is not due to lack of exposure. Indeed, in response to pressures from coworkers, Nora had attended a three-weekend *est* training, but she noted proudly that it didn't "change" her. Nora does not present herself as a person on a quest for happiness, searching for cultural resources that will help her find and preserve it. Rather, she is already happy, and this happiness is answer enough to whatever questions life poses.

It is not that Nora Nelson is so secure that she has no need to think about her marriage. Like almost all those I interviewed, she is aware of the prevalence of divorce. She and her husband agreed before they married that marriage should be permanent, but "it isn't always. But anything can happen, but we started out that way. I see a lot of divorces in my practice. I see my patients over and over so I know how many divorces there are." Nonetheless, her reaction to the ever-present possibility of divorce is non-committal: Marriage should be permanent, but "I guess if I found out I didn't love I wouldn't feel this way either." She can see that "you can feel differently about a person after a few years, or whatever," or, indeed, "find out you didn't want marriage in the first place, because I didn't think I ever wanted to be married. I guess I would have felt maybe this really isn't right."

Nora's willingness to contemplate not loving her husband or not wanting to be married has to be considered in light of her frequent affirmations of her married life: "Well, I am as much in love now as when I was first married" ; and repeatedly, "I just like being married. I can't see myself being single." Far from being detached from the culture she uses, she is strongly committed to a few basic ideas which she finds sufficient.

The narrowness of Nora Nelson's cultural range can be highlighted by contrast with Teresa Dreyer, a twenty-eight-year-old homemaker. Married five years, she is the mother of two small children. Teresa, like Nora Nelson, is a devout Catholic whose happy marriage is central to her life. Yet her cultural understanding of love is much more richly elaborated than is Nora's.

Teresa Dreyer and her husband, a struggling salesman, are both active in their church. They have attended Marriage Encounter, where they learned "communication techniques" that they use "in trying to keep [their] feelings known to each other and keep things open." In her down-to-earth view of love, "keeping lines of communication open" is "something you have to work at."

Like Nora, Teresa sees her life as the one, right kind of life for her. But she justifies this life in both personal and general moral terms. She stopped working when her children were born, not just for convenience or because she likes children but because she believed it was right.

> I have always felt that way, ever since I was a little girl. I guess it was my upbringing. That's the way my parents feel and I think that's what God feels. I think that's what God is saying in the Bible. When a woman marries she is supposed to be a wife and a mother. That's her foremost responsibility.

Contrast this with Nora Nelson's description of the decision she and her husband made not to have children:

> I guess I wouldn't have cared whether or not we had children. I never really thought that I wanted to have children. I just didn't think about it, since I never really thought about marriage that much. We didn't get married until we were 26 and 27, and I guess by that time— maybe if I had been 21 or whatever, I would have cared a little more. I was kind of set, you know, with my job and my life and had independence, and so was he.

Teresa Dreyer sees her life choice as full of meaning, appropriating that meaning from a variety of sources. Nora Nelson instead disclaims the decision, using conditional, hypothetical language to describe it and adducing idiosyncratic personal reasons to account for it.

The contrast in style appears again in Nora's and Teresa's answers to questions about whether their love will last. It is striking that they use such different language to express very similar feelings. Nora says: "I like being married. I don't know. I'm so used to being married, I would hate to think of not. I don't think I'd like to be by myself." She loves her husband, and does not anticipate that their love will change:

> I still feel as much in love as I did. Whether or not it wears off I don't know, because I haven't felt any differently. But I don't think you would fall out of love that fast, as I think you would still have to feel an awful lot for the person, if you had lived with someone long.

Teresa Dreyer uses widely available cultural meanings—both the religious ones of her church and standard therapeutic advice about communication and sharing—to construct a rich interpretation of the meaningfulness of her own life experiences:

> He's my best friend. . . . Marty knows me through and through, and he still accepts me the way I am. I mean there are little things we don't know about each other, but I know him pretty well too. I can

pretty well figure out his feelings and what's going on inside him. We can talk openly about things that are upsetting us or things that make us happy, and I love him the way he is. There are some things that I do that irritate him, and he does that irritate me, but we are each other's best friend. I can go to him and let down, and he can come to me and let down and be open and honest. I think that's the basis of it. I believe our love comes from God. He gave us each other to love and to share our life together. The love comes from Him. We shut Him out, sometimes we're not too loving toward each other, sometimes we don't act too loving toward each other, but He's basically there overseeing our love for each other and for our children.

Not only does Teresa Dreyer describe her life in richer terms than Nora Nelson does, she seems to use cultural resources more actively to guide and help her with issues in her marriage. She embraces the value of "communicating," for example, and she describes the cultural meanings that reinforce her sense of commitment to her marriage.

It seems like we've been through a lot in the past five and a half years. . . . It seems like every time we go through something that's tough, we go through it together, and we come out loving each other more at the end of it. We might have arguments and disagreements because there's a lot of tension with financial problems, but we're still keeping the lines of communication open, and trying to talk it out, and trying to work it out together, even though it might get rough sometimes. Neither one of us is about to cop out on the other one.

In contrast, Nora Nelson uses less culture partly because she seems to need less. Her marriage is fine, she loves her husband, everything has worked out well, and she is happy. These verities make further cultural exploration unnecessary.

Nora Nelson employs a few, central cultural symbols which, for her, have an obvious, commonsense truth. She loves her husband, she is happy, and she and her husband make each other happy. These truths seem sufficient to explain and organize her life. Within that frame, the details of her life—including the four hours an evening her husband works on the telescope he is building in the garage, the "support" he gives her for what she wants to do, the agreement they made not to have children, and her obligation to "try to be what you picture a wife to be . . . cooking, shopping, the things a wife would do"—all seem naturally to make sense. She sees no reason to frame them in larger or more elaborated cultural terms.

In contrast to Teresa Dreyer, who describes the hard times she and her husband have shared, Nora Nelson feels no need to work on or even shore up her self. She tells no "conversion narrative"—a story of the creation of a new self, or a new understanding in terms of which a past life and a past self can be criticized and examined. She uses the cultural categories of "love," "happiness," and even "God" to frame her life as good, but she does not actively employ them to manage problems or opportunities within it. Nora is fatalistic about life ("You don't really know what will happen. Nobody does."), and one consequence of this fatalism is that she need not make active efforts to anticipate life's demands. She felt no anxiety about getting married because in dating "there was always something there. I guess the sex when you needed it was always there, and still kind of felt secure because you always had someone. I guess I was never to a point where I didn't have somebody." Thus even her most significant life transition, her marriage, seemed to her to come naturally, without any transformation (even though by her own account she did not originally plan to marry) or even any effort on her part.

It is not that Nora Nelson lacks the cultural resources themselves. *Est* training exposed her to the ideas of "communication" and taking "responsibility" for your life, even if she resists applying them to her own experience. And God is a real presence for her as for Teresa, although she invokes God only when asked whether she goes to confession: "I don't really feel that you have to do that. I'm not sure why, because I feel now that God knows what you do." She also can make use of widely available cultural ideas when she feels the need, as when she offers a conventional argument for using contraception despite the Church's position: "I guess I feel I'm doing the right thing because if you brought children into the world and you didn't want them, I think that would be worse."[7]

Nora Nelson and Teresa Dreyer also differ in the way they relate their cultural understanding to experience. Teresa continually applies her general cultural understanding to images and examples from her own experience, integrating experience with culture. Nora Nelson more often uses general formulas to summarize her life—"I'm happy" or "I love my husband"—without using those generalizations to evoke particular memories that flesh out their meanings. Contrast, for example, Nora Nelson's repeated conviction that she and her husband are "very close," "care for each other," and "really get along well" with Teresa Dreyer's evocation of the tone and texture of her marriage when she says, in the passage quoted above, that her husband knows her "through and through," that she loves him "the way he is," that she can "go to him and let down" and he can do the same with her.

Like Nora Nelson, Teresa Dreyer tells of no "conversion." She fell in love, married, and she believes she is leading precisely the life she wants to and ought to be leading. Why, then, is her use of culture different than Nora's? How has she elaborated a richer cultural understanding of love? First, Teresa Dreyer is integrated into a wider community of discourse than are Nora and her husband. Teresa and Marty are active in their church. They have participated in Marriage Encounter and in the Christian Family Movement, which they run in their church. She speaks of having "a lot of close friends" through church, while Nora is involved primarily with her husband and her own family. Teresa thus has had practice in formulating her understanding of marriage in general terms offered by religious movements that focus on family (although, Marriage Encounter jargon—"dialoging," "love is a decision," "the World's plan versus God's plan for our marriage"—appears nowhere in the interview). But participation in a community may also play a wider role in stimulating culturally guided examination of one's life.

Basil Bernstein (1975), studying the language of working-class versus middle-class schoolchildren, has described the use of "restricted" versus "elaborated" codes (see also Heath 1983). Working-class children, he argues, speak in concrete terms, because they take for granted a small, known world of others who share the same references and assumptions. Middle-class children, on the other hand, develop elaborated codes, both more explicit and more abstract, that allow them to communicate in a public sphere with diverse others who do not necessarily share their particular experiences and points of reference. Although Nora Nelson, married to an educated professional, is in some ways more upper-middle class than is Teresa Dreyer, it may be that Teresa's wide circle of interaction has broadened her use of cultural resources for describing her experience, giving her the habit of reflexivity, of elaborating the meaning of what she does in self-conscious ways.

A second source of the differences between Nora Nelson's and Teresa Dreyer's use of culture is that Teresa defines herself as struggling and changing, needing cultural guidance in living her life. Nora Nelson, in contrast, defines her life as stable and happy. On no quest to improve herself or her marriage, she does not mobilize as much culture or use it as actively as Teresa does.

All this suggests that how much culture persons use is not primarily a matter of how much they possess. Rather, people may have very similar cultural resources—in this case, education in some of the psychological language of seventies-style self-actualization along with Catholic belief and teaching—but use them quite differently. For Teresa Dreyer, these cultural traditions seem to pervade the interview, while Nora Nelson, in possession of similar resources, simply uses less of them.

Of course, to ignore a cultural resource even if one is familiar with it, not to "use" it, also means not exploring its potential to explain or justify one's life. Thus, in the end, using culture sparingly may mean coming to have less of it. So, for example, Teresa Dreyer has applied her psychological and religious ideas to her particular situation, while Nora Nelson, by minimizing such language, has also elaborated its meanings less fully.

Segregated versus Integrated Culture

In addition to the amount of culture they use, people also differ in the ways they integrate culture and experience. This dimension is linked to the variations described in the last section in how actively people bring culture to bear on their experience. But I want to focus here on how culture and experience are integrated—whether one illuminates and sometimes changes the other, or whether they remain segregated so that cultural lessons or programs for action resist revision by experience.[8]

In this aspect of the way she uses culture, Nora Nelson resembles another interviewee, Paul Manville, even though in other respects the two are very different. Nora Nelson is happy, while Paul Manville might be described as disillusioned, even embittered. But these very different personalities share a tendency to think culturally in terms of fixed positions or "policy statements" about their lives.

In his mid-thirties and divorced for seven years, Paul Manville has a clear view of the lessons to be drawn from his failed marriage: "My previous experience was one of feeling like I'd been put in a closet. I don't like feeling like I'm owned, and I don't want to own anybody." Although he is not looking for a long-term relationship ("I have certain personal goals I want to achieve before I go out and take on a lady, on a steady basis"), he can describe what he would want:

> I would like to have a woman who can be something or someone interesting to talk to, who has ideas, who expresses them freely, but with somewhat the same attitude I do—that just because that's the way she feels, it doesn't mean I have to feel the same way, and likewise I don't expect her to have to see things the same way I do. I would hope that if I felt very strongly about the woman that she would maybe prefer to be with me than with someone else. To share in the fun times and carry some of the load.

Paul Manville is articulate, and he has a firm philosophy of life:

> I am one to allow someone their ideas or their thoughts on something. I have mine in many cases. That doesn't mean I go around and

try to sell them to everyone I run into who gives me an opportunity to state them, anymore than I'm going to ram them down somebody's throat as the only way to look at a given set of circumstances.

Paul does occasionally invoke concrete examples from his experience. He says of his wife, for instance, that she "wanted to be owned," to act "like we are one. I kept saying, no, we are two and we are working together as one." He uses these experiences, however, to ground the fixed policies with which he confronts the world. He declares to the world what kind of person he is, as if to say, "take me or leave me."

One could also describe Paul Manville's use of culture by saying that he frequently substitutes abstract cultural formulas for experience, rather than using them to understand or interpret experience. This insulation between conventionalized cultural expressions and evocation of his own life experience comes through, for example, in the following discussion of "honesty" in relationships:

> One of the worst things that can happen [in a relationship] is jealousy, and deceit. I guess some of the best things, conversely, would be openness and honesty where thoughts and emotions are concerned without fear of reprisals. To me a marriage or a good relationship would be one where I felt like the woman were one of my best friends in addition to being my lover.

Paul then notes that he can be "brutally honest": "if someone doesn't want to know then I don't think they should ask the question, because I don't want to be put into the position where I'm expected to lie to save somebody's feelings." If he had an affair and his wife or girlfriend didn't know, he would probably be honest even if he knew she would be hurt:

> I'm not going to rush right over and tell her, but if she asked me about it, I'd tell her the truth.
>
> Q.   And if she didn't?
>
> I'd probably tell her anyway.
>
> Q.   You'd probably tell her anyway, even though you know it would hurt her?
>
> Yeah. If she were to find out a year or two years later from somebody else, she's not going to feel very good about me. And I would expect that. [small laugh]

If the situation were reversed, he is unsure whether he would want to know. "There are a lot of people who advocate that if you're going to be indiscreet I don't want to know about it. If it's thrown in my face, yes, I have to deal with it. I would just rather not know about it." Does this mean that he really doesn't believe in honesty after all? No. He concludes, "I think you're better off—to be honest."

Here Paul Manville can consider the logistics of the problem of honesty—weighing the advantages and disadvantages of various tactics. This run-through of a hypothetical situation also reflects his experience, since his marriage broke up in part over the issue of jealousy and mutual trust. But this schematized drama about whether and when to be honest remains hypothetical, insulated from the personal experience whose lessons it seeks to convey.

Paul Manville's philosophy derives from his life experience, but his interpretation of that experience has hardened into clichés and formulas—"own or be owned"; "fear of reprisals"; "best friend" as well as "lover"; and many others ("If I want to smile at a pretty girl, I want to smile at a pretty girl . . . "). Such formulas convey the sense of a person belligerently presenting his exterior to the world, clarifying where he stands by declaring what he stands on. He does not seem to be using culture actively to understand his own life.

The key to Paul Manville's cultural style is his sense of certainty, which makes it unnecessary for him to revise his ideas in light of changing experience. Paul, like Nora Nelson, conveys no sense that he is actively working out how to live.[9] For several years Paul has avoided involvement, engaging only in "casual" relationships. But he has now stopped pursuing these as well, because he "got tired of being a runaround." He does not embrace his current life as fulfilling or meaningful, but he is not striving to change it either. He has learned painful lessons without yet integrating them into a new organization of action.

Paul Manville is disillusioned with his past experience of love, but he has not committed himself to an alternative (even being a "runaround") that might fully displace it. Indeed, he stands curiously distant from his current life, unwilling to invest it with wider meaning. Thus although he has elaborated a complex worldview, he is not engaged in actively revising it to accommodate or explain his ongoing experience. Rather, principles abstracted from that experience have become firm policy about what he does and does not want in relationships.

The detached but elaborated philosophy of Paul Manville and Nora Nelson's simpler culture of affirmation remain distanced from experience for similar reasons: neither is engaged in transforming a self or reworking an approach to life through culture. They use culture primarily to defend a stable orientation to the world rather than interrogating experience in light of cultural aspirations or searching for new cultural possibilities to interpret their experience.

INTEGRATING CULTURE AND EXPERIENCE

Teresa Dreyer, the committed Catholic wife and mother we met earlier in the chapter, illustrates a fuller integration of culture and experience. Perhaps the very strains she alluded to in her marriage—worries about money, occasional tensions with her husband—contribute to her sense of actively working to have a better marriage, to understand herself and her relationship, and to place her marriage in a larger cultural context.

A rich integration of culture and experience is also possible, however, for those who, like Paul Manville, don't currently have what they regard as a satisfying life. Jeannie Shore, twenty-nine and single, is still looking for a fulfilling career and meaningful romantic involvement. Nonetheless, she uses culture in a remarkably dynamic way, constantly linking culture and experience.

Settled in neither a career nor a marriage, Jeannie Shore remains tentative about the meaning of her life, invoking neither the transcendent ideals that seem to animate Teresa Dreyer nor the refrain "I'm happy" that sustains Nora Nelson. Jeannie sees herself as having little experience on which to base views of love and marriage, and she has no firm belief system to draw on. But she does actively use cultural meanings to understand her experience; and she continually reworks her ideas in its light.

Jeannie Shore selects from the commonsense culture around her to construct an understanding of love. But she also draws on interpretations of her own experience, even though she has never had what she would call a "real" love relationship. She is, instead, poised to engage a life whose outlines are not yet clear. In contrast to Nora Nelson, for whom "happiness" provides sufficient justification for an unexamined life, Jeannie Shore actively examines her life. She carries on a complex, intense—if culturally conventional—conversation with herself as she attempts to understand her experience in more general terms.

> Well, I don't think I have ever been in love. I've been infatuated. I've been very infatuated, but I don't know if it was love. . . . Puppy love, like I couldn't eat. I was constantly thinking about this person. I couldn't do anything. . . . This has happened three times. The first two times I think was infatuation because I was so—I was in a state that I knew this can't be love. . . . I think I realized it then. This isn't real love because I didn't know how the other person felt. He

probably didn't feel anything like the way I felt, so in that sense I knew it was like puppy love, infatuation. . . . I met someone [two years ago] and there was some of the same feeling, but it was a little more than that too, because I think he really felt something for me too, which in the other relationships I didn't get that much from them.

Q.   How could you tell if that was love or wasn't love?

Well, it was not a lasting relationship.

Q.   How will you know when you are in love? . . . Is it only as you said [whether] it would last for a short time?

Not necessarily. I think if you know that the other person has a feeling, that they care about your welfare, they care about you. If they express those things about you, toward you, you know, they're very concerned about you in an emotional state and physical state as well.

Here Jeannie Shore constructs a vision of love that seems quite concrete and detailed, even though she claims never to have experienced it herself.

Jeannie uses the idea of love to describe the kind of lasting, mutual relationship that can become a marriage. Indeed, with very limited first-hand knowledge, she nonetheless develops many of the same understandings of relationships as do others who speak from more experience. In describing a "good relationship," she seems to echo Teresa Dreyer, Nora Nelson, and others long married:

When two people respect each other. They respect each other as people, as individuals. They don't stifle a person or try to possess a person. They just let the person be as they are. They don't try to change a person. They accept a person as they are, with faults, without faults.

Jeannie Shore has made conventional cultural images her own. Even without direct experience, she has inserted an image of herself—her own likes and dislikes, her own imaginative anticipation of what love will be like—into her picture of love relationships. But this outline also remains deliberately indefinite, providing cultural equipment for someone who is keeping her options open:

Q.   How do you imagine a relationship with a man? What would it be like? Have you met anybody like that?

Not yet. No.

Q. And you can't think of any?

Oh, I think it would be real nice to be swept off my feet—that kind
of love. But when I mentioned before about respect; it would be
someone who has a good sense of humor and can laugh about things,
be serious when you have to be serious too.

Because from her own point of view her life is not settled, Jeannie
has given it a great deal of thought. As she sees it, her crucial problem is to
become a more autonomous person, "seeing myself as myself and not as
part of my parents' family, their daughter, but . . . developing myself as a
person, as me, not as an extension of my parents." This struggle is not resolved. "I think that's something I'm still trying to work out, to develop as
me, myself, and not as when I'm with my parents." Developing a sense of
"what I want to do with my life" includes finding a more satisfying and
more lucrative career and "developing new friendships with people, and
establishing more relationships with people."

Jeannie Shore is consciously aware of searching for cultural resources for the different possible directions her life may take. As she describes it, "I think I grew up thinking that I would be dependent on a male,
and in a sense I still am. I'm still somewhat dependent on my father finan-
cially. . . ." She had thought that at some point she would marry and then
she wouldn't "have to worry about money. But that's not true. That's probably why I'm so concerned about my career . . . because I don't know if I'll
get married, or when I'll get married, and I have to look out for myself."

With relatively little life experience but an active, if uncertain, life
project, Jeannie Shore uses culture to evaluate her life in terms of her ideas
and to reformulate her ideas to understand her life. It is not that she is an
exceptionally deep thinker or draws on an especially rich culture. In fact
she uses neither a religious tradition (she is Jewish but "not religious") nor
an explicit therapeutic ideology to understand her experience. But she
does actively rework her commonsense understanding, directly relating it
to her experience and reformulating that experience in its light. She used
to feel, for example, "that you had to look a certain way for a man to be attracted to you. . . . But then, I think, . . . some of my close friends feel this
way too, we don't have to break our backs and radically change our personality for a man. It's not really that important."

I guess I could see when I was in college, especially, there was some
guy that I really liked. I'd see the type of girls that he'd go out with,
and I'd say, how come I'm not like those girls. Then from that I think
I could see that you don't have to change yourself to be like other

people just for that person. People will see you as you. You don't have
to go around changing yourself for other people.

Jeannie's thought that perhaps she need not change herself to please
a man is only one of many small efforts she has made to redefine her sense
of self, especially in response to her changing estimate of the likelihood of
marrying. But her specific views are less important than her continuous
attempt to use culture to rethink her life.

The contrasting cultural styles of Nora Nelson, Paul Manville, Jeannie Shore, and Teresa Dreyer suggest that understanding how culture ex-
erts influence on individuals requires not only analyzing cultural content—the particular symbols, meanings, and ritual practices upon which
people draw—but also the variations in how people link culture and experience. Broadly speaking, these four people share a very similar culture,
or at least similar cultural elements. Paul Manville, Jeannie Shore, and
Nora Nelson largely agree that love requires giving the other person support without constraining him or her too much (although this is more of
an issue for Paul than for Jeannie or Nora), while Nora and Teresa Dreyer
share a deep commitment to Catholicism and to their own marriages (although Teresa has taken from her Catholicism the idea that her commitment to marriage and children fulfill God's purpose for her, while Nora
has drawn no such conclusion from her religious beliefs). Nora and Teresa
both use the language of love to describe why their marriages are good
and right; and they, like Paul Manville and Jeannie Shore, are conversant
with the dominant middle-class understanding of love as a relationship
between two people who remain separate yet share, support each other,
are friends as well as lovers, and so forth (although they vary in the depth
of their allegiance to the therapeutic ideals of honesty and communication). Jeannie, who has never had a "real" love, and Teresa, who deeply believes that she has, both see love as sharing weaknesses as well as strengths,
accepting the other person for what he or she is.

This broad agreement, however, is as much a matter of all floating
in the same cultural soup as actually being committed to any common
understandings that would constrain action. And since individuals vary
not only in what they draw from the cultural repertoire but in what they
do with whatever culture they take up, examination of these cultural
agreements and divisions must be complemented, as I have tried to do
above, by analysis of the different ways people hold and use their culture.
And full exploration of these issues in turn requires attention to how integrated and coherent versus how diffuse and divergent is the culture with
which people grasp experience.

CULTURAL COHERENCE

The more and less examined lives we have considered so far have been lived largely without reference to a conscious ideology that is expected to guide daily life. Many Americans do not have such a worldview, but for those who do, examining one's life is considered to be a continuing obligation. At the same time, not every overarching ideology in fact produces a coherent, internally consistent worldview, and some people develop basically coherent ideologies on their own. By looking first at several evangelical Christians—who are at least in principle obligated to lead their daily lives according to a coherent set of religious meanings—we may perhaps say something about what difference a strong, well-organized ideology makes in the way people link culture and experience.

Involved in her church, her family, and her marriage, Judy Crossland, a mother of two who works part-time as an office manager, leads an ideologically guided but relatively unexamined life. Raised in an evangelical church, and still close to the family and the rural community in which she grew up, Judy believes that the Bible provides an absolute standard of right and wrong to which she must adhere. Nonetheless this coherent religious tradition does not give Judy herself a unified, self-conscious worldview. She takes its teachings so much for granted that she does not feel their pressure. Morality is a given based on "the whole way I've been brought up and the Christian doctrine that I've always heard. It's all a part of both of our lives. There's no problem with what we consider right or wrong."

To Judy Crossland, her life with her husband seems precisely what her religion requires of her. Good Christians marry, remain faithful to their spouses, give priority to family life, are honest in their dealings, and do not use drugs or profanity. This conventional morality separates a Christian life from a non-Christian one. The Bible also says one should be law-abiding—"there's Scripture about if you're a servant, you are to serve your master and you're supposed to serve him as well as you can. That's applicable to the laws of the land, basically." So Christian living fits easily with conformity to the surrounding legal order.

Judy Crossland's religious beliefs do not bind her action at every point; indeed, in some quite important matters she reserves the right to follow her moral intuition even when it conflicts with God's commands:

Q.   Do you take the standard of right and wrong as being pretty absolute, like it's what the Bible says or what Christ wants you to do?

It depends on whether it's something that's fairly absolute. The Bible
is really very specific on divorce, but I'm not going to condemn
someone for getting divorced. That's not my prerogative.

Q.   But you wouldn't do it even if your marriage were pretty bad?

I can't say that. I really can't. I can't ever imagine it in the marriage
that I'm in, but if I were married to someone else, I don't know.
I would hope that I would never have to come to that decision.

Judy can thus feel religiously justified in doing what fits her commonsense
understanding, even when she cannot quite justify it religiously. Thus,
keeping someone alive "on a machine in the hospital and they are basically a vegetable, I don't see anything wrong in unplugging that machine.
Most of the times they should never have been on the machine to start
with." She knows that this violates the principle of being law-abiding, but
"even though the law says it's wrong, I don't think God intended us to do
that. That's playing God. Of course you can say not putting him on the
machine is playing God too, I suppose. I don't know."

Judy Crossland "doesn't know" how to reconcile the biblical injunc-
tions with her moral principles about euthanasia or divorce because she
doesn't need to know. She feels firmly enclosed in an upright life that as-
sures basic conformity to her Christian ideals.

Judy's Christian commitments do, however, affect her life in specific,
delimited ways; at these points she consciously uses her beliefs to guide her
action. For example, she considers it a mild sin when she goes "through a
yellow light when I know I should really stop. I drive sixty, not fifty-five,
most of the time. I tend to have a heavy toe." She is sometimes aware of
giving in to temptation, but these battles with sinfulness are small ones:

Sitting down to a good meal can feel right, but if you sit there for an
hour and keep stuffing yourself, that's a sin. I mean gluttony is a sin,
let's face it. You eat what you need to eat. There's quite often I get up
from the table and I know I've overeaten, but it sure felt good at
the time.

She can also identify specific instances of immorality and act on her obligation to avoid personal wrongdoing. As an office manager, "I wasn't responsible for it, but [my boss] wanted to do some things that I just felt
weren't really right. I made sure he knew that I felt they weren't right. . . .
Most of the time I convinced him to change it—to do it my way, if he
stopped to think of it." She also participates actively in the fellowship of

her church, driving a sick congregant to the doctor or baking cookies for a Bible-study class.

Although her life seems permeated with religious meaning, Judy Crossland operates largely within an unexamined, commonsense framing of experience. Unlike Teresa Dreyer, she does not spontaneously interpret central aspects of her life in specifically religious terms. Judy instead evaluates her life primarily in ordinary terms: "I'm happy. Is that a good enough measure? I'm not a real deep thinker, . . . I'm more a day-to-day type person. . . . I guess I'm happy and we're satisfied." She describes the meaning of her life through detailed recountings of its background. Explaining why she married the person she did, she tells the story of how she and her husband met, when and where she used to see him, when she brought him home to meet her parents, when she realized she "had never felt that way before, that going out with someone [else] was wrong," when and where he actually proposed, how they decided on a wedding date, what she wore, who came to the wedding, how they arranged the room and the pastor, and so forth. This courtship, vividly recounted after fourteen years of marriage, is deeply meaningful, but that meaning radiates out from its particulars.

Judy Crossland's Christian principles frame her life, but in a very particular way. Her religious beliefs signal her participation in a distinctive social world, set off from the surrounding society. A boundary separates specifically Christian from non-Christian conduct, and she attends to the details of daily life that mark that boundary.[10] The boundary is defined by adherence to traditional morality, which emphasizes the importance of a stable marriage and the priority of family life, among other things. Thus she finds it anomalous that the man she works for can be both "Christian" and less family-oriented than she: "He works twenty hours a day. . . . He's a Christian guy also, but right now, that's his focus." But for Judy, ideology relaxes inside the boundary of a Christian life. Her way of life is right and good, demarcated from specific, wrong ways of living. Yet her faith has little to say directly about most of what happens within that life.[11]

Does a self-conscious ideology then necessarily make a difference in the ways people formulate their experience? How does Judy Crossland's use of culture differ from Nora Nelson's? Each uses culture to justify a commonsense world, but for Judy the frame is much more substantial, and therefore has a more constraining influence on the life it frames than does Nora's commonsense culture of "happiness" and "love." For Judy Crossland, her belief system stands out in her everyday world, given salience by her church's explicit attention to faith and practice. Her belief system is also more sharply drawn, so that at particular points her beliefs make specific demands on her life. Nonetheless, Judy's religious beliefs mainly affect her by sustaining her general conviction that the life she leads is a Christian one (see Sikkink 1998).

Judy's husband, Howard Crossland, an earnest agronomist, applies his Christian faith more pervasively to regulate the details of his daily conduct. Unlike his wife, Howard tells a unifying "conversion narrative," a story of how, as a youth, he lacked sufficient self-control and risked damnation, and of how his acceptance of a personal relationship with Christ has helped him "do good to your fellow man, to refrain from immorality, to refrain from illegal things."

Like his wife, Howard Crossland draws a broad social distinction between a proper Christian life, the kind he leads, and the worldly values that surround him. As for Judy, this distinction between Christian and non-Christian living is tied to adherence to conventional morality. Thus when a colleague at work claimed to be a Christian, "it became obvious to the best of my judgment that he was not," when the man lost control under pressure, using "foul language and abuse to people."

But Howard Crossland's Christianity does more for him than draw a boundary around a world ruled by convention. It provides a unifying belief system that he attempts to apply to all aspects of his daily life. Howard seeks out opportunities to remind himself of the demands his religion places on him. He is thus frequently aware of his religious convictions as a guide to day-to-day action. Law-abidingness—paying his taxes honestly, for example—and keeping control of his emotions both seem to him direct consequences of his faith. A coworker, he explained, "couldn't figure out why I hadn't completely blown my top when they blew about a three months' research project for me." But while "through human levels" he may be tempted to lose his temper, his religion teaches him not "to try to change things that are unchangeable."

The most important demand Howard Crossland's religion makes is the obligation to love others selflessly. He says, "I have a sign hanging in my bedroom, 'Love is when another's needs are greater than your own.'" He watches for conflicts between what he wants to do and what would help others, the boundary between Christian and worldly conduct, so that he can enact his obligation to love others:

> I usually try to consider somebody else's needs instead of my own. A typical example, after setting up this appointment [with the interviewer] it would have been more convenient for me to have had it in the evening. I assumed it would be better for you, . . . and I thought, no, it's O.K.

> I do this in my work relationships. I tend to take a more difficult road for myself within reason, if it works out better for somebody else.
>
> [Judy] called me asking about eating [dinner out] together [to celebrate a promotion]. It kind of messed up my evening and some other things, but she came up and we went out to dinner. She had something to celebrate and she wanted me to celebrate with her. I'm not highly emotional. I could have gotten along just fine by going home and fixing me and the kids something, but we went out to eat.

This vigilance makes Howard's religious ideology a continuous presence, infusing his daily life with meaning. Despite a settled sense that "I've changed avenues a little bit, but I've always known who I am, and a general idea of where I'm going," Howard's beliefs require a great deal of him. He frequently reminds himself that he could behave selfishly, that he could be tempted to lose his temper, that problems in a marriage could make it easy to walk out. Thus he continually regenerates the experience of moral choice, finding opportunities to interpret his life in religious terms.

This search for moral issues that highlight adherence to Christian principle is, of course, a professional pastoral activity for evangelical Protestant ministers. They attempt to mobilize a community and delineate its boundaries through both external and visible as well as internal and personal experience. These ministers illustrate both the attempt to articulate a coherent, all-encompassing worldview and the ways even such a professionally managed ideology can lose its coherence in accommodating itself to everyday life.[12]

One evangelical pastor described all the problems of modern society in Christian terms. The "looseness and a lowering of standards," the high divorce rate, and working mothers were all problems that Christian commitment could avoid. But for him, adherence to Christian faith also promises practical benefits. "The ones that I see, that I find satisfied and fulfilled and happy, are the ones who have tried to apply their faith to their marriage and lived out their faith." He moves cheerfully from the deepest symbols of his faith to the certainty that life will be better for the committed Christian:

> It was love that caused [Christ] to give His life to make atonement for man's sin. That's part of our belief. Scripture says, husband love your wife that way. So it's giving of oneself toward one's mate. Well, when a man treats his wife that way, most women respond to that warmly. . . . When I see couples applying such Scripture in their marriage with an emphasis on a love that gives of itself to the other person, I find them

happy and fulfilled and able to handle the stresses of life much better than the ones who don't have that kind of foundation.

Such an ideological specialist is, of course, experienced in casting his commonsense observations in the terms of his faith. Thus he recognizes that problems occur in marriages "in five or six major areas, again and again." One member of the couple may be more religiously committed than the other; sexual infidelity, alcohol, financial difficulties, and lack of communication can all disrupt marriages. But these problems either have "a spiritual basis," as do infidelity and alcohol use, which can be overcome by commitment to Christ; or, like misunderstandings within marriages, they can be resolved by the pastor's intervention to help the couple communicate about "the differences they have brought to their marriage."

Here the use of religious meanings serves as a pastoral strategy, promising a better life and describing in religious language the vicissitudes that common sense would describe in slightly different terms. He emphasizes that Christians are different by suggesting that their faith can resolve the personal difficulties that baffle others.

When the evangelical pastor was asked how the young people in his church differed from older generations, he used religious ideology to define away troublesome experience:

> I'd say the ones that are mature in their faith that basically their values
> are the same, because it's based upon the truths of the Holy Bible,
> which are for us timeless. They haven't changed. . . . If a Christian has
> accepted Christ as his personal savior, as the one who brings him to
> a right relationship with God, and has accepted the Bible as an objec-
> tive standard of authority for faith and practice, and that's been so for
> two thousand years, then there really should not be any difference be-
> tween a couple in their fifties and a couple in their twenties, because
> both of them accept the fact that love . . . is going to be patient and
> kind and not bragging, giving the other person the benefit of the
> doubt.

This sort of surface ideological coherence, apparently produced for public consumption, sacrifices resonance with everyday experience in favor of theoretical principle.

Another evangelical minister pursued ideological coherence in a different direction. While he too found it necessary to make compromises with worldly interests and ideas, he pushed hard the attempt to apply a consistent ideology in everyday life. He argued that "there is a love that we can have for other people that is generally selfless. We have to learn it. It's actually a matter of the will." He offered several examples of applying the principle of love even in difficult circumstances, attempting to teach people to live out the implications of their faith. He described one church member who was being forced out of an upper-management position in a large corporation because of a conflict with one of the higher executives:

> And I'm trying to help her to see how to love that person. . . . I said, "O.K., in the way that you love him you're going to have certain thoughts, because you may be right. It really may be unjust. But according to the teaching of the Bible . . . you don't always take your right when it's your right. . . . As Jesus showed it, there are some times when you yield a right out of love for the other person, because that's part of the sacrifice. So I say, you can start loving this guy."

The pastor accepted that even his unified belief system must sometimes accommodate the demands and opportunities of the secular world. Asked whether in competing for promotion within a company the Christian should lovingly stand aside, he replied,

> I'd say, let's talk about that and try to get some wisdom on that. Because on the one hand, I would say, "O.K., I think you ought to consider just saying to that person, 'You have a lot of good qualities and that job is a possibility for you. I'm going to commit myself not to step on you to try and get this job because my belief in what God wants is more important than my personal ambition.'" At the same time, there is room, I think, for positive, healthy competition. . . . I think you could love that person and say, "I'm really going to try for this position . . . because I think I can do it." So I think you can blend them, and sometimes this is very difficult.

Although trying to live out a coherent worldview is especially characteristic of ideologically ordered communities such as Christian sects or radical political movements (Berger 1981), such attempts can be found in more mundane settings. A construction worker, Ben Carpenter, for example, is deeply dissatisfied with his present way of life. He aspires to an ideal of independence, self-reliance, and contact with the outdoors that he is currently unable to realize. But he has a remarkably coherent image of what a good life should be. Approaching his thirtieth birthday, he finds he is not where he wants to be—"you know, where I thought I would be when I turned thirty." He wants to change jobs and move to a more rural area:

> Quality of living. I don't believe that my children have the quality of living that could be provided in a less populated area. I keep thinking

about all those rats that they experiment with, and they go crazy
when they're overpopulated.

Describing a job he wanted but did not accept because the area was too
isolated for his wife, he combines lyrical appreciation of nature with a love
of independence:

> Where I had my job, I was going to be running an [operation] with
> only the [absentee owners] above you, and it was all rolling hills with
> pine, with tons of pine trees and lakes everywhere, Indian reserva-
> tions. It was dynamite, in the mountains.

Ben Carpenter's belief in independence pervades his views on many
subjects. He rejects what he sees as the hypocritical religiosity of his parents, saying, "I'm religious, but I don't go to church. I pray at home by myself. I don't need a church anymore." He wants to teach a kind of skeptical independence to his children:

> Responsibilities? Well, I have responsibility now with children that
> came with marriage because we both wanted children, and I have the
> responsibility to raise them to be thinkers. I don't want them to grow
> up believing everything they see. I want them to be able to reason. I
> want to set a good moral example if I can so that they'll be morally
> good children—won't be criminals and crooks.

Ben shares the individualist voluntarism that is common among
these interviewees, but he holds it more consistently and carries it further.
Asked what people owe those they love, for example, he says,

> I owe them my love. That's all I owe them. I don't owe [my wife] any-
> thing and [she] doesn't owe me anything. We're together mutually
> because we want to be. It's not because I owe her. . . . Anything we
> give we give because we want to, not because we have to. Like I didn't
> have to come home from work today to take care of the kids. I
> wanted to so that she could get some rest.

Ben Carpenter sees himself as consciously trying to live out a particular moral vision. Asked whether he wants any more children, Ben replies,
"No, two is enough. Two is morally just. I just don't think it's right to have
more. Too many people." He longs to get away to the wilderness where he
can hunt and fish. He hates having to take orders. Yet he is insistent on giving priority to his family, even though it meant sacrificing the job in the
isolated rural environment he craves. But asked what would constitute an
ideal society, he replies, "A true socialist society, utopia. I'd like to see no
more big business. Big business tramples on individuality, as much as they

claim they're for individuality. I don't mean communism. I mean socialism, where everyone contributes what they can and everyone receives what
they need."

Many elements of Ben Carpenter's worldview come from the same
pool of ideas that other interviewees share—he believes that trust and
communication are central to a good marriage, that "if you love someone
you have to trust them" and that trust includes accepting that his wife is
"an adult" who "has a right to grow and that goes with the trust." He accepts that if both people in a relationship are to grow "you have to make
the relationship change to make it work or otherwise it will fail." And he
echoes Ted Oster in his summary view of right and wrong: "If I feel good
then it's right. If I don't feel good, then it's bad."

Nonetheless, for Ben Carpenter the usual elements of an individualist worldview jell in a particularly unified and consistent way. He doesn't
just adduce various individualist formulations in accounting for particular elements of his life. He actually pursues a relatively coherent philosophy of life that he consciously attempts to follow. Sometimes, certainly, he
makes compromises. He wasn't able to take the wilderness job he wanted
because his wife was too afraid of the isolation. He has held his construction job for seven years even though he hates the lack of autonomy. But he
applies a kind of unified individualism consistently across many areas of
his life, from the nonchurch religious training he gives his children, to the
hunting and fishing trips he loves, to his systematic plan for eventually getting his family out of what he regards as the corrupting, unhealthy world
of the city.

People vary greatly in how much their cultural resources are linked
under a unifying ideology. While even the most impassioned ideologues
tolerate some slippage between their ideas and their lives, nonetheless
some people do make conscious attempts to fit their lives to their worldviews. Still others operate with much more fragmentary and incomplete
systems of ideas, working less hard to make ideas and experience correspond. Starting from a unified cultural tradition maintained by a cohesive
group is one way to come under the sway of a coherent belief system, but
the case of Ben Carpenter illustrates that cultural coherence may also be
developed by employing available cultural elements in a particularly consistent way.

CONCLUSION

To think about the relationship between ideas and action, we may return
to the work of Max Weber (1968), who most closely examined when and

under what circumstances ideas become a powerful force in human action. For Weber, culture influences action by shaping people's motives—the ends they seek and the means they deem adequate to achieve those ends. But not all culture is equal in the way it shapes action. Ideas have greater influence when they develop a "rational image of the world and [represent] a stand in the face of the world" (Weber 1946a:282). In Weber's view, ideas that remain unsystematic and fragmentary are likely to have little independent influence on action (see Bellah 1964). Only relatively rationalized systems of ideas are autonomous and coherent enough to channel people's psychological and practical motives in the direction demanded by the ideas. Cultural and religious systems also vary in the degree to which they encourage, or even make possible, applying ideas to specific aspects of everyday life. Calvinism (Weber 1958a) was unique not only because it was a highly rationalized, unified worldview but because it generated powerful motives for applying religious meanings to daily life.[13]

If the Weberian approach to cultural analysis makes sense, the dimensions of culture we have examined here—how much culture people use, how much they integrate their culture with their experience, and how coherent or unified is the culture they employ—ought to be crucial ones.

I have tried in this chapter to suggest a range of connections between culture and experience, or rather a range of patterned ways that people use culture to structure that experience. I have argued that various kinds of abstract culture—ranging from common sense, through traditional cultural symbols, to systematic ideologies—may be used to bracket experience, to infuse it with multiple layers of meaning, and sometimes to transform it. I have also explored some instances where culture remains segregated from experience, rather than penetrating it.

I have suggested reasons why some of the people I interviewed used culture differently than others did. Culture seems, for example, most disengaged from experience when people have, in some sense, frozen their sense of self in relation to the world, and when they are socially more isolated. Greater interpenetration of culture with experience seems to occur, at least for these middle-class Americans, when there is an attempt to change the self (or to maintain a changed self) and when a person is a member of an active community of discourse that both permits and forces its members to articulate wider meanings. We have also seen how even a more systematically articulated ideology, like that of evangelical Protestantism, can be used in highly "settled," conventionalized ways, to separate the church community from the wider society and to reinforce individual Christians' sense of commitment to their faith.

Earlier chapters have tried to show that people keep "on tap" much more culture than they actually use. Thus people possess culture of very different sorts—that which is actively part of current experience and that which is held in reserve, so to speak. In this chapter, I have suggested that people vary also in the ways they integrate culture with life experience, and that they may change over time and across life spheres in the ways they draw connections between culture and the lives they actually lead. But before we can understand how culture influences people, even in so intimate and important a sphere as that of "love," we must examine what people use their culture for. Only when we understand culture's uses will we be in a position to consider when and how culture actually governs experience, when it simply provides the color or tone to everyday events, and when and why in some circumstances people adopt culture that actively, directly shapes their conduct.

CHAPTER 4

CULTURED CAPACITIES AND

STRATEGIES OF ACTION

Why does culture make a difference in human action? If cultures provide diverse tools or repertoires of meanings that people use in varying ways, and if people differ in how seriously they take their culture and how richly they deploy it, to understand how (and when) culture shapes action, we need to analyze how people actually make use of culture—what they use it for.

This will temporarily take us away from the analysis of love talk, since how people use culture to organize actions, emotions, and decisions concerning love depends in part on how they use cultural materials to construct a self in the first place. Thus this chapter focuses on materials that highlight self-forming, the way culture is used to construct, maintain, and refashion the "cultured capacities" that constitute actors' basic repertoires for action. In later chapters we will see how those cultured capacities are mobilized in the realm of love.

People use culture to learn how to be, or become, particular kinds of persons. Such self-forming (see Greenblatt [1980:1–9] on "self-fashioning") utilizes symbolic resources provided by the wider culture. Through experience with symbols, people learn desires, moods, habits of thought and feeling that no one person could invent on her own.[1] Symbols also provide people continuing access to their inner lives—awakening, stimulating, or heightening capacities for judgment and sensibility. Culture equips persons for action both by shaping their internal capacities and by helping them bring those capacities to bear in particular situations.

It may seem strange that one needs culture to learn how to be a certain kind of person. But people do use culture, sometimes self-consciously, to become the persons they aspire to be.[2] Howard Crossland, the self-sacrificing agronomist we met in the previous chapter, describes just such a process in the development of his Christian faith. Raised in an evangelical Protestant church in a small, Midwestern farming community, he used its teachings to discipline himself. During his high school years, he accepted religious training on pragmatic grounds: "I think all of us kids went to Sunday School at least until the high school age, so I did too." He "needed the training" to control "a little more drinking than I should of" and "a little hell-raising," potentially threatening vices: "my father—usually almost exclusively restricted to the weekends—would drink heavily.... [T]he weekends were not the happiest part of the week for us. Some of this stuff [religious training] would build a foundation on how you would avoid some of this."

In college, however, this serious young scientist came to feel differently: "I had not been living up to my religious teachings, and certainly didn't have a one-on-one relationship with Christ. And I guess in all fairness I would say ... I always had a little fear of death out there, and I guess I probably initially accepted Christ and the Christian faith partially out of love and partially out of fear—eternal damnation." His earlier religious training had left a gap. It "maybe left my life, shall we say, this is sort of a paradox, a little freer to do as I pleased the rest of the week. Whereas the relationship which I developed then, I could see it had to be part of every minute of each day, and I could see a greater help through prayer and through simply following the teachings of the Bible, help to make various decisions." The help he needed was moral, like the firmness not to cheat even a little on his taxes, making "the fine line a little more black and white." But he also needed help in controlling his feelings—not losing his temper or being misled by the ups and downs of human emotions: "Because I've the Bible to study, it points out it's not really relying on your emotions. There are certain facts presented and you accept the facts. Like God loves me, even if I'm having a lousy day and I don't feel like He loves me, but it says in there that He loves me, so I can accept that as a fact." Thus an aspiration for self-control—seen as the alternative to dissolute living—led this young man to seek out religious experiences that could justify, motivate, and sustain a disciplined life. Of course, his very notion of the disciplined self he could be, the possibility of having and thus desiring such a self, also depended on culture. Without his childhood religious experience and the polarity it established between moral laxity and self-restraint, he might never have sought the inner discipline his deepened relationship with Christ could offer. But when he sought to sustain and strengthen that self, he used culture to do it.

This strict Christian asserted that he could not accomplish his goals alone: Getting your "life all put together . . . is pretty close to impossible doing it on your own. . . . First of all you accept God, then he gives you help to do this—to do good to your fellow man, to refrain from immorality, to refrain from illegal things." Howard's insistence that he relies on God's help conforms to evangelical Christian doctrine, but what his religious understanding makes explicit is true of all cultural experience. Becoming a certain kind of person is learned, practiced, and sustained through culture.

CULTURED CAPACITIES

What, then, are the capacities cultures impart to their users? The first, as I have already emphasized, is the capacity to be a certain kind of self. Trained capacities to think and feel, what Geertz (1973b) has called "moods and motivations," enable one to adopt a line of conduct and carry it out. To be guilt-ridden about wrongdoing, passive before authority, or infuriated by insubordination may be crucial parts of a self that can carry out particular lines of action (Greenblatt 1980). More important still is the internal organization of the self (see Swanson 1971)—whether, for example, one resonates to the moods of others and can enter a trance state at ritually appropriate moments (Geertz 1973b; Swanson 1978) or resists blending the edges of the self into the psyches of others (Elias 1994; Taylor 1989: 305–90; Arditi 1998:54–85). Such internal capacities shape the kind of life one can construct.

Second, culture helps people internalize skills, styles, and habits. These include all the things one can be "good at," from practical skills like knowing how to dress in a suit, converse with a new acquaintance, or take a standardized test; to subtler matters such as keeping a poker face when enduring social humiliation or exploding in violence when one's honor is violated.[3] Indeed, such skills and habits constitute much of what we actually mean when we observe that someone differs from us culturally or when we feel culturally out of place in an unfamiliar environment. Not knowing how to bow correctly in Japan, or worse, not having any habitual sense that bowing is natural or appropriate; not thinking to discover who in a group is older or younger than oneself and to modulate one's forms of address appropriately; feeling violated when one's privacy is invaded, or rather when there is no privacy—all these are important signals that one

lacks the cultured styles, skills, and habits that fit one for a particular social world (Hamabata 1990:1–25; Kondo 1990).[4]

Habits are hard to build and easy to take for granted. But without
appropriate habits one can have great difficulty adopting a particular line
of conduct. To take a regular job, for example, one must ordinarily have
habits of time-consciousness. That means owning a timepiece and remembering to look at it, setting the alarm at night, getting up and dressed
in the morning, having a reliable way of getting to work, and so forth.
Without such routines, meeting a regular schedule can be a daunting task.

Harder to see, but just as significant, are skills for evaluating the social and material world, from the way fifteenth-century Italian merchants
gauged the volume of odd-shaped containers (Baxandall 1972), to the cali-
bration of obligation and loyalty or honor and insult,[5] to what is so important to middle-class Americans—the assessment of individual character.

Much of our active engagement with art, literature, sports, story-
telling, and gossip involves exercise of such cultural skills. When Kenneth
Burke (1973) writes of "literature as equipment for living," he does not
mean that people use the plots or characters of novels as direct models of
how to live. But if a homemaker who reads gothic novels is not in fact
learning how to be a terrified virgin heiress, and teenaged moviegoers are
not studying to be vampires and robots, at least some of their pleasure
nonetheless comes from exercising cultural skills important for their ordinary life activities, particularly those of evaluating the character of individuals. From the most serious fiction to the most implausible soap opera,
our dramas revolve around crises and challenges to character.[6]

We enjoy analyzing personality and interpreting motives because
character matters to us. In a voluntarist, market society, we present ourselves to others as individuals with a certain kind of character that guarantees our performance, trustworthiness, or inclinations (in the same
sense that knowing someone's lineage might be thought to guarantee his
conduct in a more family-based society [see Collier 1997; Derné 1995]).
We also depend upon our ability to evaluate the character of others. In
most fictional dramas, of course, there is ultimately an "answer"—about
what kind of person someone is, how she will behave at a critical moment
of decision, what will destroy or redeem her—in a way there seldom is in
real life. But these urgent questions about what kind of self one has, and
how to interpret other selves, are highly charged for us because so much
rests on them. Cultural experience sharpens those capacities of judgment
and response important to our everyday lives.

Third, as Margaret Archer (1988) among others has suggested, culture marks group membership. People use culture to delineate group

boundaries and to signal membership to other group members (DiMaggio 1987), to differentiate themselves from others (Bourdieu 1984; Lamont 1992; Lamont and Fournier 1992; Waters 1990), and to establish and maintain alliances (Barth 1969; Cohen 1974). As with the evangelical Protestants we saw in this chapter and the last, the use of culture to mark group membership can reinforce its power to shape distinctive kinds of selves.

Finally, culture offers ideas and images that constitute a view of the world. In some cases, people organize their lives according to elaborate theories of what the world is really like. But others with more interpersonally rooted lives (based, for example, on loyalty to allies or friends) may find such a larger ideology both unnecessary and uninteresting. As Geertz (1973b:99–108) has argued, worldviews—including scientific theories, religious beliefs, and folk wisdom—give persons the continuing conviction that they know enough about how the world works to act with some confidence within it. But in stressing culture as the antidote to the chaos of meaninglessness, Geertz again overemphasizes cultural coherence. It may be much less important for people to have a coherent worldview than to have enough different beliefs to adapt to most contingencies without losing the conviction that somehow the world makes sense.

It is easiest to see how culture works where people use it most explicitly and self-consciously.[7] Art Townsend, co-pastor of a liberal Protestant church, sees himself as "modeling" for his congregation the new ways of acting that he has discovered through Marriage Encounter and other brushes with the ethics of personal authenticity. Indeed, a full description of his worldview would recapitulate much of the self-actualization ideology of the "me decade" of the 1970s (see Tipton 1982). In this youthful minister's description of his stance toward life, we can trace out the complex cultural retooling—a new sense of self, incorporating altered ways of feeling and judging experience; new styles, skills, and habits of action; and changed views of the nature of the world—that allowed him to enact new ways of being in the world.

Self

Art Townsend attributes his changed mode of action to a new view of himself as a minister, a "professional lover": "the thing that is hardest for me to do is . . . to love myself, to allow myself to be lovable." Learning to love himself then changed his attitude toward everyday problems: "It means that when I mess up I do not go through my own neurotic trip of beating myself up. I simply have at it again. I simply get up on my feet and go forward, and don't judge myself for having made a mistake."

Sustaining a confident self that will not be hampered by its mistakes is a matter of active cultural work—involving a new model of human nature and new rituals for untangling the knotted parts of troubled selves. Art encourages a new emotional attitude toward "problems." For a confident self, eager to "grow," "problems become the playground of consciousness. . . . There are some days I just feel really jazzed up and excited about problems. It's like 'Yum, yum, give me another problem!'" He confronts sadness, guilt, and self-blame with a belligerent cheerfulness epitomized in his advice to "lighten up" as the road to "enlightenment." He refuses to accept congregants' moral self-denunciations, their "cross of roses." "If they keep crucifying themselves again and again, they are not going to find a whole lot of support. They come in with that hang-dog look and all that suffering, and I say 'How wonderful! How great! That really is spectacular!'"

Art Townsend teaches those who organize their conduct around moral rules and guilt over transgressions to think and feel about themselves in new ways. Accepting, loving, and also laughing at oneself are the beginnings of a recycled humility, in which one is readier to admit weaknesses because they do not seem so drastic. More important, one gives up guilt and accepts "responsibility" for one's life. "Responsibility" means thinking of the self not as "right" or "wrong" in terms of objective moral rules but as having "choices." Speaking of his work as a marriage counselor, Art notes that many couples come to him when one spouse has already decided to leave and just wants out "without getting anything on them." He counters by emphasizing responsibility for choices:

> What we begin to explore is first all the baloney that "I did everything I could." Because nobody has done everything they could, ever. Even when things are working, they haven't done everything they could. So let's get off of that and enable people to experience their own feelings and get in touch with their own desires, and decide what they want, and what they are willing to do.

The helpless self has no place in Art Townsend's scheme; what really counts are the choices people make. Indeed, the responsible self is nearly omnipotent. "It's up to everyone to decide their own path, you see, because you can do life in such a way as to end up getting yourself smashed, if that is your unconscious desire, and the truth is that you don't have to do that."

Art Townsend wants his parishioners to learn a differently organized sense of self, to "shift out of the mode which has expectations into the mode which has intentions." He attempts to "place strategic dynamite charges around expectations—blow the expectations aspect to smithereens," because expectations are "doomed to be disappointed," while "an intention empowers your life." He suggests that a coherent moral life can emerge from knowing clearly what one wants (an intention "will unfold, and you'll have a sense of whatever is . . . appropriate for that intention"), rather than from moral rules about what one should do or be.

Styles, Skills, and Habits

The new self Art Townsend proposes is connected to new social skills and styles. Accepting oneself and nonjudgmentally loving others supports a particular style of dealing with conflict. This style depends on a changed interactional etiquette even as it redefines such elemental concepts as "thoughts" and "feelings."

The neatest trick in the culture of authentic communication is the redefinition of "feelings." In part a redescription of the self's interior, it is even more a rewriting of the rules and a reeducation in the skills and habits of interaction. A feeling "is different from a thought or a judgment. The problem is that most of the time I was using the words feel and think interchangeably." A feeling is simply an internal state, and in that sense one person's feeling need not threaten, frighten, or upset another. If, for example, a couple have "a commitment to explore feelings together and to experience what the feeling feels like to the other person," then sharing a feeling—even one like revulsion or anger—can draw them together rather than drive them apart:

> Tell your mate what it feels like: "Where do you feel it in your body? Does it have a temperature? Does it have a texture?" You get into a deeper level, and what happens is that feelings draw together . . . and you actually, literally feel the feeling the same way the other person feels it. And when you do there is a shift, there is a zing, and it is like the two become one.

The counterculture of the 1960s left a legacy of "psychobabble"—a language about "communication," "sharing feelings," and "hearing" one another (Katriel and Philipsen 1981). In Art Townsend's explication, we can see how this language supports new interactional skills, which in turn permit new ways of dealing with others (see Swidler 1979; Tipton 1982). These skills are bathed in a global style of optimism, directness, and careful attention to others, marked by such interpersonal habits as gentle smiles, extra eye contact, and welcoming nods in situations that might produce grimaces of irritation in more conventional interactors.

Worldview

The new style Art Townsend advocates is sustained by the doctrines of a large, if loose, worldview.[8] As he tries to reeducate his parishioners (and the interviewer) in new habits of thought and feeling, he shows how a new worldview can foster the styles, skills, and habits for a changed self. In Art's vision, honestly communicating selves can ultimately reach interpsychic agreement—the "zing" in which "the two become one"—because they are in fact parts of a mystically unified cosmos. He argues, "if . . . you honestly try to connect who you are with who the other person is, you cannot lose. You see, the joke is that we are all connected anyhow on a level that we do not see. . . . When you and I have a struggle and disagreement and want to go to war, what I am doing is punching myself in the nose."

Happily borrowing from Eastern mysticism, Christianity, and the pop culture of the 1970s, this liberal Christian believes that the world is fundamentally good. His mystical monism supports the notion that he is responsible for everything, since everything is ultimately him. But he also experiences this responsibility as a psychological truth: When he feels hurt, "It is my hurt. How is it going to be theirs? I may have helped them to precipitate behavior that I have chosen to be hurt in response to. But it is my hurt." In what is perhaps a distant reverberation of Calvinist predestination, he also believes that whatever happens to people is ultimately for their benefit. "If I feel hurt, there is some part of me that needed to feel that. I have experienced in my life that there is nothing that happens to me that is not for my own fulfillment—for the fulfillment . . . of my higher self."

Art Townsend slips easily into a half-heretical Christianity, positing a benign world in which the possibility of evil has been all but eliminated. In this cheery mysticism, the full flowering of the good in every person is only a matter of time: "Somebody that says, 'I don't need other people yet . . . I have not an appreciation for other people,' simply hasn't reached the level where they have discovered that yet." Everyone is "growing," even those who seem not to grow fast enough to find their better selves in this life. "Sharing some of my weirdness in terms of . . . traditional Christian orthodoxy . . . , if I thought God were such a being that He would waste a human soul on the basis of its mistakes, essentially in a fifty- or sixty-year period, that would be a little limiting."

STRATEGIES OF ACTION

Someone like Art Townsend, who is in the process of trying to incorporate (and teach others) elements of a new cultural repertoire, exemplifies important ways people use culture: to become a certain kind of self; to learn styles, skills, and habits; and to support these with a larger worldview. Now we must return to the question of how culture actually influences people, shaping their social relations and their thoughts, feelings, and action.

For Clifford Geertz (1973b, 1973d), the central aspect of a culture is its "ethos"—a mood or feeling, embodied and reinforced by symbols, made to seem reasonable by a worldview that it in turn makes plausible. The tone, mood, or feeling of a people's life is a pervasive tint, like the filter that suffuses a film in rose tones, lights it with golden highlights, or shades it a menacing gray. But the cultural influences in the lives of the people we have examined so far do not seem to operate in this indirect, all-encompassing way. These people switch the cultural framing of a problem, often in midstream. They are passionate about some things, laid back about others. They use culture to evoke some moods and suppress others, to bring some capacities of the self to the surface while others are kept in reserve, to work at solving some life problems while leaving other issues unexamined. The implication that culture affects action largely by shaping its ethos, coloring life by diffusing outward from a few intensely hued ritual moments, implies a culture both more unified and less complex in its operation than the culture we actually observe.

An alternative view, which traces its lineage from Max Weber's work on the social effects of ideas, suggests that culture influences action by shaping the goals or ends people seek and the means they think will get them there. In Weber's famous metaphor, ideas are like "switchmen." While interests provide the motivating force or engine of action, ideas frequently determine "the tracks along which action has been pushed by the dynamic of interest" (Weber 1946a:280). In this formulation, human beings are goal-oriented actors, pursuing their interests as they understand them. But their culture shapes the ends they seek and the means that they think will attain their ends. Thus culture affects action by providing its ends and constraining its means.

The Weberian view of culture's influence became dominant in American sociology through the work of Talcott Parsons, who adopted Weber's basic analysis of how culture shapes individual action. For the "ideas" that concerned Weber (complex historical entities like Protestant doctrine or the Confucian worldview), however, Parsons (1951, 1961) substituted "values," ultimate ends of action that provide the ever-unreachable ideals that define particular societies. Sociology made an essential contribution to the analysis of action, in Parsons's view, because the economic image of a rational actor was incomplete without a sociological account of where actors derive their ultimate ends and their beliefs about which means are legitimate.

The Parsonian view of how culture influences action is enormously appealing intuitively because we often think of ourselves as goal-oriented actors and, especially in America, we are likely to give an account of why we act the way we do by speaking of our "values." But as sociological explanation, such a view is theoretically implausible and empirically inadequate (see also Joas 1996:148–51). First, the assumption that culture shapes people by shaping their values is not supported by evidence. If deep, enduring values were dominant factors in individual behavior, we should expect people in changed circumstances to continue to pursue traditional values, perhaps using new methods to achieve their goals. In fact, we observe precisely the opposite. People change their ends relatively easily in new circumstances—for example, immigrants seeking individual wealth and prestige in market societies, while they may have sought family continuity and family honor in their homelands. What tends to have more continuity is the style or the set of skills and capacities with which people seek whatever objectives they choose (see Swidler 1986).

Values-based explanations of how societies differ face similar empirical difficulties. Western scholars used to take satisfaction in explaining Western economic development by contrasting Western values—achievement orientation, egalitarianism, universalism—with the more otherworldly, particularist, ascriptive values of non-Western or "traditional" societies. Weber argued that Protestantism, especially its Calvinist variants, channeled the desire for salvation into a distinctive set of motives that encouraged rational, methodical action to master the world. Protestantism contributed to the development of rational capitalism by encouraging accumulation of wealth as a sign of salvation while restraining the enjoyment of that wealth, by fostering methodical economic calculations of profit and loss, by promoting honesty and predictability in business practices, and by encouraging hard, disciplined work. In contrast the otherworldly, mystical Eastern religions led away from rational economic action by focusing human motives on mystical escape from the world and devaluing methodical action in the world (Weber 1958a, 1968; Marshall 1982; Schluchter 1981).

But it is precisely here, in the comparative analysis of economic development, that cultural explanation focused around ends or ultimate values has failed most dramatically. Researchers in the Weberian tradition have been embarrassed by their success in finding functional equivalents to the Protestant ethic in non-Western societies that Weber would have considered otherworldly, mystical, or otherwise averse to rational economic activity. If there was an initial triumph in discovering independent religious sources of a transcendental, ascetic, and potentially rationalizing ethic in one remarkable non-Western modernizer, Japan (Bellah 1957; Ikegami 1995), the replication of such parallels has undermined the very argument for the unique causal influence of Protestantism (see Eisenstadt 1970a).

Is culture then unimportant? Far from it. Non-Western societies' encounters with the West have everywhere produced a surge of cultural activity (see Wuthnow 1987:221–47)—from the cargo cults of Melanesia (Worsley 1957), revitalization movements among Native Americans (Wallace 1956), and revivals of religious traditionalism in new nations (Geertz 1973j), to the Marxist ideologies of China, the Soviet Union, and much of the Third World. Faced with the challenge of the modern West, late-developing nations have *constructed* ascetic, this-worldly, modernizing ideologies, fusing borrowed elements with cultural resources their own traditions made available (Gerschenkron 1966; Wuthnow 1980). Chinese Communism (Schurmann 1970; Madsen 1984; Walder 1986), Islamic scripturalism (Geertz 1968), and other nationalist ideologies (Gourevitch 1979; Hannan 1979) have developed as indigenous movements for ascetic rationalization.[9] Cultural fervor—ideological and religious—has everywhere propelled the transformations modernizing societies seek.

Culture, in fact, drives contemporary social change, but not in the way conventional sociological models suggest. Rather than pursuing enduring traditional values, many contemporary Third World nations have generated powerful, transformative ideologies. Culture shapes these societies not through values but by furnishing a repertoire of capacities for action that can be mobilized to achieve new objectives.[10]

The argument that culture influences action by supplying its ultimate ends or values is also problematic on theoretical grounds. To claim that people act so as to maximize culturally determined values is misleading in somewhat the same way as the claim that they maximize "interests." Both views see human beings as choosing their actions one at a time, in light of their interests or values. Both views also assume that having the skills or capacities to act in a certain way is unproblematic, so that all persons need ask themselves is, "What do I really want?"

Hans Joas (1996) has formulated an alternative to the model of action as goal oriented. Drawing on the work of John Dewey and the American pragmatist tradition, he argues that goals and means are in fact chosen reciprocally. "Only when we recognize that certain means are available to us do we discover goals which had not occurred to us before" (p. 154).

Joas conceives "perception and cognition not as preceding action but rather as a phase of action by which action is directed and redirected in its situational contexts" (p. 158). The implication of this view is that "our perception of the world appears to be structured by our capacities for, and experiences of, action" (p. 158). For Joas, the human body is the basis of "pre-reflexive aspirations and tendencies" which orient people to situations. "It is the body's capabilities, habits and ways of relating to the environment which form the background to all conscious goal-setting, in other words, to our intentionality" (p. 158). Action, in this understanding, is inherently situational. "Every habit of action and every rule of action contains assumptions about the type of situations in which it is appropriate to proceed according to the particular habit or rule. . . . [S]ituations are not merely a neutral field of activity for intentions which were conceived outside of that situation, but appear to call forth, to provoke certain actions" (p. 160).

People do not, indeed cannot, build up a sequence of actions piece by piece, striving with each act to maximize a given outcome. First, people would be crippled if they had to think about each action they performed. Like dancing, but much more complex, orchestrating one's day-to-day life must be learned so that it "comes naturally." People develop habitual ways of acting, so they do not trip over their feet while deciding what steps to take (Camic 1986; Joas 1996). Culture provides the capacities that make such complex orchestration possible. Second, people organize action over time. Individual actions do not make sense by themselves, but only as parts of larger patterns. And culture has its effects not by providing the ends actors pursue but by shaping the patterns into which action is routinely organized.

I call these larger patterns "strategies of action." These I define as ways actors routinely go about attaining their goals. Thus my focus is on "means" rather than ends. I argue that the skills and capacities necessary to pursue a line of action have greater influence than their objectives in determining how people will actually act in new situations. (In stable situations, strategies and ends of action may appear so fused that one cannot disentangle them.) And, finally, I emphasize the flow of action over time. Culture affects action by shaping that repertoire of routine, natural styles, skills, and habits that together organize and sustain a strategy of action.

Strategies of action are general solutions to the problem of how to organize action over time, rather than specific ways of attaining particular ends. Relying on alliances with family, developing one's individual capabilities so as to do well on the job market, joining a gang and protecting its turf, developing a wide network of casual acquaintances, building a group of fictive kin with enduring mutual loyalties—all these are characteristic strategies of action of some groups or individuals in our society. But few people rely exclusively on one such strategy. A person may, for example, cultivate capacities that make her good at her work, but at the same time develop informal relations of mutual help and support that are likely to make any given job more secure. In the American middle class, people prepare themselves to earn a living, maximizing their individual marketability, while also maintaining kin and community ties that provide the solace and security that markets do not (Hewitt 1989). Often the demands of varying strategies of action conflict (as investments in marriage versus career often do for women [Gerson 1985] or heading for college versus maintaining street-corner attachments did for Italian slum youth [Whyte 1943]). Nonetheless, both individuals and groups attempt to maintain diverse repertoires of strategies of action, within the constraints set by the investments and commitments each of these strategies demand.

A strategy of action provides one or more general ways of solving life's difficulties—solutions that may be applied to a variety of problems.[11] I argue that a person's available strategies of action shape the kinds of goals he or she pursues, instead of the other way around.

The phrase "strategy of action" may seem to imply rational calculation, or a utilitarian model of action in which actors are motivated by the pursuit of interest. But I mean the phrase in just the opposite sense. What people want is a product of the cultural shaping of their capacities for action. And those capacities for action are organized into generalized strategies of action.

Strategies of action necessarily depend on culture. Cultural experience shapes the sense of self, the styles and habits of acting, and the larger beliefs about the world that allow individuals and groups to construct and enact particular life strategies. Culture then influences social action because it supports or limits the strategies of action people can pursue.

Strategies of action are also inherently social. Not only do people depend on the wider society for cultural resources that shape their capacities for action; strategies of action make sense only within a social world. A strategy of relying on kin may depend upon distinctive cultural capacities—the ability to feel guilt and induce it in others, skill in mobilizing family rituals that reinforce bonds of loyalty and obligation, a sensitivity to others' hurt feelings. But such a strategy makes no sense except where others share similar expectations and where the aspirations and obligations one feels can be reciprocated. Similarly, the skills and capacities of a market actor make little sense without a market. But the strategies-of-action perspective differs from more usual anthropological interpretations of the "fit" between culture and social organization. It stresses that individuals maintain cultural capacities for varied strategies of action which they mobilize differently in different situations; and it suggests that the cultural influences individuals and groups carry into new situations are those that form their capacities for action—not their ends or goals.

ACTION

To see how a set of cultured capacities can be mobilized to support a new strategy of action, we may return to the articulate, self-actualized pastor, Art Townsend. The new cultural capacities Art has learned make possible changed patterns of action. As he describes it, "integrity and responsibility" mean not evading problems but dealing with them as they arise. Sharing feelings, converting expectations to intentions, and practicing integrity and responsibility support new strategies for dealing with the social world.

The most concrete manifestation of these new strategies is Art Townsend's changed relationship to his church. "The shift is that I no longer treat the church as an employer.... An employee does not keep telling the boss about his inadequacies . . . but the church is really a part of me and I am part of the church, and my shift professionally has gone from how can I please them and make them like me so that I can keep my job and get a promotion, to how can I love them. . . . How can I help these beautiful special people to experience how absolutely wonderful they are." A new formula is then at work: having learned to love himself, Art no longer hides his fears and failings, but joyously shares them as a source of "enlightenment" for his congregation. "I tell them on Sunday morning what is going on. It fills the church with this wonderful energy . . . and everybody is laughing. I mean they laugh out loud. Lightening up is one of the steps to enlightenment." This youthful pastor's willingness to express vulnerability makes him a confident teacher, rather than an anxious employee of his congregation. In the ultimate service profession, Art Townsend has developed a new basis of pastoral authority over his flock.

Art Townsend also uses his new style to resolve difficulties more general than those of marriage or ministry. To see the ethic of "integrity and responsibility" in use, it is instructive to examine this pastor's account of an incident in which he "acted without integrity": His church had agreed to host one of a series of interdenominational retreats in collaboration with other churches in the area, having repeatedly made clear to the church hierarchy that, since their facilities were small, they could invite only another small church. After weeks of negotiation, despite "a very,

very clear, polite no, explaining the reasons why," the hierarchy simply informed them that the retreat was set with a much larger church. Art reported:

> So I came in this morning, and rather than dealing with the issue and sorting it out, what I did was to stomp around for a while saying "they can't do . . ." See already my shift, "*they* can't do this to us." See already the thing starting to crumble, and wasted about twenty minutes of energy stomping around, calling people on the phone, and kicking asses, making them wrong. What I experience now is that wasn't necessary. It didn't move toward a resolution of the dilemma. And some part of me even knew at the time that what I was doing was not contributing to a solution, but contributing to the development of the problem.

The alternative approach Art favors involves a willingness to pick up where one is and move on, not trying to affix blame but looking for ways to solve the problem. Perhaps people could eat out in the church courtyard, or they could borrow the facilities of a larger church up the street. But the possible solutions are less important than his view that his righteous anger "was wasted energy. It was wasted energy."

This fluid strategy substitutes empathetic communication of needs for fixed expectations and obligations. It thus presumes an essentially benign context of similar, sympathetic others, with whom it is possible to reach mutually satisfactory understanding. Indeed, this strategy of action is an ideal addition to the repertoire of a middle-class service professional like Art Townsend, who deals almost exclusively with others like himself (see Tipton 1982). This style may also appeal to his Silicon Valley parishioners, who must manage complex social relationships in a fluid social world, with variable, hard-to-define standards of conduct. They may particularly appreciate devices for psychic self-restoration in a world where anxiety over possible failures or regret for past mistakes can be a debilitating drain on one's energies.

Art Townsend, who makes his living by talking about how to act, articulates with unusual clarity the cultural supports for a strategy of action. He describes learning to see himself in a new way, defining new feelings and experiencing new moods and motivations. He also expresses a new style of interaction, framed in language borrowed from the human potential movement. He has learned skills and habits that allow him to reorganize his own conduct (through forming "intentions" while refusing to become bogged down by "problems") and to negotiate relations with others (by sharing feelings without judging; by searching flexibly for solutions rather than "making them wrong"). And finally he has developed a new world-view, in which the underlying harmony of a unified cosmos guarantees the eventual fulfillment of human possibility.

The new culture Art Townsend has learned has reshaped his action not by providing new values or goals but by giving him new capacities to act. (And, indeed, as the examples above show, his new strategy of action is an addition to his existing repertoire; he can still "kick ass" as well.) A strategy of action involves a characteristic way of solving problems and characteristic sets of problems to be solved. Such strategies depend on skills, styles, habits, and capacities for organizing self and action that are learned through culture. Such skills, I have argued, are essential for pursuing a line of conduct and for adopting the interests or values that one could maximize in that line of conduct. Culture constrains action because people can most easily construct strategies of action for which they already have the cultural equipment. When people develop lines of action, they start with the repertoire of things they already know. Implicitly they ask, "Who am I? What am I good at? What do I know how to do?" [12]

Despite its rational sound, a strategy of action does not imply rational calculation. Once a person has integrated the elements of a strategy of action into his or her behavior, they become ways of orienting oneself to or evaluating situations. A strategy of action may lead one on occasion to make elaborate calculations—"Should I invite my cousin's boyfriend, and risk my friends feeling offended that their boyfriends were not invited as well? Or should I invite my cousin without her boyfriend, knowing that she will be hurt, even though she would never say anything?" But it is organizing one's life in one way versus another—through a network of reciprocal obligations to kin and friends, or through an individualized career—that constitutes the strategy of action. Outside the context of such a generalized life strategy, particular calculations based on either "interests" or "values" make little sense.

Within an established strategy of action, however, "values" do come into play as important guides to action. Indeed, one of the cultural resources that help people to enact a strategy of action is a set of "values" that orient important choices within that strategy. If a person's strategy of action is to develop professional competence in a world based largely on back-scratching and mutual favors, he may frequently consult his "values" to remind himself that the pursuit of professional competence comes first. Values *are* important. But values are not the reason why a person develops one strategy of action rather than another. They are not, so to speak, the originator of the chain of "reasons" why someone acts as she does. Instead, values are one of the many cultural resources, like other skills and habits, that allow persons to enact strategies of action. Commitment to particular values, including the ability to consult them and to apply them to specific choices, is one of the cultured capacities that make a strategy of action possible, rather than the cause of the adoption of that strategy.

The model I propose might also be called an "identity" model of how culture works. The fundamental notion is that people develop lines of action based on who they already think they are. This is true in two senses. First, as I have been saying, actors' capacities shape the lines of action that they find possible and promising. The second sense in which mine is an identity-based model is that a great deal of culture operates by attaching meanings to the self. The term "identity" usually implies a more unified self and a more inward-looking psyche than I wish to evoke. Precisely the point of an adequate identity model would be to point out that what is experienced as the "self" and its cultural resources or capacities is constructed very differently in one historical period or social situation versus another. Natalie Davis describes, for example, the "autobiographies" of sixteenth-century French women who wrote about themselves (in the third person) within histories of their families (actually their husbands' lineages) (Davis 1986). But even in a world in which (exaggerating a bit here) lineages are real and individuals aren't (see Meyer and Jepperson 2000), the acting, experiencing person will be engaged by matters that affect the group with which she or he is identified (see Honess and Yardley 1987; Hogg and Abrams 1988; Abrams and Hogg 1990, 1999).

Identity in contemporary popular understanding refers to some essence located deep within the person. But of course most identities are much more institutional and collective than that—one's identity is one's totem, tribe, lineage, nation, or village. As will become clearer in chapter 8, the focus on a personal identity that contemporary Americans take for granted results from social codes and practices that define us to ourselves and others, not from anything inherent in individual personhood. Nonetheless, a great deal of culture is organized by and about identities, both individual and collective. The self's capacities for action and the capacities for action of collectivities shape potential strategies of action and thus in turn influence the ends they are likely to pursue.

Strategies of action are the major links between culture and social structure. Culture powerfully influences action by shaping the selves, skills, and worldviews out of which people can build life strategies—strategies made possible in turn by culture. But in periods of social change, when new cultural understandings and new strategies are being tried out simultaneously, culture persists when the strategies it helps to sustain can flourish within extant social-structural constraints. It is in this sense that culture and social structure exist in complex, but not impenetrable, interdependence. In the next chapter we will investigate the different ways culture is binding (and thus independently influences action) in stable versus less stable periods.

CHAPTER 5

SETTLED AND

UNSETTLED LIVES

Culture shapes the diverse capacities out of which people build strategies
of action. But the way culture influences action—and
the way people use culture—differs in two kinds of situations, which I call "settled" and "unsettled." In describing individuals, we may think of settled and unsettled
lives; in describing societies, of settled and unsettled periods. The contrast is intended to differentiate situations
in which new strategies of action are being developed
and tried out (unsettled) from situations in which
people are operating within established strategies of action (settled).

Culture influences action in both settled and unsettled situations, but its influence is of a very different
sort. When people operate within well-established strategies of action, they can live with a loose fit between culture and experience. In unsettled lives, however, culture
is more visible—indeed, there appears to be "more" culture—because people actively use culture to learn new
ways of being.

American teenagers, for example, often live, rather
than simply listen to, their music (Frith 1981; Gaines
1991), while many adults retain the musical tastes established when they were young. After young adulthood,
music, like existential questions about the meaning of
life, becomes more a pastime and less a passion. Being
swept away by cultural experiences, from religious conversion to rock concerts, seems mainly an activity of the
young.

Young people are voracious culture consumers because they are still trying out (and trying on) the possible selves they might become. They are in the process of forming and reforming strategies of action, developing the repertoire of cultured capacities out of which they will construct the patterns of their adult lives. They seek out the shaping, and the shaking up, culture can offer. Both the chameleon-like cultural involvements of adolescents, in which they try out multiple styles,[1] and the intensity of those involvements, tell us something important about how culture works in unsettled lives—for people who are in the process of constructing or reconstructing strategies of action.[2]

This intensified use of culture to reconstruct one's life is evident in the experience of Brian Palmer, a successful San Jose businessman. After his wife left him, he began to rethink his life, using culture in new ways:

> I live by establishing plans. I had no plan for being single, and it gave
> me a lot of opportunity to think, and in the course of thinking I read
> for the first time in many, many years. Being an English major, I ob-
> viously liked to read. I got back into the habit of reading—to the
> point of reading two novels a week. Got back into classical music for
> the first time since my college years. I went out and bought my first
> Bach album, and a stereo to play it on.

When he was shaken and unsure, but also free to consider new opportunities ("young bodies parading around the swimming pool," "smoking grass for the first time in my life," and "mostly the thinking process of being alone and relating to my children"), Brian was drawn to cultural pursuits that had not engaged him during his settled adulthood.

Brian Palmer's story also illustrates the limitations of the usual ways we think about culture's influence on action. After a period of unsettledness, this successful business executive underwent what he describes as an important change in his "values"—tied closely to a new marriage to a woman very different from his first wife. From focusing exclusively on career success, he committed himself to family life:

> Two years ago, confronted with the work load I have right now, I
> would have stayed in the office and worked until midnight, come
> home, gone to bed, got up at 6:00, and gone back in and worked until
> midnight until such time as I got it done. Now I just kind of flip the
> bird and walk out. My family life is more important to me than that,
> and the work will wait, I have learned.

Thus values, at least in the sense of the goals around which he organized his life, were not the major sources of continuity in Brian Palmer's life. What persisted were old strategies with which he pursued his new values. In fashioning a new life, he drew on his existing repertoire of cultured capacities—the self, skills, and worldview he already had available. He continued, for example, to organize his life in terms of challenges to be met. The man who explained his career success by saying, "I decided I would really like to test myself in the big league," then tested himself in other arenas: "I have two stepchildren living with us now, and my three natural children, and I try every day to do something with each one of them. Just to share a little bit because it makes me feel good and it makes them feel good. I like it."

This driven executive's response to the breakup of his first marriage reflected his usual approach to problems. "Being a compulsive problem solver I analyzed the failure. I don't like failure. I'm very competitive. I like to win. So I went back and reexamined where the thing broke down and found that I had in fact contributed at least 50 percent and, depending upon the vantage point, maybe 99 percent of the ultimate demise of the institution." This rethinking and the "humbling" experience of being the single parent of "three big boys" led to a reassessment of his values, but in a way that drew on his existing cultural style:

> I was operating as if a certain value was of the utmost importance to me. So I asked myself how important is that value in relation to, say, value B, and the answer was, hey, it's not really all that important, so let's quit playing that silly game with ourself.

The greatest challenge of all was his second wife, Maryellen—a "human dynamo" and, that "anachronism," a "practicing Christian." "I just became totally enthralled with her entire being. She's a very creative and artistic person. She paints. I like to paint too. She's a much better painter than I am. She can do anything."

> Whereas I felt intellectually superior—superior in almost every way—to my ex-wife, I feel no better than a peer, and in many cases inferior [to Maryellen]. She's a challenge in every way. Just to keep up with her is a challenge. . . . If I had six of her on my staff, I could get rid of twenty people. That's how efficient she is. It's just unbelievable, and I admire that in people. . . . While dinner is cooking she'll write a letter, bake a cake, write [another] letter, and sew cuffs up on a pair of pants. . . . While I'm cooking dinner, I cook dinner.

Brian's values shifted from concentration on his own success to sharing both time and love with his new family. But his way of organizing his life—around challenges—and his style of understanding that experience—full of lists, percentages, and priorities—remained very much intact. Thus Brian Palmer illustrates both the way culture becomes more salient when people are seeking to reorganize their lives and the way in which even such reorganized strategies draw largely on an existing repertoire of cultured capacities.

Nan Pfautz, a divorced woman in her forties with a secure administrative job, provides another example of how people's cultural involvements intensify when they are reordering their lives. But she also demonstrates how incompletely new cultural capacities alter people's repertoires, which continue to include older cultural styles and strategies which they seldom fully replace.

Nan Pfautz, like Brian Palmer, reacted to the breakup of her marriage by turning to the wider culture in search of insight. "*The Prophet* by Gibran—his thing on marriage is that you don't become one, but you're two pillars, standing side by side in support. I thought, now that's what I believe. I really believe that, instead of this 'as you get married you put your two candles together to become one candle,' that you're one person, and all this old concept." Her new view seemed true from her own experience—"I knew that wasn't right for me anymore. You can't become one, because I'm the one that loses the one. I'm the one that's the zero."—but she could formulate it only when she had found the right cultural terms.

Helped by *est* and Fritz Perls, *Passages* and *The Prophet,* Nan Pfautz developed a new style, and a new strategy, for dealing with love relationships. "I don't think it was a conclusion that I came to on my own at all. It was a slow process from these various things that I was hearing." For years she kept a quotation from Fritz Perls on her wall:

> I do my thing and you do your thing. I am not in this world to live up
> to your expectations, and you are not in this world to live up to mine.
> You are you and I am I, and if by chance we find each other, it's
> beautiful.

Nan was trying to get over the earlier pattern that had dominated her relationships: "I seemed to want to hang on to people too much. . . . I wanted them totally to be mine, and I wanted to be totally theirs, with no individuality." She had seen the Fritz Perls quote and "I looked around until I found a copy of it. . . . I studied that for so many years, and I think I needed it at the time." Later, however, she came to feel that "there's a hole in it": "A real relationship to me is that you care enough to keep checking in on how the other person's feeling, and how they're doing, how they're growing, what's going on—and caring about that." At one time in her life she had needed the Perls quote: "I really needed to keep my individuation, and I felt that was how I did it, was to keep reminding myself." After she had consolidated a greater sense of individuality, she grew dissatisfied with Perls' image of relationships without commitments. As did Brian Palmer, Nan Pfautz made active use of cultural materials when she was reorienting her life. When her line of action became more settled, her cultural involvements became more muted and less visible.

These reformulations of Nan Pfautz's understandings of love relationships took place against a background of other cultural assumptions that were never brought into question. Thus, even during a period of personal struggle to change her way of dealing with relationships, most of her cultural repertoire remained unchanged. For example, like many middle-class Americans, she took for granted that what happened to her as a child—parental love or the lack of it—shaped her adult life in inescapable ways. This popular Freudianism provided one apparently natural way of understanding self and others, and of acting on the self to solve problems. Thus in thinking about the painful "fantasies" a current love relationship inspired, Nan debated whether those feelings were irrational legacies of a rejecting father, or were instead accurate signals of "something that I really need to realize isn't right for me." She assumed that accurately reading her psyche's unconscious messages would help her know what to do. While such assumptions rested on clear cultural foundations, they no longer required active cultural support. Psychological self-scrutiny was part of her established repertoire of commonsense ways of dealing with life.

Culture takes a more explicit, coherent form when people are reorganizing their strategies of action or developing new ones. For most people, major life transformations—the shift from adolescence to adulthood or the readjustment after a divorce—inspire some cultural rethinking, although people also continue to rely on their existing repertoire of personal and social capacities. Thus both Nan Pfautz and Brian Palmer reacted to divorce by becoming more active culture consumers, even while they used elements of their existing repertoires to fashion modified strategies of action. Brian Palmer retained his competitive, ambitious style, even when he sought satisfactions deeper than those he had found in work. Nan Pfautz developed a new independence, but she maintained both her psychological assumptions about the self and her therapeutic strategies for dealing with personal difficulties.

MODES OF CULTURE'S INFLUENCE ON ACTION

Culture works differently in settled and unsettled lives. In settled lives, culture is intimately integrated with action. Culture is ubiquitous, yet it is difficult to disentangle what is uniquely "cultural" since culture and life experience seem to reinforce each other. It is settled culture about which a theorist like Clifford Geertz (1973b) writes so persuasively: culture is a "model of" and a "model for" reality; culture fits with and expresses ("materializes") a sensibility and a way of life; cultural symbols reinforce an ethos and a worldview, so that each seems to validate the other. William Sewell Jr. (1992), using similar imagery, has written of the ways cultural rules or "schemas" constitute social structures. Actors abstract schemas from familiar structures and then use those schemas to reproduce the structures. I have argued that the fit between culture and structure or experience is in fact much more disjointed and less seamless than Geertz or Sewell imply. But the apparently unproblematic (if almost always also incongruous) integration of culture and experience, in which contradictions and inconsistencies cause no difficulty because no one feels the need to examine them, is characteristic of settled lives—and of the "immethodicalness" of "common sense" (Geertz 1983a:90; see also Billig 1992).

In unsettled lives, in contrast, people use culture to organize new strategies of action and to model new ways of thinking and feeling. Cultural work is more active and its influence is more visible because the new patterns are in tension with previous modes of action and experience.

This contrast is not, of course, absolute. Even in settled lives, people do active cultural work to maintain and refine their cultural capacities. Conversely, even the most fanatical ideological movement, which aspires radically to revamp the cultural capacities of its members, will inevitably incorporate many tacit assumptions from the surrounding culture. There are, nonetheless, more and less settled lives and more and less settled cultural periods. Individuals in certain phases of their lives, and groups or entire societies at certain historical moments, are involved in constructing new strategies of action. It is for the latter situation that conventional sociological models of culture's effects are most inadequate.

Ideology, Tradition, and Common Sense

We may distinguish a continuum of cultural embeddedness ranging from ideology, to tradition, to common sense.[3] Ideology, tradition, and common sense vary in how explicit and self-conscious versus implicit and taken for granted their meanings are.

Comaroff and Comaroff (1991) have made similar distinctions between what they call "hegemony" and "ideology." Insisting that culture is diverse and often fragmented, they "take culture to be the space of signifying practice, the semantic ground on which human beings seek to construct and represent themselves and others—and hence, society and history" (p. 21). But, they insist, not all culture works in the same way. Hegemony and ideology are the "two dominant forms in which power enters—or, more accurately, is entailed in—culture" (p. 22). "Hegemony" is "that order of signs and practices, relations and distinctions, images and epistemologies—drawn from a historically situated cultural field—that come to be taken-for-granted as the natural and received shape of the world and everything that inhabits it" (p. 23). Drawing from both Gramsci and Bourdieu, they see hegemony as the "*dominant* conception" of the world, "an orthodoxy that has established itself as 'historically true' and concretely 'universal'" (p. 23, emphasis in original).

Ideology is more explicit, less embedded, and more open to challenge. The Comaroffs (1991:24) accept Raymond Williams's (1977) definition of ideology as "an articulated system of meanings, values, and beliefs of a kind that can be abstracted as [the] 'worldview'" of a social group. Hegemony and ideology differ in the extent to which they have been "naturalized": hegemony "consists of constructs and conventions that have come to be shared and naturalized throughout a political community," while ideology "is the expression and ultimately the possession of a particular social group, although it may be widely peddled beyond" (p. 24).

The Comaroffs (1991) make one additional point that is relevant to our discussion here. They insist that ideology and hegemony are not to be understood existentially as different types of culture but rather as "two modalities, each associated with a characteristic form of empowerment, within any cultural field," with cultural field understood as "a fluid, often contested, and only partially integrated mosaic of narratives, images, and signifying practices" (p. 27). Ideology and hegemony exist along a continuum of more and less conscious or unconscious, "seen" or "unseen," "apprehended" or "submerged," "cognized" or "unrecognized" (p. 29).[4] The fact that what has been explicit ideology can become naturalized, blending into the authoritatively self-evident hegemonic, and that what has been only partially recognized in experience can be articulated as explicit ideology, makes the distinction between hegemony and ideology dynamic and fluid.

I have dwelt at length on the Comaroffs' distinctions between hegemony and ideology because the continuum they imply is the same one along which I wish to place ideology, tradition, and common sense. Indeed, "common sense," as I use it, is very close to what they call hegemony, and my notion of ideology is also close to theirs. But I also add a third element, tradition, which shares some features with ideology and others with common sense. Like common sense, tradition may be taken for granted, structuring and framing life rather than providing its direction. But like ideology, tradition is very much visible, explicit, palpable, and even sometimes contested. Such distinctions among cultural modalities are not just theoretical niceties. Culture influences action very differently when it operates as ideology, tradition, or common sense.

An ideology is an articulated, self-conscious belief and ritual system, aspiring to offer a unified answer to problems of social action. Traditions, on the other hand, are articulated cultural beliefs and practices, but ones that present themselves as fixed, expected parts of life. Even the "invention of tradition" (Hobsbawm and Ranger 1983) is invention of a distinctive sort. Proponents of a newly invented tradition attempt to "naturalize" it by investing it with the prestige of established usage—not to make it invisible like common sense, but to make it the received vehicle through which social aspirations, including collective identities and individual interests, can be articulated.[5]

Diverse rather than unified, partial rather than all-embracing, traditions may not inspire universal enthusiasm. Some couples have church weddings while others marry before a judge; some adhere to traditional beliefs and practices, others reject them. Some families gather for Christmas and Thanksgiving, while others eat out with friends; and major collective rituals like Fourth of July picnics or Memorial Day parades may be celebrated by only a tiny minority, even if the ritual forms are widely known. A traditional wedding ceremony may seem flat, forced, or even embarrassing. Any given wedding may not "work"—that is, inspire the appropriate emotions or go smoothly. But weddings still provide an established ritual vocabulary in which a new social bond can be forged, group solidarities symbolized, and social loyalties rehearsed—as well as one through which insults can be conveyed, group exclusions marked, and social inequalities displayed.[6] Traditions, whether the routine ones of daily life (Goffman 1959, 1963, 1967) or the extraordinary ones of communal ceremony, establish expected forms of conduct, even when people consciously feel quite disaffected from those traditions.[7]

Common sense, finally, consists in assumptions so unselfconscious as to seem a natural, transparent part of the structure of the world, objectively real and needing no explicit support or elaboration to be true (Geertz 1983a). It is not that everyone agrees about their commonsense observations. Indeed, common sense is replete with contradictory aphorisms, incompatible platitudes, and fluctuating interpretations (see, e.g., Billig 1992). But common sense carries the assumption that people share common terms in which these interpretations can be made.

Ideology, tradition, and common sense are sustained in different ways by practices, and they have different relations to group life. An *ideology* usually defines a community. A group defending its boundaries will develop greater self-consciousness and intensity about its beliefs. The explicit practices demanded by the ideology (distinctive clothing, codes of secrecy, specialized jargon, or ethical strictures) help members differentiate themselves from the surrounding society (see Kanter 1972). In pure form, an ideology is almost always the expression of a sectarian community, whether a commune, a religious community, a political movement, or a nation state.

Traditions also help to define solidary groups. From headgear, to cuisines, to family stories, traditions can display and reinforce group ties. But these groups need not be closed and exclusive. Rather, most traditions display and regulate degrees of loyalty, reciprocity, and obligation. Such rituals as weddings, for example, provide widely shared systems for signaling loyalties and memberships—deciding who will be invited, who will sit at which table, whether the wedding will be held in the bride's hometown, and so forth.[8] Other traditions, from a school's colors to the expectation that the teacher will sit at the head of the class, also emblematize social relationships.

By their solemnity or drama some rituals may also impress the importance of social obligations upon participants. But those loyalties and memberships are usually multiple and overlapping. The groups they define are often not formal communities but informal networks of obligation and loyalty. And while their forms may be standardized, it is the potential for variability within a repeated framework that makes them useful as ways of establishing or renegotiating relationships of membership, relative prestige and power, or personal alliance.

Many traditions are maintained long after their original rationales are forgotten. Like rings exchanged at a wedding, costumes at Halloween, or decorated eggs at Easter, traditions may be given varied interpretations (Fernandez 1965). There is no tight "fit" between tradition and a larger worldview. Traditions are thus sustained more by practices than by beliefs. And the practices are often those that define informal groups (DiMaggio 1987), establishing both hierarchies and solidarities.

Common sense is also sustained by practices, but not practices exclusive to a particular group. Although common sense is partial, fragmentary, and often internally contradictory, it is also pervasive. Common-sense understandings are often shared across group lines—or at least, since common sense proclaims its self-evidence, there is the assumption that it ought to be shared, even if that assumption is rarely tested. Common sense provides the coin of the microworld of face-to-face interaction.

Indeed, what makes it seem true despite its internal inconsistencies is that it is not the exclusive possession of any group.[9]

The practices through which common sense is maintained are those of ordinary conversation. Thus those who have no occasion to speak to one another may have incompatible forms of common sense without being aware of it. But even those who talk frequently tolerate a wide range of observations, ideas, and experiences as common sense, without demanding rigor or pursuing contradictions (Geertz 1983a; Bourdieu 1990). For those settled into established patterns of action, common sense is unexamined; inconsistencies never emerge clearly and are considered unimportant, so that uncertainties and disagreements slip by without requiring a resolution.

Particular cultural conceptions can vary in explicitness and self-consciousness. A religious belief, for example, may be held by some people as ideology, by others as tradition, and by still others as common sense. The scientific worldview, which at its inception was a powerful ideology, has become unquestioned common sense. Over time, ideology can generate both tradition and common sense, but the reverse movement can also occur. Traditions may, under certain historical circumstances, be reactivated as ideology. Geertz (1968:61) describes this process in modern "ideologized" Islam, where people come to "hold" rather than be "held by" their beliefs. Ideology, tradition, and common sense may thus be thought of as phases in the routinization of cultural meanings.

At a more complex level, the distinction is one between more and less fully objectified or "reified" cultural meanings. Culture that seems real, independent of the efforts individuals make to maintain it, is common sense. Common sense appears not to need to be shored up by rituals or enacted by believers in order to remain true. It is "common" precisely because it is accessible to everyone and appears to arise naturally from experience (see Geertz 1983a:91). Common sense has no church or cult.

Traditions, on the other hand, both define and are sustained by collectivities. They require collective effort or group participation. A God demands periodic affirmation from his worshipers. A high school prom or a family reunion retains its power only as long as some group makes the effort to enact it. Traditions like the American belief in individual rights or Jewish traditions of community philanthropy are self-consciously maintained, enshrined in word and deed.

Finally, ideology is the product of continuous, explicit construction. Existing understandings of the world are recast in its terms. Ideological proponents insist that the world be altered to fit the ideology's picture of the true and the good (Mannheim 1936) or they do "ideological work" to bridge the gaps between beliefs and actions (Berger 1981). But ideologies and ideologized religions are also subject to continuing struggles over their meanings and implications. Indeed, any cultural system that insists on a tight fit between beliefs and reality is necessarily vulnerable to challenges.

Unsettled Lives

Periods of social transformation seem to provide simultaneously the best and the worst evidence for culture's influence on social action. Established cultural ends are jettisoned with apparent ease, while ideologies proliferate, influencing action in powerful, direct ways (see, for examples, Geertz 1968; Schurmann 1970; Eisenstadt 1970a; Walzer 1973; Madsen 1984; L. Hunt 1992; Schama 1989; Sewell 1996). In such periods, ideologies—explicit, articulated, highly organized meaning systems (both political and religious)—establish new languages and styles for new strategies of action. When people are learning new ways of organizing individual and collective life, practicing unfamiliar habits until they become familiar, then doctrine, symbol, and ritual directly shape their action.

Ideological communities often demand that members live according to their beliefs. Adherents of a religious cult wear orange, share their property, or attempt to transcend the boundaries of their egos because of their religious ideas (see Berger 1981; Zablocki 1971). Early Protestants simplified worship, scrutinized their conduct, and worked in a calling because of their faith (Weber 1958a). Doctrine and casuistry tell people how to act and provide blueprints for community life. A larger worldview defines the community's special place in the world and gives it a sense of shared mission.

In such situations of ideological contention, matters of ritual practice or doctrine become highly charged, so that statuary in churches (Baxandall 1980), the clothing and preaching styles of ministers (Davis 1975; Zaret 1985), or the sexual mores of countercultural communards (Berger 1981) become fraught with meaning. Rituals and symbols acquire such significance because they reorganize settled habits and modes of experience. When developing new strategies of action, people depend on explicit cultural models to learn ways of organizing selves, relationships, patterns of cooperation and authority, and other capacities for individual and group life.

Such overt, ideological cultures might well be called "systems." While not perfectly consistent, they aspire to offer unified answers to questions of how human beings should live. Adherents seek a close fit between their life experience and their cultural understanding. Culture thus has greater, or at least more obvious, influence over action in unsettled than in settled lives. We shall see, however, that the intense influence of such ideological culture is influence of a peculiarly limited sort.

Art Townsend, the liberal Presbyterian minister we met in chapter 4, provides a good example of both the power and the limits of ideological culture. He is an exception to the general principle that ideologies are worldviews shared by a group, since his views are an admixture of bits and pieces cobbled together from various sources. But he is like other ideologists in that he sees his program of cultural change as setting him apart from the world as it is and pointing toward a new and better day.

Art Townsend is exceptional among my interviewees in the coherence and unity of the cultural commitments he espouses. In part, of course, this is a consequence of his professional responsibilities. Charged with "modeling" for his congregants a new way to live, he articulates this ideal with unusual clarity. But his culture is coherent for another reason—precisely because it is "new." And that newness suggests that his culture does not fully encapsulate him, despite its apparent coherence.

Even Art Townsend's articulateness strikes an odd note. It is as if his views are too self-conscious, too clear, too pat. We sense that a self whose cultural supports are so visible cannot be quite as solid as it seems. And indeed, as Art makes clear, his is a conversion that is still in progress. He can express new ways of feeling and acting—"It's my hurt. How could it be theirs?"—precisely because he simultaneously holds other assumptions—that those who hurt me cause my hurt, for example—which still come quite naturally.

Conventional habits of thought and feeling thus lie just behind Art Townsend's rhetoric, showing us that he is not a Zen monk but a young American newly taken with (and in the business of demonstrating to others) unfamiliar styles. He comes equipped with conventional, middle-class expectations about how people will experience themselves and treat others. These include blaming oneself for one's mistakes, expecting others to accept blame for theirs, and assuming that "feelings" are to be dealt with by doing something about their causes rather than by sharing them as psychic experiences. As he makes clear, he staves off his earlier ways of thinking only with effort, as he struggles to make a new approach his own.

> It's something that is simple, but not easy, and there are some people
> that have incredible difficulty with it, in trying to internalize it and
> make it real for themselves.

Art Townsend's cultural system is "simple, but not easy" because it is doing something for him that we do not always expect our culture to do. He is trying to learn new routines, new habits, new skills, rather than simply exercising those he already has. He is using culture to retool himself, to integrate within himself the equipment for new patterns of action. Thus, his worldview, his optimistic mood, his engaged yet nonjudgmental style, all seem a bit exaggerated—more active, more coherent, more self-conscious than they would be for one to whom this way of organizing action came naturally. His culture has not yet been made comfortable by being lived in, and it carries the burden of building, rather than simply supporting, a style of action. But this is precisely the ideological style of teenagers, converts, and others who are making the effort to assimilate new patterns of action, to establish their routines and shore them up with appropriate beliefs and feelings. Ideological thought—self-conscious, clear, articulate, standing out against ordinary experience rather than settling within it— is the mark of culture that is not fully comfortable and familiar.

We can thus see in Art Townsend both the extent and the limits of ideology's effects on action. Ideologies—highly articulated, self-conscious systems of belief and ritual—claim unified sway over the actions of their adherents. But the intense demands of ideological cultural systems mask the fact that these ideologies are in competition for their adherents' loyalties. In conflict with other cultural models, ideological cultures are coherent because they are defined against existing worldviews, assumptions, and habits.

Ideological systems are thus causally powerful, but in a restricted sense. Rather than providing the underlying assumptions for established ways of life, ideologies make explicit demands in a contested cultural arena. Their influence on action is strong but not deep because, at least initially, such ideological movements do not provide a complete cultural repertoire. Even as they construct new patterns of action, many of their unquestioned understandings of the world and their unexamined cultural practices still depend on tradition and common sense. An ideology thus adds new elements to an existing repertoire of cultural capacities, but, however demanding, it does not supplant (though it may suppress) the existing cultural repertoire of its adherents.

Over time, as an ideology becomes established, it may extend its claims increasingly into taken-for-granted areas of daily life. The contemporary feminist movement, for example, has gradually extended its critique of gender inequality from inequalities in the home and workplace to such issues as violence against women, pornography, and sexual harassment—making matters that were traditionally unnoticed in the wider culture issues of explicit ideological attention. By insisting on changing such mundane matters as forms of address and gendered pronouns, it has transformed ideology into accepted practices. Nonetheless, whatever the new ideology does not tackle directly remains under the sway of the old order. Old orders are resilient, hiding their premises in the minutiae of daily life.

Ideology's influence on action is limited in a second way as well. Ideologies, often carried by social movements, model new ways to organize action and to structure group life. Such ideological movements are, however, in active competition with other cultural frameworks—at the least, in competition with common sense, and usually with alternative traditions and ideologies as well. Explaining cultural *outcomes* therefore requires more than an understanding of an ideology's direct influence on action. As Robert Wuthnow's *Communities of Discourse* (1989) brilliantly demonstrates, explaining outcomes also requires explaining why one ideology rather than another triumphs (or at least endures). Such explanation depends on analyzing the structural and historical circumstances within which ideological movements struggle for dominance (see Skocpol 1985).

Ideologies may, however, influence the outcome of such historical struggles, since different ideologies may give their adherents very different capacities for creating and sustaining social organization. In the early modern period, for example, those armed with ascetic Protestant ideologies very often won their social battles. Protestantism seems to have given its adherents advantages in group conflicts. It directly supported innovations in social structure (the "transformative capacity" of which Eisenstadt [1970b] speaks), such as the popular egalitarianism of Cromwell's Puritan army. It also facilitated distinctive forms of collective action, such as the activist voluntary associations E. P. Thompson (1963:350–400) describes, or the more systematic forms of political authority Puritans favored (Walzer 1973). Mary Fulbrook's *Piety and Politics* (1983), noted for its argument that the political implications of "precisionist" Protestantism varied in different structural contexts, also shows that whatever their political orientations and alliances, in the cases Fulbrook studied, precisionist Protestants won out politically. And Philip Gorski (1993; forthcoming) shows that Calvinist discipline conferred enormous advantages for modern state building.[10]

Any theory of ideology's causal significance must then deal both with the immediate effects of ideologies on the actions of their adherents and with larger explanatory questions about why an ideology develops in particular directions, why certain groups adopt it, and why those groups ultimately succeed or fail.

To take the example of Protestantism again, Weber (1958a) traces the powerful direct effect of Calvinist belief upon those who held it. But

Walzer (1973) explains that in England Calvinism appealed to those displaced clergy and insecure gentry who were looking for new ways to exercise authority and for a new ethos to regulate their conduct as elites. Calvinism succeeded in attracting powerful converts precisely because it satisfied elite interests. But Calvinist ideology played an independent causal role by providing elites with a new understanding of what their "interests" might be—and by teaching the styles, skills, and habits that allowed them to pursue these newly defined interests. Only a person who had adopted the new ideology would aspire to exercise authority in a newly rational, methodical, just, and God-fearing way—becoming a "good magistrate" at the head of a Godly commonwealth (rather than, say, demanding renewed respect for traditional authority).

Culture has independent causal influence in unsettled cultural periods because it makes possible new strategies of action. People use it to constitute new actors (selves, families, corporations), shape the styles and skills with which they act, and model forms of authority and cooperation. In a wider and more long-term explanatory frame, however, an ideology's appeal may depend on the strategies of action it supports; and the specific historical situations in which these contested cultural models are enacted may determine which take root and thrive and which wither and die. Thus, we cannot look to the characteristics of the ideology alone for a full understanding of its causal significance.[11]

Settled Lives

In settled lives much of culture's role in supporting strategies of action is nearly invisible. Using well-established strategies, people draw from a complex and contradictory cultural repertoire to deal with the small perturbations of life, so culture seems to exercise little direct influence on action. An idea here, a belief there, an old saying that proves false—none of these wrinkles in cultural life are likely to make much difference to people who have well-established life patterns. For Nora Nelson or Judy Crossland, for example, cultural experience is everywhere in the accounts they give of their lives, but that culture is diffuse, inconsistent, and unclear in its effects.

Culture's influence in settled lives is obscured by the "loose coupling" between culture and action.[12] People profess ideals they do not follow, utter platitudes without meaning them, and express cynicism about conventional ideas with the assurance that the world will go on just the same. Such gaps between the norms, worldviews, and rules of conduct individuals espouse, on the one hand, and the ways they habitually act, on the other, create little difficulty within settled lives. People naturally "know" how to act—that is, their cultured capacities have come to seem "natural." Cultural experience may reinforce or refine the skills, habits, and attitudes important for common strategies of action, but these strategies do not visibly depend on cultural support.

Within settled lives, people sustain multiple capacities for action, further weakening the apparent connection between any particular cultural belief or practice and action. A disciplined individualist, oriented toward a major life goal, may still enjoy occasional bouts of hedonism without altering his basic life strategy. Established traditions may be neglected, altered, or disdained without changing the ways people actually live (and the same traditions may be taken up again with enthusiasm, having never really disappeared from the lives of their disaffected adherents, as, for example, when parents of young children revive their earlier religious involvements [see Roof 1978]). Catholics like Nora Nelson, for example, may remain firm in their conviction that they are good Catholics even though they use birth control (Greely 1989).

In settled lives culture and social structure are simultaneously too disconnected and too fused for easy analysis. That is because culture is diversified, by being adapted to varied life circumstances, and has gone "underground," so pervading ordinary experience as to blend imperceptibly into it. Settled cultures are thus more encompassing than are ideologies, since they are not in open competition with alternative models for organizing experience. Instead, they have the undisputed authority of habit, normality, and common sense. But such culture does not impose a unified pattern on action. Rather, settled cultures constrain action by providing the set of resources out of which individuals and groups construct strategies of action.

What, then, is culture's causal role in settled lives? First, settled cultures provide a "tool kit" of resources with which people can construct diverse strategies of action; the limitations of that tool kit necessarily constrain action. Second, constructing such a strategy means appropriating cultural elements (both such tacit culture as attitudes and styles and, sometimes, such explicit cultural materials as rituals and beliefs) that give specific shape to that strategy. For example, a man may draw on the symbols of married love, learning to "communicate" and remembering anniversaries, as part of solidifying his marriage. In such a case, culture cannot be said to have "caused" the choice he makes, in the sense that both the cultural elements and the life strategy are, in effect, chosen simultaneously. Nonetheless, the available cultural resources make it easier to put together some strategies than others.

An example of such a cultural effect comes from the work of Gisela Schonrock (1984), who has shown that the decline of widely accepted ritual stages of courtship in America from the 1950s to the 1970s (going steady, becoming ringed, pinned, engaged) made it more difficult for couples to negotiate the increasing commitment leading from dating to marriage. Cultural change had reduced dating couples' resources for monitoring whether a relationship was moving toward marriage and for negotiating increasing levels of commitment.

Thus culture is causally significant both because the cultured capacities individuals possess constrain the strategies of action they can construct, and because available cultural resources allow individuals to initiate and cement such strategies. Thus, for example, the culture of "falling in love" provides the dominant organization of experience through which people in contemporary America find life partners. That culture of love shows those who are searching for a life partner how to do it and thus is not a purely independent cause of their action (exposure to the same love culture has no such effect on the rest of us). But the existence of such a patterned cultural drama facilitates and frames the individual's quest. Such cultural materials might, for example, direct a person's attention to her inner emotional state as a way of monitoring the progress of her courtship, give her a language in which to negotiate greater intimacy and commitment (by saying "I love you," and seeing whether the commitment is reciprocated, for example), and allow her to enact, psychologically, the dramatic transition of marriage. Thus cultural resources affect action in settled lives by providing the materials out of which strategies of action can be constructed. But that influence is *facilitative* rather than determinative, and it does not operate by imposing particular norms or valued outcomes on individuals. Rather it makes some patterns of action more enactable than others and provides a ritual vocabulary in which such social transactions can be negotiated.

Culture's influence in settled lives can be observed in what is usually called "cultural lag"—the reluctance to abandon established strategies of action. People do not readily take advantage of new structural opportunities that would require them to abandon established ways of life. This is not because they cling to cultural *ends*, but because they are reluctant to discard familiar strategies of action for which they already have the cultural equipment.

Of what does this "cultural equipment" consist? It first comprises the cultured capacities of individuals—for example, an ability to organize the self to make choices (see Tobin, Wu, and Davidson 1989:151–53), to resonate with the enthusiasms of others, or to insulate oneself from the surrounding environment. People may have multiple capacities of this sort, but such things are difficult to learn and require continuing exercise; a person's tool kit or repertoire necessarily remains limited.

A second kind of cultural equipment for forming a strategy of action is a set of public codes in which social relationships can be negotiated. The tradition of Christmas gift-giving (Caplow 1984), for example, provides a code for signaling attachment to various members of one's friendship circle and kin network. Rituals and traditions convey meanings—and thus can carry a variety of messages (Bourdieu 1977). The tradition of becoming "engaged" can make a young woman realize that she does not want to marry or it can help her move toward a marriage. Such a ritual system does have independent influence on action (aside from its influence on activities such as buying rings): the availability of such codes facilitates building and maintaining some kinds of social relationships and not others. For example, the absence of certain ritual complexes (like annual ceremonies honoring local saints) in American life makes it harder to build stable strategies of action around, say, attachment to an ancestral hometown. The available cultural codes for negotiating and cementing social relationships do not compel any particular relationship, but they facilitate the formation of some strategies of action rather than others.

Another kind of cultural resource that shapes possible strategies of action are values themselves. In chapter 4 I argued that enduring cultural values do not guide action. But values *are* sometimes important in maintaining strategies of action, especially in settled lives. In unsettled lives, values do not usually determine how people act. Indeed, people are likely to change their values while still holding on to the strategies with which they go about achieving their ends. In settled lives, however, values— both "terminal" and "instrumental" (Rokeach 1973)—may play a significant role. A man preoccupied with juggling the demands of wife and children against those of his work may well have developed a settled policy about whether "happiness," "an exciting life," "self-respect," or "social recognition" is more important to him. He may even refer to those values in making particular choices. Indeed, values are important pieces of cultural equipment for established strategies of action, since operating with a strategy of action means, in part, having ways of making the choices that normally confront one within it.

In this way, we can recognize the significance of values for action, not as determiners of ends but as tools for fine-tuning action within established life strategies. Values are another cultural resource that allows people to construct and operate within strategies of action. The availability of culturally defined values thus makes some strategies of action easier to construct—easier in the sense that one has available more of the relevant cultural equipment—than others.

To summarize the argument: culture affects action, but in different ways in settled and unsettled lives. When groups construct new strategies of action, they do so through ideologies. Ideologies are highly organized, and they aspire to coherence and comprehensiveness. They provide guidelines for action and have strong, direct influence on their adherents. They also supply rituals, symbols, and worldviews that teach adherents a new ethos and new ways of acting in the world. Those who are learning the cultural supports for a new strategy of action may strictly follow the ideology as they try to establish patterns of action that are unfamiliar or are in contention with competing ideological systems.

Ideologies directly shape the actions of their adherents, and they make history by bringing new possibilities for action into being. But their ultimate effects on action are often limited, because wider structural and historical factors determine how ideologies fare against competitors. We may, for example, analyze the "effects" of Protestantism based on its system of doctrine and ritual practice. But such an explanation will be inadequate without an account of why Protestantism attracted adherents, how it changed in its struggles with competing ideologies and social movements, and why those armed with the new cultural capacities Protestantism created succeeded in institutionalizing new strategies of action (see Wuthnow 1989).

In settled lives, in contrast, specific elements of tradition and common sense have relatively weak direct influence over action. People draw on multiple, often competing cultural traditions, and they easily find ways to justify quite varied actions. But culture nonetheless plays an important role. It ingrains, reinforces, and refines the "cultured capacities"—skills, moods, habits, and modes of thought and action—out of which people construct strategies of action. Culture thus shapes long-term continuities in the style or ethos of action, in the typical strategies groups or individuals use to organize action, and in paradigms for collective action.

The diverse, less consistent, less coherent culture of settled lives is powerful because it is pervasive and taken for granted. Thus its modes of organizing action are "ready to hand," shaping the basic capacities with which people construct varied lines of action.

PART III

Culture from the Outside In:
Love and Marriage

CHAPTER 6

LOVE AND MARRIAGE

*I*n this chapter I ask how multiple cultural framings of the same issue can coexist side by side. I ask first what maintains the plausibility of a cultural worldview, even when people are directly critical of it. And I ask a related question: What larger institutional demands anchor each of the dominant understandings of love? Discerning what circumstances lead people to invoke one of their cultural understandings rather than another is a critical step in untangling the complex relations of culture and social structure.

The middle-class adults I interviewed are not passive victims of popular romance.[1] Indeed, most greet the romantic love mythology with skepticism or outright disdain. Yet I shall show in this chapter that the same interviewees who reject the "movie image" of love use it repeatedly in their own thinking. I will try to account for the persistence of mythic understandings of love in the midst of a dominant, self-conscious "realism." We will begin to see here how culture is organized less by what goes on inside people's heads as they analyze their experience than by the external contexts with which they have to deal.[2] This analysis of two cultures of love, which persist simultaneously even in the minds of the same people, will suggest that culture may be organized as much from the "outside in" as from the "inside out."

LOVE MYTHS

To understand the inner dynamics of the romantic love mythology, it is valuable to trace its origins in European cultural history. Scholars agree that courtly love poetry, which emerged in Europe at the end of the eleventh century, created a fundamentally new vision of love, self, and society (Lewis 1959; R. Bloch 1977; M. Hunt 1994). Sung by troubadours in the courts of feudal France, it told of knights made virtuous by love and of heroic deeds performed in the service of noble ladies. In courtly poetry, love became an ennobling passion rather than the dangerous appetite familiar to Greeks and Romans, or the tormenting temptation described by the early Church fathers. Instead, the love of a knight for an exalted noble lady was what "makes a man virtuous and causes him to perform many heroic deeds" (Capellanus 1957:41, excerpted in Stephens 1968). Love could transform the self, forging noble character.

The other side of courtly love was a tragic vision, in which the love that inspired virtue could also lead to betrayal and death (Rougemont 1956; Lindholm 1998). The paradigmatic courtly love story is that of Tristan and Isolde. Like the later stories of Lancelot and Guinevere or Romeo and Juliet, it portrays an ill-fated love that violates social obligations. A magic potion makes Tristan fall helplessly in love with his king's betrothed, so that only death can ultimately unite the lovers and end their betrayal. Courtly love powerfully reshaped the European imagination. It envisioned a new moral complexity in the relationship between individuals and the social world (R. Bloch 1977; Elias 1994).

For the courtly tradition, love was (1) a sudden and certain passion ("love at first sight") for (2) an idealized lover. Love could (3) transform the self, making a person virtuous; but it also (4) separated individuals from society, leading them to defy social conventions in pursuit of a more personal destiny. The separate self and a conception of virtue in tension with social commitments is central to the appeal of the love myth.

Courtly love and its accompanying ethic of chivalry remained the code of the European nobility for centuries (Elias 1994; M. Bloch 1961). But the courtly ideal of love comes to us reshaped by the bourgeois culture of early English capitalism. As Ian Watt (1957) has argued, that culture took its quintessential form in the eighteenth-century English novel. The writers and publishers who created the novel form courted a newly literate, middle-class reading public and sold their wares in a new kind of cutthroat literary market. Both readers and writers were steeped in the individualism of the world's most capitalist and Protestant nation. Love became the focal myth of that individualism.

The novel that founds the bourgeois tradition of romantic love is Samuel Richardson's *Pamela*.[3] In *Pamela,* the essential drama of courtly love is preserved, but with crucial changes in its meaning. Pamela, a virtuous servant girl, resists the determined advances of her employer, Mr. B. In defending her virginity, the physical integrity of her body, she proves the integrity of her character. Her virtue is rewarded when Mr. B. finally abandons his efforts at seduction and marries her instead.

Love in the novel remains a drama about virtue. But rather than simply inspiring heroic deeds, love becomes a test of individual character. In bourgeois love stories, individuals still discover and defend their integrity. But rather than betrayal and death, the bourgeois love story ends with a marriage in which the autonomous individual finds his or her proper place in the social world.[4] Bourgeois love thus alters the tension between individual morality and social demands, reconciling the two through a love that tests and rewards a person's true merits.

In the novel, love both reveals and reforms character. Pamela shows that she is truly virtuous, down to the last fiber of her being. She resists and eventually overcomes not only her employer's lust but all the social forces arrayed against her. While Pamela's character is tested, Mr. B.'s is transformed by love. Pamela's goodness redeems him, and in loving her for her virtue he becomes virtuous himself. Thus love is the drama through which individuals find and define themselves. Individuals who preserve the self against social forces are rewarded by finding a place in the social world.

In the bourgeois myth, then, love is a matter of individual integrity. Love is, first, a clear, decisive, and unwavering choice. Love crystallizes the self, so that discovering whom one "really" loves is discovering one's true self (as in Jane Austen's novels, for example, where heroines outgrow their immature willfulness, learn to know themselves, and then can recognize the true value of their beloveds). Love must thus be certain, as the core of the self is certain.

Second, true love must be unique and exclusive ("one true love"), embodying the uniqueness of the individual self. The loved one is idealized in the sense that only true love could justify an exclusive choice. Third, love can overcome obstacles both personal and social ("love conquers all"). Through love individuals assert their integrity in the face of social forces (marrying for love, not money, for example).[5] Finally, love is enduring, even as the self is enduring. The love story has a decisive ending ("happily ever after") that resolves the dramatic struggle of the individual to define his or her self within the social world.

In sum, bourgeois love is (1) a clear, all-or-nothing choice; (2) of a unique other; (3) made in defiance of social forces; and (4) permanently resolving the individual's destiny. To put it in different terms: "They met, and it was love at first sight. There would never be another girl (boy) for him (her). No one could come between them. They overcame obstacles and lived happily ever after."[6]

REAL LOVE

When the middle-class adults I interviewed talked about love, they debunked precisely this mythic vision. "Movie" love is intense, overwhelming, and sure, they said, but real love is often ambiguous, gradual, and uncertain. Indeed, if we examine what people actually say about love, it is almost the opposite of the mythic ideal: (1) Real love is not sudden or certain. It grows slowly and is often ambivalent and confused. Love does not require a dramatic choice but may result from circumstance, accident, or inertia. (2) There is no "one true love." One can love many people in a variety of different ways. (3) The kind of love that leads to marriage should not depend on irrational feeling in defiance of social convention, but on compatibility and on practical traits that make persons good life partners. The fewer obstacles people have to overcome, the happier they are likely to be. (4) Love does not necessarily last forever. Love and marriage do not settle either personal identity or social destiny. Rather than guaranteeing that one will live "happily ever after," love requires continuing hard work, compromise, and change.

I call this antimythic view of love "prosaic-realism." It is just as "cultural" as the mythic view it claims to debunk. It appears both in autobiographical accounts, when people describe how they came to love or marry as they did, and in general observations on what love is or should be.

Betty Dyson, a middle-class homemaker, has been married eleven years and has two children. Actively involved in the Baptist church, she reflects a view of love fairly common among the people I interviewed. For her, love was not a sudden, inexplicable passion:

> As for why I married the person I did, he was the right person at the
> right time at the right place. We met while we were going to school
> and we spent a lot of time together and we decided fairly quickly that
> we wanted to be married and share our lives.

Far from claiming that her husband was uniquely right in some ineffable way, she lists quite straightforwardly the traits that make them well-suited:

> He's an awful lot like my father. I'm an awful lot like his mother. He
> was the kind of person I felt I could share a lot with, who had similar

ideas and a similar outlook on life. We were very compatible. We enjoyed doing a lot of the same things. We were good friends.

There was no love at first sight. Indeed, she insists on describing as un-
hurried what was, by some standards, a whirlwind courtship. "It grew
very gradually. Well, we were going to school, and he was hanging around
a lot . . . and I was avoiding him a lot, but within two months we decided
to get married." Rather than describing a decisive choice, she describes
her marriage as something she and her husband fell into without really realizing what they were doing. What a novelist might romanticize, she
seems almost intentionally to make prosaic:

> I tried to avoid him, but he was fairly persistent, and the more I got
> to know him, it was all right. . . . He was attracted to me, but I don't
> know if you would call it love. Maybe. He was on a rebound, I think,
> a little bit, having been rejected by somebody else. He was just look-
> ing for somebody to be friendly with, but as I say, within two months
> we had decided that we did want to be married.

This homemaker describes love not as an intense, all-or-nothing
passion but as an experience grounded in the small ups and downs of
daily life. She is not avoiding emotion in her description, but she reserves
intense feeling for the prosaic, everyday kind of love. She is "much more
in love" with her husband than when they married because, for her, real
love develops only over time. "It's partly just living together and sharing
your lives and getting to know each other, and partly because I know more
of what love is." Love is "a growing thing" that "will change and will manifest itself in different ways." It involves "caring for each other and the
concern and the willingness to share your life and to be part of another
person's life, and to take responsibility for that."

For this active Baptist, real love is permanent, but not because one
inevitably lives happily ever after:

> I think if you love someone enough and you commit your life to
> them in marriage you'd make it permanent. There will be times when
> you don't feel like you're in love, but since you've made a commit-
> ment and are willing to honor that commitment then you will work
> towards bringing back the love."

Thus for Betty Dyson, as for many of the people I interviewed, love
involves hard work rather than sudden passion. It depends on such ordinary things as compatibility, sharing, and common interests, even when
"physical attraction and romance" are also important. If there is a central

organizing principle to her view of love, it is an ideal of maturity. She is "much more in love with [her] husband now," because you can love someone more when you have shared a life together. Far from being a sudden and certain choice of a unique other that resolves the problems of life, love for the prosaic-realistic culture starts out as gradual, uncertain, and conventional and deepens over a lifetime.

PERSISTING MYTHS

At times, even the most prosaic view of love can suddenly shift, however, revealing a mythic understanding quite impervious to the "realism" that dominates ordinary experience. Remember, for example, Donald Nelson, whose arguments (see chapter 2) for "respect" between independent spouses were swept away by an image of all-or-nothing love when he contemplated what he would do if his wife were ill: "Nora is the most important thing in my life. . . . [S]he's important because she's—I love her." This interview was somewhat unusual—both because this rationalist engineer was so resolutely unromantic and because the question may have invited a histrionic answer. But this reemergence of a mythic vision of love occurred over and over in other interviews, even if in less dramatic ways. It was as if something were pulling at the experience of these conventional, middle-class interviewees—something that eluded their commonsense view of the world.

This lurching back and forth between mythic and prosaic views of love also affected Ted Oster, the successful lawyer we met in chapter 2, who had "really flipped" over his wife. In his case conflicting views of love showed themselves as an internal debate he could not seem to resolve. He described having fallen for his wife, in something very much like love at first sight. But he vacillated between the mythic view that there is "one right person" and what he himself saw as the more rationally persuasive idea that many people could be acceptable spouses, with circumstance and accident determining whom one actually married. He reluctantly accepted the "realistic" view after breaking off an earlier engagement: "I suppose . . . I had developed the feeling that nothing is perfect in that there wasn't just one person I could be with." But he could not quite abandon the idea of one true love, despite its implausibility: "Maybe I just didn't rationalize it as being simply impossible. It can't be [true] because that many coincidences couldn't happen all the time. You see a lot of people successfully married." Yet despite his rational reservations, he found himself clinging to the belief in one right person. "I had been told, and I really did believe because I wanted to believe the idea, that, boy, when you meet that one special person you'll really know it. I guess maybe there's more than one special person. Maybe there's quite a few. Maybe there are quite a few people with whom you could be equally happy in a different way, but you have to find somebody from that group." For this young lawyer, the mythic idea remained somehow true, despite his conscious skepticism.

How can we understand the alternations in Ted Oster's thinking—and in that of almost every person I interviewed—between a "realistic" and a "mythic" view of love? Let me first try to describe more clearly what I think is happening, before offering an account of why it happens. I do not think that people are simply responding to a culturally induced myth—a kind of brainwashing. As is evident in the quotes above, the prosaic-realistic ideal of mature love is every bit as cultural as the romantic myth. The language people use to reject infatuation and insist that love grows slowly or requires hard work is just as stereotyped as that in which love solves all problems. But what we observe is not just a compromise between mature realism and mythic romance. People seem instead to alternate between different frames for grasping reality, suddenly slipping into a mythic vocabulary at variance with the ways they normally think. While vehemently rejecting "infatuation" or "movie-star love," they periodically invoke images of love—as all-or-nothing, certain, enduring—that violate the commonsense understandings they normally use.[7] These are not delusions or mistakes, however. Instead, there is a structural reality behind the mythic view of love which continually throws people back on a way of thinking they may consciously reject.

MARRIAGE

The "mythic" view of love is grounded, I believe, in a structural reality. People recognize that it poorly describes the uncertainty, ambiguity, and impermanence in their own experiences of love, yet they continually return to its way of interpreting certain experiences. That structural reality is marriage. (Even for those who do not marry, or those like gays and lesbians who are denied the legal right to marry, the structural features of marriage provide the dominant model for love relationships.[8] As I make clear below however, those who truly bypass or abandon a marriagelike model of relationships may also stop thinking of love in mythic terms.[9])

As an emotional state love may not be all-or-nothing, unique, heroic, and enduring. But despite the prevalence of divorce, marriage still has this structure: One is either married or not (however ambivalent the underlying feelings may be); one cannot be married to more than one person at a time; marrying someone is a fateful, sometimes life-transforming choice; and despite divorce, marriages are still meant to last.[10]

The dual character of marriage lies behind the conflicting ways people use the concept of love. Much of the time, they use ideas of love to manage and interpret ongoing relationships. Here they employ a prosaic-realistic view, which is not realism in the sense of a neutral assessment of experience. It is shaped by conventional formulas and ideals, especially that of maturity. But it does attend to psychological variability, and to the ups and downs of daily life, more than does the mythic view. It is an ethic about *being* married (or "coupled"), offering suggestions about how to manage an ongoing relationship. The prosaic-realistic view has its own romantic ideal—of down-to-earth, gradually evolving love. But its fundamental concern is with established relationships—describing how people can get along, understand each other, and work out their difficulties. As Betty Dyson, the middle-class homemaker, put it, "it's not essential at the beginning of a marriage for there to be love, but it is essential that it be a growing relationship and that love will develop from that."

The mythic view persists because it answers a different set of questions—questions, I would argue, about a decisive choice, implicitly the choice of whether or not to marry, or stay married. It reproduces the institutional features of marriage, recasting them as matters of individual volition.

A Decisive Choice ("Love at First Sight")

In a revealing exchange, Betty Dyson responded to a vignette—about a woman who must decide whether or not to stay with her severely depressed husband—with a peculiar, but acute, observation. She insisted that the wife's decision could not depend on "how much" she loved her husband:

> It's a yes-or-no situation. You're either for him or agin' him. I don't
> think there's a measure on love. There are times when you feel more
> romantic. There are times, you know, when I hate him. You have a lot
> of emotions involved, but the underlying feelings, the commitment,
> are always in there.

Earlier she had acknowledged that love can vary in degree or intensity (she loves her husband "more" than when they married), and she asserted it again as a psychological truth: "There are times when you feel more romantic. There are times . . . when I hate him." But she nonetheless subscribed to one of the central mythic properties of love—that it is an all-or-nothing phenomenon, that you can't put "a measure on love." And of course she is right—not that love cannot be measured, but that the choice of whether to stay with someone or leave is pretty much a "yes or no" decision.

The dual properties of marriage—as relationship and as institution—also account for the dramatic alternations in the thinking of our sober engineer between prosaic and mythic love. In talking of his marriage as an ongoing relationship, Donald Nelson described such things as getting along, understanding each other, and respecting each other's independence. But a question about what he would do if his wife became ill raised the issue of marriage as a commitment. When the choice was between staying or leaving, the answer was "Nora is the most important thing in my life. . . . I love her."

I do not mean to argue that choices about whether to marry, or whether to stay married, are actually determined by "love"—or even that the question of love plays a significant role. People may stay married out of convenience; loveless marriages often endure; and many apparently loving ones fail. It is rather that the culture of love—precisely in its mythic form—gives people a way of talking about the all-or-nothing consequences of choices they may be quite confused and ambivalent about making.

It is the decisive consequences of choices about marriage that make the love myth compelling, even when people find its particulars implausible. If a friend seeks advice—about whether to marry, whether to break off a relationship, whether to divorce—we may listen to the psychological and circumstantial particulars, but then find ourselves asking, "Well, do you love him (or her)?" We may know perfectly well that our friend is confused about precisely this point—or she may say, yes, I still love A but I love B too. But none of this knowledge, nor even a distaste for this whole way of thinking about love, is likely to prevent us from acting as if the problem were whether or not she "really" does love A—because in the end she is either going to stay with A or leave. The mythic understanding of love recognizes the structural reality of just such choices.

A Unique Other ("One True Love")

The love myth also posits one perfect mate for each person. (This accompanies the ideal of "love at first sight," in which recognition of the "right" one is instantaneous and unwavering.) My interviewees, however, did not describe their courtships or their mates in such romantic terms. While the

young lawyer "flipped" over his wife, and others reported swift engage-
ments, what is striking is how little most interviewees had to say about
why they married the people they did:

> Well, because he was the one I met, I guess. I could have married
> someone else had I met somebody else. . . . It wasn't love at first sight,
> but it was like a steady growth of support and friendship and love.
> [thirty-eight-year-old nurse, married seven years, one child]

> I always assumed I would get married, there was no question about it
> in my mind, and I thought I was awfully late at the time. . . . I felt very
> lonely much of the time between I suppose getting out of high school
> until I got married. . . . I couldn't find somebody that I was happy
> with. And vice versa, that she would be happy with me. . . . It has
> worked out very well. [forty-four-year-old engineer, married seven-
> teen years, four children]

> We kind of grew on each other, I guess. . . . Tough question. I love
> her. Why her and not anybody else? I guess it's just her personality.
> She's up all the time. [twenty-six-year-old accountant, married one
> year, no children]

> We met at a time when, I don't know, I guess we just happened to be
> right for each other at the right time." [thirty-four-year-old travel
> agent, married nine years]

The word that recurs consistently in these descriptions is "right"—
the right person, the right relationship, and the right time. But the word
"right" operates in two very different senses; bridging two distinct meanings. One is the prosaic attitude: "There were no fireworks; it just seemed
right." The other is the mythic experience in which one's beloved is "just
right," special, perfect.

In their everyday experience people see their relationships as contingent, imperfect, and ordinary. Yet in one sense the myth of "one perfect
love" is true—true of the structural experience of an exclusive, long-en-
during relationship. One may not marry the uniquely perfect person, but
that relationship does become unique. One's marriage partner becomes
irreplaceable, not because one could not have had an equally happy mar-

riage with someone else, but because one could not have had this marriage, these experiences, this love.

This sense that one's marriage is now the only reality explains why most people give such feeble accounts of why they married the persons they did. It is hard to give reasons for what in retrospect seems inevitable. Indeed, when recounting their decision to marry, many couples describe it as hardly having been a decision, but as having developed naturally out of the relationship itself. One couple, married for twelve years, were high school sweethearts. When they married, the husband said, "there wasn't a lot of discussion." His wife was "the kind of girl I wanted to marry," and "somewhere along the line I just made the assumption that that's where our relationship was headed." But despite this prosaic account, there was a "rightness" that was almost like romantic destiny. The wife said, "I asked my sister . . . about love. . . . I was looking for a definition of love because I felt, at eighteen, how could I know that I was in love. But even her words didn't really put it. I knew that's where I was." The husband, too, "spent a lot of time trying to figure out what love should be." But in the end, "I felt so good about us that that's probably what it was. If it wasn't that, I wasn't really concerned about it because that just felt good enough that [that] was the right feeling, the right place."

The young lawyer's reasoned opinion that "there wasn't just one person I could be with" is in this sense less true than his mythic ideal of "one special person." The person one marries is special—legally and institutionally unique, however ordinary or extraordinary his or her personal attributes. A thirty-five-year-old, self-employed businessman explained how being married to someone makes her "right" in the sense that she is both so uniquely perfect as to be irreplaceable and so familiar that her virtues are impossible to describe: "I guess because I've been married for twelve years, and the person I love is my wife, and I don't really remember any other relationships that much. Because this is the only one that really counts." The social organization of marriage makes the mythic image true experientially, whatever the facts.

Overcoming Obstacles ("Love Conquers All")

Very few interviewees described heroic struggles to marry against social or family opposition. Indeed, even where a prosaic remark hints at possible drama ("Even when . . . I was trying to date somebody else in college . . . I knew I was in love with [him]"; or Betty Dyson's "He was hanging around a lot . . . and I was avoiding him a lot"), the drama seems underplayed.

There was an occasional marriage against parental opposition, but little was made of it.[11] These interviewees on the whole seemed perfectly content to have married just the kinds of people their parents wanted for them, and indeed, they frequently said just that.[12]

Heroic struggle to marry has largely disappeared from the accounts my interviewees give of their lives, but it has been replaced by another powerful heroism—the heroic effort necessary to keep relationships together. Interviewees insist that one must "work at" a relationship.[13] Even more, they assert that a whole range of virtues—from honesty and a willingness to face change, to stamina and a willingness to stick by one's commitments—are necessary to preserve a modern marriage. Thus love again becomes a test of character, but it tests a different kind of character than that of the rebellious youth fighting for his or her true love. This is the mature heroism of adulthood (see Swidler 1980). Its virtues are self-knowledge, honesty, and a willingness to face difficulties squarely.

The heroic themes of the love myth have thus been transposed from the drama of choosing to the drama of sustaining a marriage. In some ways, this violates the pattern in which mythic love is invoked when people think about forming or leaving a marriage, while prosaic realism flourishes when people consider how to manage day-to-day relationships. The secret of this apparent reversal is that the institutional structure of marriage— all-or-nothing, exclusive, requiring a decisive choice—has been partially transformed by the difficulty people have in staying married. The mundane problems of getting along in a relationship continually raise the more decisive question of whether the partners remain committed to work at getting along (see Illouz 1997:193–96).[14] Thus prosaic love requires heroic commitment. The institutional insecurity of modern marriage introduces a mythic element right into the heart of marital mundaneness, making ordinary, everyday actions heroic tests of individual character.

Here prosaic love and mythic love meet. Interviewees insist on the ordinariness of their love relationships as a transmuted myth of the heroic. In this view, even the frequent pettiness and indifference of daily life ("There are times where I don't even think about his day"; "you're living together, see each other every day, you don't sometimes pay attention") simply demonstrate the demanding moral struggles love requires. Love "conquers all" not by overcoming social obstacles but by meeting the mundane demands of ongoing relationships.

I have been arguing that the mythic culture of love relocates the institutional features of marriage—exclusive, all-or-nothing, transformative, enduring—in the interior of individual psyches. The prevalence of divorce has left the institution of marriage intact but has changed some of its social meanings. The prosaic-realistic culture of love is made plausible by this change in the institutional significance of marriage.

Ted Oster, the young lawyer, like almost all the people I interviewed, thinks of marriage at least in part in terms of the possibility of divorce. Asked whether love "is forever," he responded immediately by stressing the need to "work at it to keep it going forever." His sensitivity to the mundane details of relationships, his interest, for example, in making sure he and his wife regularly find time to "communicate," reflects this sense of vulnerability. "It makes me nervous at times because I know that I'm not, or perceive that she's not, working hard at it, or working in the right way, or that I don't have the energy level or the whatever to do what's necessary." The prosaic culture's critique of mythic love comes from its insistence that the really heroic moral struggle is that which occurs within ongoing relationships.

Love Lasts Forever ("Happily Ever After")

Despite its fragility, the institution of marriage makes plausible the fourth, and arguably most implausible, element of the traditional love myth: the ideal that true love lasts forever. This, of course, has been the stuff of poetry for centuries—from "Love is not love which alters when it alteration finds" to "I'll be yours for endless time"—as poets find ever new ways of saying "forever." [15] (It is also the stuff of ironic poetic reaction as in Andrew Marvell's "Had we but world enough, and time"; Carole King's "Will you still love me tomorrow?"; or Edna St. Vincent Millay's "I loved you Wednesday, yes, but what is that to me?")

The people I interviewed vacillated about whether true love endures. As we have seen, many insist that love does not last by itself, that "You have to work at it." Indeed, they are haunted by the fragility of marriage. Divorce is an evident danger, as well as a continuing option. They recognize that feelings of love are transient, so that, as Betty Dyson said, "There are times when I hate him." And finally, many interviewees responded to the vignettes by saying that a person should leave a relationship when it is no longer satisfying, as long as she or he has made honest efforts to work out the difficulties. While one can pledge love that lasts forever, apparently one cannot be bound by such a promise.

Nevertheless, these interviewees still valued enduring love. Indeed, there is evidence from studies of college students that from the 1960s to the 1980s young people became more "romantic," seeing love as a crucial prerequisite for marriage (Simpson, Campbell, and Berscheid 1986:366–67).[16] Furthermore, these college students also regard love as necessary for sustaining a marriage. Among my interviewees, those who were married used the prevalence of divorce as a cautionary lesson. Rather than assuming that they themselves would divorce, they talked about what they must do to avoid it: work on their relationships, keep growing together, or share a commitment to Christ—and, of course, "communicate."

More surprising, these interviewees persistently employed a mythic sense of the word love in which real love *must* last forever. Thus, without in fact believing that love does last, and while recognizing the fragility of contemporary relationships, they spoke as if love that ends could not have been "real" love in the first place.[17]

For these middle-class Americans, what is "real" love can only be decided after the fact. Sam Woods, a self-employed businessman, married twelve years, sees marriage as a lifelong commitment, sanctioned by God. For him love is not real love unless it is enduring. A vignette about a man tempted to leave his wife for a woman he loves more led him to argue that the man cannot know "which is real love . . . until it's tested." Love must be "tried, have difficulties come into the relationship. That's when you find out what really love is. What he's experiencing is the exciting part of love, of a love relationship. He feels good; he's excited; he's turned on. He maybe feels younger or whatever." But this is not "real love."

A very different man—a divorced and remarried thirty-two-year-old real-estate broker proud of his "communication skills"—made exactly the same distinction between infatuation, which feels like love but does not last; and love, which may feel like infatuation, but is enduring. Describing his early relationships, Thomas DaSilva said,

> I had about four or five relationships prior to [my first marriage] with women I had considered myself to be in love with. I had this image of this ideal love that was perfect, that was made in heaven, and that nothing could touch it, and everything was going to be fine.

But when those relationships failed, it was evident to him that they had not really been love. And when his marriage failed, rather than concluding that love can die, he simply revised his conception of love itself. By examining in detail how this smooth salesman redefined love, we can see more precisely why mythic love remains plausible even in the face of contrary experience. We will see how even one who considers himself thoroughly disillusioned reproduces a mythic understanding of love, because "love" defines not a unique feeling but a unique structural slot in his life.

TRUE LOVE

Thomas DaSilva's youthful image of love combined idealistic expectations of married life with a "purely glandular" excitement. "I just felt physically, you know, I felt this rush. A feeling I couldn't even describe. It was overwhelming." He also thought of love as missing someone when they were gone. "All of a sudden when I was taken away from somebody, or they went away, I wanted to be back with them. That was love." Love was also acting like husband and wife:

> Man's function is to put bread on that table, take care of the wife,
> protect the wife. Her job is to make sure that she runs the household
> properly. She raises the children. She basically does what you say. . . .
> Love was when that happened and everybody smiled and was happy
> with it.

When he married, he was certain that his marriage would last. "It was great. . . . I was elated. I am going to provide for this person. I'm going to go out and set the world on fire." "I'd see people being a certain way, and I'd say, 'Boy, they're in for trouble. Look how great we are. Aren't we wonderful.' It just appeared to me while I was married to my first wife that, boy, we had the ideal relationship. This was perfect."

After the crushing breakup of that marriage, Thomas DaSilva moved temporarily into a new pattern of relationships—one not oriented toward marriage, and that made no use of the idea of love:

> How can I explain this? I didn't make any differentiation between be-
> ing friends and having a sexual relationship. In fact being friends with
> someone led to sexual relationships and sexual relationships led to
> being friends. I felt, you know, that I made a lot of good friends in
> that kind of situation, and I would talk about it in that sense. I don't
> think the subject of marriage came up too often. The three or four
> times it came up were people who felt that they wanted to get mar-
> ried, and I had to tell them that I didn't.

Thus during a period when he had temporarily banished thoughts of marriage, he needed a new framework for thinking about relationships. He replaced the ideal of love with friendship. Friendship allows intimacy but has very different structural characteristics than does marriage: it is not exclusive; it grows or declines, but is not all-or-nothing; and it requires no decisive choice or commitment.

Despite his disillusionment, however, this energetic bachelor retained an ideal of "love," precisely, I would argue, because he still envisioned the possibility of marriage. He did not preserve the content of his earlier beliefs about love, but he reopened the structural slot "love" had occupied.

> I think what I was looking for was "what is it that I am looking for?" In the back of my mind I was thinking that I would know it when I saw it. At that time I was still believing largely in the sense of "I'll know it when I see it. It'll hit me and I'm not looking for it particularly. I'm just going about what I do normally."

What then was the "it" he was looking for—this something so special that, although it could not be described, he would know it when he saw it? His original image of love had proved false. Neither passionate emotion, nor traditional marital roles, nor happiness-ever-after had worked. But disappointment did not end his quest for "it." He had given up the specifics of his original ideal of love, but not the structural shape of the love myth. He was still searching for a unique, exclusive, special "it"—because only such a love could correspond to the institutional properties of marriage.

After his divorce, Thomas DaSilva had transcended the ideal of one right person:

> I had this narrow thing I was looking for before. And all of a sudden I became aware of the fact, jeez, there isn't anything in particular to look for except that you want to find a person. . . . All of a sudden that concept of a single person started to dissipate. It went away. All of a sudden, I said, jeez, that's kind of silly. You could take seven, eight, nine, or ten of these people and you know that you could be married to any of these people and have a marriage that is a good one, maybe different from your other one.

But despite his experience that "as I got to know more and more women, I liked them all," the quest for someone mythically special did not disappear, even though "They were all so different in different ways. I liked this about this person. I liked that about that person." But after dismissing the mythic idea (more decisively than the young lawyer could bring himself to do), he described his second wife, Melinda, in just such terms:

> Q. So then what was it like when you met Melinda?
>
> Melinda was so different than anybody I had ever met before. I was struck immediately by Melinda, but I was so guarded about

that. "Wait a minute now. Where have you ever seen it like this before?"

Q.   How was she different?

She was so damned perfect.

Love had certainly acquired new meanings. "Infatuation" was still enjoyable, but Thomas DaSilva had developed a more mature, realistic view of love. He and Melinda "had a lot of things in common about what [they] liked and didn't like." They found that their "families were very similar in a lot of ways." He had changed, so that he liked her independence, the fact that she would not expect him always to take care of her. "I could cry with her. I could be other things than what I was able to be with other people. She was able to be the same with me." Indeed, he explicitly contrasted his understanding with his earlier conception of love. "I felt that it wasn't a lonely feeling when I was away from her as much as it was a feeling like I can get more out of my life with this person with me. . . . I know that with this person my life will be fuller because there are so many things here that we can do and work at."

Thomas DaSilva changed his conception of love. After divorcing and dating many women, he had adopted the prosaic-realistic culture of equality, emotional sharing, communication, and "working at" things together. He had stopped thinking that there was "a single person" he could be married to. But the underlying structure of the love myth reasserted itself with compelling force as he talked about the woman he did in fact marry.

Actual love stories, of course, do not always end in marriage. That is what makes novels, movies, or TV dramas exciting. But it is the structure of marriage as an institution that makes the love myth plausible. Even when lovers are separated, the mythic story asserts that there is one right person. Even if fighting for that person fails, there is a decisive choice in which the hero finds out what she or he really wants. Even when love stories are about relationships outside of marriage (or about the loss or rediscovery of love within a marriage), they embody the ideal of a single, exclusive love, a unique relationship to one other person, a heroic fight against obstacles, and the possibility of an all-or-nothing certainty about that choice.

My argument is that the features of the love myth—an exclusive, unique passion, a decisive choice that expresses and resolves identity, a struggle to overcome obstacles, and a commitment that endures forever—correspond neither to personal experience nor to the observations people make of others they know. But its power is not an illusion. Rather, the love myth accurately describes the structural constraints of the institution of marriage. These constraints affect those who marry and those who divorce or remain unmarried, as long as they are implicitly or explicitly asking of every relationship whether it is the "right" relationship—one that is, or could be, or should be a marriage.

LIFE STRATEGIES

What can we learn about culture more generally from this analysis of the culture of love? Although the domain of love is a specialized one, the relationship between institutional constraints and cultural meanings that we have found here has wider implications. By examining how people organize action around institutional demands, we can develop a broader understanding of what reproduces cultural meanings, how people use culture to construct lines of action, and what sorts of "realities" culture actually describes.

Cultural Persistence

This chapter has shown how images of romantic love continually resurface even among people who consciously disavow them. When cultural understandings persist in this way, culture critics have argued that a dominant ideology holds people in its thrall, either because of manipulation by the culture industry (Gitlin 1983; Thompson 1990) or because the ideology is so hegemonic that no one can envision an alternative. But if ideological hegemony means the unthinking acceptance of dominant views, that is clearly not the case here. If it were, researchers should not find widespread cultural dissent (see Abercrombie, Hill, and Turner 1980; Mann 1970), such as the rebelliousness of the working-class London boys in Paul Willis's *Learning to Labor* (1977) or the skepticism Americans express about the availability of the "American dream" (Mann 1970; Huber and Form 1973; Rainwater 1974; J. Hochschild 1981:114–47; Kluegel and Smith 1986:53–73; Reinarman 1987; Swidler 1992).

As our analysis of love has shown, criticism alone will not dislodge contested culture. Middle-class Americans are sharply critical of the romantic love myth. In fact, they insist that such beliefs are dangerously misleading (see Illouz 1997:158–60). And they counter the romantic love myth with an alternative, prosaic-realistic imagery.

But if the love myth is not hegemonic, if respondents are not brainwashed by popular culture, why does mythic love persist? I have argued that the institutional features of marriage make mythic love plausible, even when people reject it as a guide to ordinary experience. Let us examine this claim more closely.

Mythic love persists because, while the prosaic view is more realistic as a description of experience, description is not the only or the most important use to which cultural meanings can be put. Culture does not describe external reality so much as it organizes people's own lines of action.

Two cultures of love persist, neither driving out the other, because people employ their understandings of love in two very different contexts. When thinking about the choice of whether to marry or stay married, people see love in mythic terms. Love is the choice of one right person whom one will or could marry. Therefore love is all-or-nothing, certain, exclusive, heroic, and enduring. When thinking about maintaining ongoing relationships, however, people mobilize the prosaic-realistic culture of love to understand the varied ways one can manage love relationships. Prosaic love is ambiguous, open-ended, uncertain, and fragile.

The institutional demands of marriage continually reproduce the outlines of the mythic love story. Neither hidden ideological hegemony nor brainwashing by mass culture is necessary. Indeed, the institutional properties of marriage may explain why dramas of love retain their popular appeal.

Evidently people can live quite nicely with multiple, conflicting ideas about the world (and with huge gaps between beliefs and experience [see Swidler 1992; Schlozman and Verba 1979]). Criticism of a dominant ideal will not eliminate it as long as it still provides a useful guide to action. Thus students of ideology would do well to examine the institutional encounters that lead people to reproduce even discredited parts of their worldviews. After all, it was Marx and Engels (1970:60) who said that the true communist does not seek "merely to produce a correct consciousness about an existing fact" but rather to "[overthrow] the existing state of things." Only if we discern how people actually use ideas to organize action can we understand why some ideas are enormously resilient while others fail to take hold.

Culture and Action

It is not quite correct to say that mythic love describes the institution of marriage. Rather it describes the inner contours of individual action (and feeling) oriented to marriage. The basic structure of the love myth corresponds to, and helps organize, the lines of action individuals construct when deciding whether to enter or leave a marriage (or relationship modeled on marriage). People learn to ask themselves whether their feelings for another person are "real love"—love that can be exclusive, certain, life-transforming, and enduring. They thus reconstitute the institutional characteristics of marriage as intrapsychic states. The love myth answers the question, "What do I need to feel about someone in order to marry [commit myself to] him or her?"

Culture develops capacities for action, and culture proliferates where action is problematic. Recently problems of "structure and agency" (Giddens 1981, 1984; Archer 1988; Sewell 1992) have preoccupied sociologists. Many scholars have pointed out that social structure is itself constituted by culture and that culture exists only when it is enacted in concrete forms, so that no firm line can be drawn between culture and structure (Williams 1973; Sewell 1985, 1992; Meyer, Boli, Thomas, and Ramirez 1997; Boli and Thomas 1997). But I would like to depart to some extent from this current conventional wisdom. From the point of view of individual actors, some parts of the social world stand as obdurate structures with their own reality, while other arenas are left to be organized by individual action. (It might be better here to say "organized by actors," acknowledging that actors and repertoires of possible actions are themselves institutionalized, so that actors may be tribes, nations, or families, not just individuals. In the contemporary West, the individual person is constituted as "the actor." This is one of the core institutionalized realities around which Americans must organize their actions.) Marriage is an institution persons may accept or reject, seek or avoid. But its structure is at least provisionally fixed, from the perspective of individual actors. Courtship, however—the process of finding a person to marry—is something the individual has to do on his or her own. She cannot simply apply for a license, go before a judge, and have it done. While both individual choices and institutional structures are cultural, the way they are cultural differs.

Love and marriage provide a perfect example of this relationship between culture and institutions. Individuals, I have argued, develop strategies of action that provide them with a basic life organization. An institution like marriage solves many problems of life organization simultaneously. In general, marriage settles one's living arrangements—with whom one shares a household, and usually income and expenses; one's sexual obligations and opportunities; with whom one socializes; who will care for one if one is sick. Marriage defines a life-partnership, a unit that produces joint rather than purely individual goods. Marriage changes one's public status (and sometimes one's name) and it defines a unit in the larger social world.

Marriage is thus an institution that decides, or at least redefines, important elements of one's life organization. But at the same time, forming a marriage is left almost entirely up to individual initiative. There is no institutionalized path to marriage as there is for finding a college or career—fill out an application, take a test, be called for an interview, wait for a letter of acceptance or rejection. Even matchmakers, families, or brokers who arrange marriages can only introduce people to each other, not actually arrange the marriage itself. Thus it is up to individuals to form marriages, to link their life strategies to the institutional structure marriage provides.

The culture of love flourishes in this gap where action meets institution. In order to marry, individuals must develop certain cultural, psychological, and even cognitive equipment. They must be prepared to feel, or at least convince others that they feel, that one other person is the uniquely right "one." They must be prepared to recognize the "right person" when that person comes along. In addition, people must mobilize the psychic energy to make the life changes that marrying involves, from sharing money and living arrangements to sharing such things as a social identity, a dinner hour, a kin network, or children.

Love, then, is the quality of "rightness" that defines the particular, unique other that one does marry; it is the emotion that propels one across the gap that separates single from married life; and it is "commitment," the psychological concomitant of the all-or-nothing, exclusive, enduring relationship constituted by a marriage. The popular culture of love both prepares persons for and helps them to organize and carry through the aspects of marriage that depend on individual action.

In more general form, I am arguing that culture is elaborated around the lines of action institutions structure. As we saw in describing settled and unsettled lives, people consume and create more cultural "stuff"—that is, they elaborate more self-conscious symbolic meanings—when their lives are unsettled, when they must construct new lines of action. In this sense culture provides complements or reciprocals to institutional structures. The aspects of institutional life that are firmly structured do not require cultural elaboration. Individuals instead develop cultural supports for lines of action that link them to institutions. The culture of love flourishes because, while marriage is institutionalized, the process of getting married (or deciding whether or not to leave a marriage) and—in the contemporary period, the procedure for staying married—is not. As marriage has become more fragile, no longer fully settling the lives of those who rely on it, a second culture of love, prosaic realism, has blossomed alongside the old. This new love culture helps people be the kinds of persons, with the kinds of feelings, skills, and virtues, that will sustain an ongoing relationship.

Thus people create more elaborated culture where action is more problematic. As institutions constrict discretion, they reduce the need for cultural elaboration. So those who are anxious about maintaining enduring relationships actively consume "love culture." They buy self-help books on love, watch Leo Buscaglia, attend Marriage Encounter weekends, visit therapists and marriage counselors, and read *The Road Less Traveled*.[18] Other aspects of social life, such as receiving payment for the work one has done or keeping others from taking one's possessions (see Colson 1974), are the focus of enormous cultural and ritual elaboration in societies without formal governments and legal institutions, but they are much less culturally elaborated in our own.[19]

Culture then flourishes especially lushly in the gaps where people must put together lines of action in relation to established institutional options. Culture and social structure are thus, in the widest sense, reciprocal. People continue to elaborate and shore up with culture that which is not fully institutionalized.

What Culture Describes

The sociology of culture has often run aground on the problem of what culture describes, or, to put it differently, what makes culture plausible. It is clear that culture is in some sense "about" the world, and that a culture that no longer fits the world around it may be discarded. But what kind of "fit" do cultures have to their world?

The culture of love I have described does fit. But it does not directly fit experience or observation of the world. Rather it describes persons' own organization of action, one that is simultaneously culturally constructed. That organization of action is, in turn, constrained by the external world, but it does not correspond to it feature for feature. Think of an actor as a hiker ascending a mountain, with culture as her description of the path she follows. The mountain's topography will certainly affect her route. She will pay attention to a boulder she must cross or go around, to steep or flat places, to openings in the trees. But other features of the mountain that do not directly affect her climb may be irrelevant. She may misconstrue the larger shape of the mountain, yet well describe her own path.

Of course, thinking of culture as "description," even description of our own organization of action, is clearly inadequate. Culture also describes (and helps to constitute) the personal capacities and resources the actor will use as she follows her path. Thus her knowledge of the strength of her legs, the energy she brings to the task, even her ability to jump over boulders is integral to her organization of her own line of action.

Culture then describes our own organization of action. And multiple cultural meanings remain in suspension as long as we have many kinds of action to organize. The fact that as descriptions of the world, or even of our own experience, such cultural meanings may be contradictory or incomplete does nothing to undermine their plausibility. As long as cultural meanings help people mobilize the internal and external supports they need for action, the culture is "true." It is in this sense that both the insurance executive and the successful lawyer found it true that there was one right person different from all the others. The woman Thomas DaSilva married was different in a different way than other women were different because she filled that slot in his life for which there could be only one, unique occupant. The lawyer kept his belief in "one right person" even though he knew "it couldn't be true" because he found the one person who became uniquely right in the sense that, as another businessman said, "she is the one I did marry, so this is the only one that really counts."

For these men, as for most respondents, "real love" remains mythically enduring because love that does not last is, in retrospect, not real love. That is, the belief that real love lasts forever does not describe the world. My interviewees would be the first to insist that love dies all the time. But the culture of love does describe the line of action my interviewees are trying to sustain. That line of action involves keeping themselves and their partners committed to an enduring relationship. And here "love" serves as the all-important term for cultivating that set of feelings, that reading of one's own psyche and the psyche of another, that internal propagation of firm decision and perpetual vigilance that can sustain a marriage. Love describes reality, but its reality is the internal contour of our own action. We take into account features of the world as those features impinge on or structure our own lines of action.

Sources of Cultural Coherence

I began this book by insisting that culture is not organized into unified systems, but that people keep on tap multiple, often conflicting cultural capacities and worldviews. But in this chapter we have seen that culture can sometimes be more coherent than it might appear at first glance. Even though experts on love offer multiple, competing kinds of advice (and many people listen indiscriminately to all of them [Lichterman 1992]) and beliefs about love range from practical homilies to transfiguring inspirations, consistent themes can be discerned beneath the chaos. But where does this "consistency" or coherence reside? I have argued that institutions provide coherence because many persons shape their action around the same institutional constraints. They then resonate to very similar cultural formulas. Standard institutional dilemmas produce coherent cultural strands, even when each individual's worldview taken as a whole may seem incoherent. Coherence resides in the cultural supports for particular lines of action, and consistent patterns appear in the culture of many individuals when they all confront similar institutional constraints and organize action around those constraints.

The effects of marriage on the culture of love provide one of many examples of how culture can be structured from the "outside in." Even when individuals are confused about what they believe, when their culture contains many inconsistent beliefs and strikes a cacophony of discordant notes, the effects of culture can sometimes be quite coherent. But to understand why culture can have systematic effects even when it is not systematic in the minds of individuals, we must examine sources of cultural coherence operating outside individual psyches.

CHAPTER 7

Ties That Do Not Bind

This chapter explores the prosaic-realistic culture of love. That culture flourishes, I have argued, as marriage becomes more fragile. It answers the question, "How can I make my marriage last?" The prosaic love culture offers not only practical solutions to the difficulties of married life (make love often; keep separate checking accounts; eat out occasionally without the kids) but a description of the general moral nature of love relationships and, implicitly, of other social bonds as well. Looking closely at how middle-class Americans think about love reveals broader understandings of how social ties are formed and how, in turn, relationships can be preserved, reformed, or improved.

At the level of specific beliefs and attitudes, even the fairly homogeneous group of white, middle-class Californians I interviewed thought about love and marriage in very different ways. Some held strongly that divorce is morally wrong, for example, while others, even those who believed that their own marriages were destined to last, saw no moral objection to divorce. Some thought that love relationships thrive on lots of talk, communication, and sharing; others felt that respect for the other person's independence is the key to a successful marriage. Some rested their conviction that their own marriages would survive on their sense of commitment to a wider community of Christian faith; others relied on personal compatibility to preserve their relationships. Some felt the need to think about their relationships a lot—to read books, consult friends, and develop theories about love; others took their marriages more for granted, assuming that what had made the relationship work in the past would keep on working.

Underneath this diversity of personal experience and cultural style, however, are striking commonalities. Interviewees share a vision of social bonds as products of voluntary individual choice. Indeed, the assumption that individuals choose their relationships is what makes both deciding to marry and maintaining a relationship so culturally problematic. Both mythic love and prosaic love acknowledge the fact that people must choose whom and whether to marry and whether or not to stay married.

This voluntarism, the assumption that individuals create social ties by their free choices, has long been considered a central feature of American culture. In this chapter we explore in greater depth what sustains this resilient cultural pattern. I first draw out the common themes that lie behind apparently diverse understandings. We will see that while interviewees differ in beliefs about the commitments and sacrifices necessary in love relationships, and while they may disagree profoundly about the moral understandings that ought to guide individual action, ultimately those differences boil down to differing conceptions of the selves who choose, and thereby constitute, relationships. Because social bonds are dependent on individual choices, beliefs about personal traits and predispositions and theories of what changes or stabilizes the self are critical to these middle-class Americans' theories of relationships.

Second, this chapter will illustrate how the voluntarist understanding of relationships implies a common cultural logic, even when it is employed by those with differing assumptions and divergent ends. That logic starts from the self whose ability to create social bonds rests on its capacity for autonomous individual choice, and it delineates the conditions necessary for such a self to make authentic, and therefore valid, choices.

Third, the chapter examines the commonalities across apparently diverse cultural understandings. Does some deeper structure underlie the variegated culture that appears in people's conversations? Given people's differing aspirations and purposes, why does voluntarist imagery seem so dominant? I shall try to demonstrate that even here, in what seems to be the deep structure of American culture, the encompassing institutional matrix rather than any simple unity of belief or cultural discourse accounts for the shared elements of a common culture.[1]

WORK ON THE SELF

We may think of the American focus on the self as a cultural technique for constructing strategies of action—especially strategies that create social bonds. Americans are unlike members of other cultures who ensure social relations by building up the family patrimony, subordinating themselves to a patron, or negotiating exchanges with potential allies.[2] For those trying to stay married, the problem is that the autonomous choice that initiates a marriage can always break it up again. Different cultural understandings provide different techniques for trying to reconcile enduring commitment and individual autonomy.

The Utilitarian Individual

The baseline model underlying varying moralities of the self is the utilitarian individual who maximizes his or her self-interest. As in the economic marketplace, individuals create ties to one another by contracting for mutually beneficial exchanges. For a pure utilitarian, what is right is whatever benefits the individual. As Ted Oster, the successful lawyer with a romantic view of marriage, put it:

> I've always loved that thing that Mark Twain said about something moral is something you feel good after, and something immoral is something you feel bad after. Which implies that you got to try everything at least once. I guess I'm pretty result oriented, and whatever produces a good result must be right, and whatever produces a bad result must be wrong.

Brian Palmer, the competitive executive, employed this same utilitarian logic when he justified his choices by saying that he does what gives him "satisfaction." Actions are right because of the benefits they produce for the actor. The individual actor, in turn, is one who has preferences or values and can make choices based on them.[3]

To solve a problem, to make a change, to improve life, the utilitarian individual must first clarify what she or he wants. This is what the lawyer meant when he said, "you got to try everything at least once." Unless you find out what you really enjoy, you will not be able to make decisions that maximize your self-interest.

After the failure of his first marriage, Brian Palmer (whose style and language we have already examined in chapter 5) reevaluated his priorities. He asked himself, "Why am I behaving in such and such a way? Why am I doing this at work? Why was I doing this at home?" His answer was that he was "operating as if a certain value was of the utmost importance" to him. Changing his life simply required changing his priorities, recognizing that "hey, it's not really all that important." Straightening out his life, finding out what went wrong, involved working to clarify what he really wanted.

For Brian, choosing to spend more time with his family was not a "sacrifice." "It's a conscious decision that I make that says, 'I got two alternatives. There are so many hours in a day, and I've been given the option to choose.'" But why is his family more important than career success? "I just find that I get more personal satisfaction from choosing course B over course A. It makes me feel better about myself." There is no larger reason why one course of action is better than another. Preferences can be justified only by the satisfaction the individual gets from them.

In this utilitarian understanding, individuals form connections to one another because they are mutually beneficial. One cannot impose one's own values on another person. Each individual's preferences are equally valid. As Brian noted, "One of the things that makes California such a pleasant place to live is people by and large aren't bothered by other people's value systems as long as they don't infringe upon your own." The corollary of this is that in cases of disagreement, or when the interests of two parties conflict, all individuals can do is to make sure they have their own priorities straight, communicate their desires clearly and honestly to others, and then negotiate the best mutually satisfactory arrangement. Human relationships are not structured by wider obligations or purposes, which might, for example, impose an order on marriages apart from the preferences of the individuals involved (based on beliefs that it is natural for people to live as couples, or that God commands indissoluble marriage and the roles of husband and wife). Only the benefits freely choosing individuals exchange with one another sustain human relationships.

The strategies of action supported by the utilitarian view involve work on the self, but it is work of a fairly simple sort. The first and most important thing individuals must do, for their own happiness and for the success of their social relationships, is to examine their own priorities and, as Brian Palmer did, bring their behavior into line with what they really want. To form social relationships, individuals can find others with whom they share common values or mutual interests. Only individuals who know their own priorities can form strong, mutually satisfactory ties to others.[4]

The central moral demand of utilitarianism is honest communication. Only through communication can people express their interests and negotiate effectively to meet the needs of others. Brian Palmer stressed the importance of "openness and communication. Communication is critical not only to a man and woman relationship, but it is the essence of our being on this planet in my opinion." He rejected absolute values, except for one: not lying, because lying interferes with the all-important ability of individuals to resolve their differences through communication:

> Being able to express how you feel about something to another human being, to another country, to another race, and being able to understand how they feel and reflect objectively as to why they feel that way, especially if there is conflict of how you feel about something. Given open communication and the ability to think problems out, most problems can be solved.

Utilitarian imagery about individuals making rational choices to maximize their interests can justify enduring commitments as well as temporary relationships based on expediency. Remember, for example, the contractarian terms in which Donald Nelson (the sober engineer we met in chapter 2) defended lifelong marriage: "If you don't want that kind of a relationship, you don't have to get married." Even if the marriage becomes boring, he argued, one chose to marry and that choice commits you to staying married. "Like I say, you don't have to get married."

The Disciplined Self

Those seeking enduring relationships may also work on the self by emphasizing the role of will. Fred Rowan, a stably married schoolteacher, raised a Catholic, stressed how this kind of work on the self can strengthen relationships: "I really feel strongly that almost any two people in whatever situation can really get along if they both make some effort to get along." Individual choice is primary, but individuals can shape what they want by effort or acts of will.

A stress on will begins to solve one of the greatest difficulties of the pure contract-utilitarian view of human relationships. Since there is nothing to guarantee that people's preferences will remain stable, there is in pure utilitarianism nothing to guarantee that any given relationship will last. Hervé Varenne, in *Americans Together* (1977), points out how this affects the structure of group life in America. When a group, like the Farm Bureau Federation branch Varenne studied in the small town of Appleton, ceases to fulfill the needs of its members, they feel free to dissolve it. But the opposite side of this coin is that a group's members must continually reaffirm their common bonds in order to keep the group alive. This, Varenne argues, accounts for the continuing dialectic in American life between individualism and conformity. Individuals must have unique preferences in order to form groups in the first place; but group members must avoid disagreements that might dissolve the group. Thus conformity, politeness, and the suppression of conflict reign within groups, while group members pride themselves on the individuality or nonconformity that justifies their choice of unique, like-minded others.

In a voluntarist understanding, one way people can stabilize relationships is by stabilizing the selves who enter into them. Simple willpower, the conviction that people can control what they "want" (as in Marriage Encounter's slogan, "Love Is a Decision"), offers a way to create more enduring social ties by stabilizing individuals' preferences.

Some Christians take the same principle even further, stabilizing selves by attaching them to what is eternal and unchanging. Although they offer a powerful critique of modern society's preoccupation with the self and its wants, they still describe a voluntarist understanding of social relationships.

Les Newman, the business-school graduate we met in chapter 2, is in his late twenties has been married for seven years. He used his perspective as an evangelical Baptist to offer a sophisticated critique of contemporary individualism:

> I guess in the divorce rate the biggest thing there is commitment.
> A lot of people are just taking it lightly. That's an offshoot, I think,
> to the large extent that our American society is becoming very self-
> oriented, or very individual-oriented: What's in it for me? How much
> do I get out of it . . . ? People don't look at the repercussions of their
> individual actions outside of themselves. The divorce rate, sexual be-
> havior today . . . people's attitude towards war, attitudes toward each
> other, I think they're all largely interrelated.

In this practicing Baptist's view, concern with one's self and one's own satisfaction cannot build a life, and it cannot provide an adequate foundation for relationships. Contrasting his own Christian marriage with other marriages, he describes a bond that goes beyond satisfying individual needs:

> There are a lot of people who obviously have very happy marriages
> and get along quite well. I'd say the biggest difference would be what
> purpose is there . . . ? What are we trying to achieve by being together
> and by being here? A lot of couples that I know aren't Christians are
> here to have a good time together and enjoy each other's
> company. . . . But I guess Connie and I, our number one priority is as
> a pair, as a couple, to work together in the way that we think God
> wants us to do, and it gives direction to our lives and our relationship
> that I don't think other people have.

Rather than building their relationship on changeable individual desires, Les Newman and his wife have a firmer foundation—the deeper sense of purpose they believe they have found in their Christian faith.

Les sees his life as anchored in something greater than himself. Yet if we examine his religious experience, we will see that his Christianity works largely by strengthening and stabilizing his self.

> One of the things I've gotten out of the Christian teachings and my personal relationship with Christ is the sense of commitment. In the sense that so much of what people do has got to be by a conscious decision. You can just sort of let life carry you along with the stream and you go wherever it goes, or you can make a decision to do something.

Through his religious beliefs, he found this capacity to make a decision and stick to it, anchoring a self that can persist in its commitments.

Speaking of the "most significant" experience of his life, Les Newman describes his "personal relationship with Jesus": It "has sort of been the ongoing thing that has tied together a whole bunch of different things. . . . He has steadied my emotion. . . . It has strengthened my commitment in my marriage, and it's had a great deal of impact on the way I relate with other people, at work, and in church and in other places too." For him, as for other Christians, transforming one's life means a kind of religiously guided work on the self.

Larry Beckett, an evangelical minister in his mid-thirties, described the process by which Christian faith strengthens the self, overcoming the selfishness and instability of ordinary human emotions. "I think most people are selfish, and when they're looking at relationships romantically they're primarily looking at it for themselves only." In contrast, "there is a love that we can have for other people that is generally selfless. We have to learn it. It's actually a matter of the will. I have to decide to go out and love people by action and by will for their own good, not because I enjoy it all the time, but because God commands it. Jesus said, 'Love your enemies.'" Although Jesus cannot command "emotions or affections," He "can command my will and my decision process and my actions, if I allow Him to." Through such training and shaping of the will, the Christian can come to want to do what the Bible commands, as "love for God becomes the motivational source for loving other people."

This evangelical minister described the fragility of marriages founded only on individual preferences and the stability that can come from anchoring the self in Christ:

> Whether it's career, or family, or romanticism as the center . . . I be-
> lieve that those things are innately limited. . . . Sometime they are go-
> ing to change, or get boring, or die down. If God is the center and He
> is unchanging, He's eternal, He is in fact our source and our maker,
> then by definition of who He is, He is not going to change."

The need to rely on something stronger and more enduring than
oneself is particularly acute given the fluidity of human emotions. Again
invoking will and decision, Les Newman said, "Before, I thought [love]
was all heart, all chemistry. Now I know that chemistry may be a good
start, but the only thing that makes it real love that will endure, and the
kind of love that is taken into marriages, is that mental decision that you're
going to force that chemical reaction to keep going with each other."
Howard Crossland, the agronomist we met in chapters 3 and 4, described
the way his Christian faith had given him "a pretty good handle on" himself. God stabilizes his emotions: "It's not really relying on your emotions.
There are certain facts presented [in the Bible] and you accept the facts. . . .
Like God loves me, even if I'm having a lousy day and I don't feel like he
loves me."

Only in the Christian faith is it "logical," the agronomist argues, to
say "to death do us part." In any relationship there will be crises, and Christian faith allows you to "weather the storm . . . until the calm comes back."
Through a relationship with Christ, one finds the strength to overcome
weaknesses and to control one's emotions and one's actions. The process
requires "help from the other members of the congregation and the help
of the Holy Spirit. First of all you accept God, then He gives you help to . . .
do good to your fellow man, to refrain from immorality, to refrain from
illegal things. . . . I do that because I love God and He says we shouldn't
do that." The Christian thus learns through his love of God to exercise
the moral and emotional self-control that stabilizes the self and social
relationships.

Connie Newman, the homemaker wife of the youthful business-
school graduate, Les Newman, echoes Howard Crossland's experiences almost exactly. She finds that "people who are totally non-churchgoing . . .
believe that in marriage if things don't work out they leave." She is an
emotional person: "That's part of the temperament that God gave me, except that I need to let Him stabilize my emotions." She lets God help her
in many ways—to "quit being bitter and resentful," not to "feel worthless," and to maintain her "commitment" to her marriage.

> I think when we got married more of my love was emotional then,
> than as a commitment. When the going got tough and Les was

having to study hard and the children were demanding my total attention, although I should have disciplined my mind and never let
these thoughts come in, I'd think, "Well, I'm just not going to put
up with this. I'm going to leave." That's not a commitment. That's
not real love. So I've let God work through me, and soften my heart
and teach me. . . .

Thus these Christians believe that the discipline of their faith steadies the
self to help it keep its commitments.

Attuned Selves

For those who do not trust willpower alone, or even willpower aided by
faith, there is another way of working on the self, which also promises to
help individuals create stronger, more enduring social bonds. This is the
"therapeutic ethic."

The therapeutic ethic helps individuals discover their true selves, so
they can make authentic choices that reflect what they "really" want. Its
underlying assumption is that individuals who have "gotten in touch
with" their real selves, freed of the inauthentic residues of family pressures, social roles, or others' expectations, will be able to forge genuine
bonds to others, ties that will be strong because they satisfy genuine needs
(not just arbitrary preferences) of both parties.

Through therapeutic effort, individuals can deepen their relationships, making them last not because they stabilize their selves but because
they achieve a deeper communication that allows them continuously to
adapt to one another. In this understanding, what threatens relationships
is not the fact that individuals change but that relationships die when they
no longer engage the authentic selves of their participants.

Melinda DaSilva, the second wife whom Thomas DaSilva described
in such glowing terms in the previous chapter, is an aspiring therapist in
her late twenties. She describes how she almost lost her marriage by letting conventional roles eclipse her real self. "You love your husband, and
this was the belief that I had, you do all these things for him. This is the
way you show him that you love him—to be a good wife." But in trying
so hard, she was "putting aside anything that [she] thought in trying to
figure out what he thought. Everything was just all put aside." What she
had "put aside" was her own, authentic self—her willingness to express
her opinions and act on her own judgment, even about how best to please
her husband. Through counseling, she began to see the problems in her
marriage as due to her failure to assert herself: "I began to realize when
Thomas and I went in [for counseling], I wouldn't voice my opinion, and

I was doing things just for him and ignoring things for myself. He viewed me less favorably, and I was doing it to get approval from him." Thus, losing oneself can threaten relationships by making one a less valuable, less interesting person.[5]

Even more important in the therapeutic view, one must be an autonomous person in order to create valid ties to others. Melinda DaSilva could "give a lot to [her] marriage" only when she "felt better" about herself. Indeed, really loving someone implies an active, free involvement that is incompatible with obligation, conformity to social roles, or even acting from a desire to please one's beloved. "The better I feel about myself, I feel I have a whole lot that I can contribute to Thomas, so I can value him more as opposed to idolize him. . . . You can be 'in love' with someone you idolize, but you can't 'love' someone you idolize."

A therapeutic understanding of love would seem to weaken relationships, teaching each partner to put the development of his or her autonomous self ahead of the relationship. Yet Melinda DaSilva learned, for example, that being "selfish" could be compatible with loving: "doing something just for yourself, which I never thought you can and still love." This new selfishness, she quickly makes clear, was also a way of becoming closer, sharing more of herself with her husband—"just thinking about myself and sitting and telling Thomas. . . . just when he comes in, saying I have to talk to him and sit him down and talk to him. . . . There are times when I don't even think about his day, but I can still love him."

In this therapeutic ideal of marriage, both partners have richer, more fully developed selves to share, and they can both give and receive more from each other. As Melinda came to see it, in a "good relationship" it is important "first for both people to be able to be strong and weak together at different times": "Our relationship, our marriage, changed as I became stronger. . . . That allowed Thomas to be able to come home and say, 'My job was horrible today'; or 'I was really upset'; or 'I was in a situation where I got anxious again.'" Knowing themselves more fully, they can share their strengths and weaknesses, developing over time a deeper, more satisfying relationship.

More clearly than either the utilitarian contract or the Christian marriage, the therapeutic relationship requires continuous work on the self to bind individuals together. In a sense, the richer and more elaborated the selves who come together in a relationship, the more they have to communicate, to exchange, to share. But the therapeutic ethic also attempts to deal with the problem left unresolved by pure contract imagery: Why would two people who come together to satisfy their own ends stay together? The therapeutically attuned acknowledge that selves change continually, but they make change the virtue out of which enduring relationships can come.

Melinda DaSilva describes how the difficulties she went through with her husband helped her understand the kind of lasting bond her parents shared. "I never understood until the past year, after Thomas and I had gone through counseling and everything. We shared experiences together. It's different than being in love. It's real different—because we have shared things together, time and experiences, all that." Her husband describes the "reassuring" quality of a relationship that has survived difficulties and developed psychological intimacy. "It's growing. It's a sense of growing together, that nobody else knows about. Just you and her. Just Melinda and I." Intimacy and shared experiences do not guarantee that a relationship will last, but they are, for the psychologically engaged, better insurance than simple self-interest, or the social glue of rules, roles, and expectations.

Deeper selves and richer communication cannot guarantee enduring relationships. But that is a risk the psychologically inclined are prepared to take. Thomas DaSilva continues, "I like knowing that we're growing and moving together although, hell, I'm scared a little bit. What if something happens again? No way. Well, you just deal with that." But dealing with life's difficulties becomes more likely, Thomas believes, when a couple share the skills required to remain attuned as they grow together toward an uncharted future: "A lot of communication. A lot of checking in. Lot of feedback. Lot of talk. That's absolutely essential." There may be risks, but the purpose of therapeutic intimacy is to create stability—stability that comes, paradoxically, from not rigidly resisting change. Another husband, Fred Rowan, the teacher who married his high school sweetheart, notes, "You keep the relationship dynamic that way, otherwise you don't grow, you just stagnate. People who have gotten divorces oftentimes focus in on one thing that was to remain constant throughout the relationship." Remaining more fluid in one's expectations provides a kind of stability through flexibility that may, in the therapeutic view, keep people together by keeping them attuned as they change.

Communication and sharing can also stabilize a relationship in another way, by making it continually new and exciting. The infinite richness of therapeutically enlightened selves and the excitement of continual change mean that relationships need never grow stale. Art Townsend, the liberal Presbyterian minister we met in chapter 4, described the rich communication he shares with his wife: "I mean there is so much more to that lady than I could possibly experience in twelve years, even intensely sharing." Fred Rowan reflected on the excitement of a dynamic marriage: "I want [our relationship] to keep changing. I don't want it to stay exactly the way it is. Even at moments when I am just overcome with how great our relationship is, I don't even want it to stay that way. . . . I don't want it to be stagnant or boring." Fred and his wife, Marge, did not insist that their relationship must last forever, although they both said that they "expect" it to. They stressed instead their willingness to accept change. "But," said Fred, "I feel pretty secure about our relationship, and if one of those changes happens to be something that our relationship ends, then that's probably the way the relationship was headed anyhow." This acceptance of both the excitement and the risks associated with change is the therapeutic ethic's answer to the fragility of relationships based on autonomous individual choice. Rather than obedience to divine authority, or mutual advantage in utilitarian exchange, individuals rely on sharing, communicating, and growing together to create dynamic stability in an ever-changing world.

I have argued that three very different American ideologies—utilitarian individualism and its theory of contract, fundamentalist Christianity and its theory of obedience to divine authority, and the therapeutic ethic with its theory of the authentic, expressive self—develop images of how to create enduring relationships. What these three images have in common is that they suggest ways of building relationships by working on individual selves. For the utilitarian, individuals must be clear about their own wants and communicate them honestly to create relationships advantageous to all parties. For the Christian, individuals must accept Jesus and obey Him in order to stabilize themselves in face of the vagaries of human feelings. For the therapeutically inclined, individuals must share the richness of their inner selves, to stay in tune with those they love.

In all three of these understandings, the key to enduring connection is work on the self, although the nature of that self differs. The utilitarian self is composed mainly of wants. It risks mistaking those wants (failing to "get its priorities straight") and thus not getting what it really desires. For the Christian fundamentalist, the self is the source of egocentric, sometimes unruly desires that must be tamed through will, through love of God that strengthens that will, and through obedience to God so that the self becomes a vehicle of His will. For the therapeutic individualist, the self is the seat of authentic feelings and needs that must be explored, brought to light, and expressed. Then therapeutically enriched selves will share those feelings, meet one another's needs, and create ever deepening, though always changing, bonds of shared experience.

Confusion of Tongues

Of course, views of self and relationships are not so neatly segregated as I have described them here. For some people, like the contented spouses in chapter 3, the notion that "I'm happy" provides a sufficient sense of security. The self appears so solid that there is no need (and perhaps no possibility) to work on it. And others, like the articulate lawyer in chapter 2, easily mobilize more than one cultural logic when they need to. Many others combine elements of Christian commitment with a therapeutic understanding of how God's love strengthens and opens the self. Judith Stacey, in *Brave New Families* (1990), a study of 1980s families in California's Silicon Valley, points to this "recombinant" culture, in which fundamentalist Protestants assimilate new-age feminism, or an egalitarian feminist seizes on Christian faith as a way to stabilize her marriage.

But even if people move among cultural logics with ease, or build personal edifices out of bricks and mortar from polyglot cultural sources, it is still necessary to explain why people's cultural understandings of prosaic love have as much coherence as they do. Why are there intelligible cultural logics for people to commingle, rather than simply a disordered agglomeration of cultural elements, with no particular pattern?

Both the order and the disarray in these cultural conversations can be traced back to the same source, to problems of action. On the one hand, persons do not have in their heads a single, coherent cultural stance that guides their action. Indeed, we see clearly that people resist the implications of their ideas whenever the ideas don't lead action in the direction they want. People justify their stable marriages by adding on more and more arguments from whatever source; committed utilitarians back away from the implications of their ideas when these prove unappealing; and even committed Christians argue that their marriages endure because the marriage makes them "happy."

Nonetheless, faced with a problem of action, with the need to stabilize a marriage or overcome a crisis, people reach for coherent ways to think about what to do, to be, to feel. Sometimes people adopt ideas from "experts," as Melinda DaSilva did with those she had learned from counseling. Sometimes people work to "figure out" a problem, as Brian Palmer did when he rethought his priorities. Some people may rely on relatively coherent worldviews, as did Howard Crossland, the Christian agronomist, drawing on his church's systematic ideology.[6] Anticipating a problem or looking back on a crisis, people express something like a philosophy of life, even if that philosophy is only one of many different resources they draw on, recombine, or shift around to meet the varied circumstances in which they need to act. Most people trim their philosophy to fit their action commitments and use logic to try to sweep up the remnants.

To the extent that there is coherence in the ways people organize their cultural understandings, it comes from two sources. First, coherence is imposed retrospectively (and sometimes retroactively) as people fit their understandings to the institutionalized conventions of a biographical narrative, and even more to the institutionalized pattern of the coherent self (Linde 1993). Thus they seek continuities that make sense of who they are as individuals, that seem to give their lives coherent meaning.[7] It is in this sense that at least some people will claim a coherent philosophy of life, even when they routinely make ad hoc deviations from its logic. The other source of coherence, however, is that which comes from the fact that people face consistent problems of action that drive them repeatedly to turn to similar sorts of solutions. When many people face the same action context, the same coherent culture will reappear across many individuals, even those who on the surface seem to have very different cultural assumptions. It is to the latter kind of coherence that we now turn.

No Regrets

The men and women I talked with held varied views of love and marriage, from Christian insistence on indissoluble marriage to feminist rejection of marriage as an oppressive institution. They were united, however, in a particular morality of the self. This morality commands individuals to do only what they can do willingly. The autonomous self must freely choose its actions.

On the one hand, such views seem to reflect the specific, historically circumscribed cultural style of the "Me Decade" of the 1970s. Respondents seek to discover their own, authentic feelings. They reconcile tensions between individual desires and social demands by insisting that the only real obstacles people face are intrapsychic ones. On the other hand, these views seem to echo an original American voluntarism, the same culture that announced that "we the people" could "form a more perfect union." (Remember that it was Ralph Waldo Emerson who wrote "No law can be sacred to me but that of my nature. Good and Bad are but names very readily transferable to that or this; the only right is what is after my constitution; the only wrong is what is against it." And even more unsettling to a modern ear: "But do your thing, and I shall know you" [from "Self-Reliance," 1841].) In looking at why even those who value commitment, self-sacrifice, and enduring relationships rely so heavily on ideas about the self, I would like to suggest a third possibility.

The Americans I interviewed implicitly recognize that no effective institutions now enforce the social bonds they value most. So it makes no sense to say that people "must" or even that they "should" do what they really do not want to do. Such obligations have no institutional meaning. One cannot any longer force a spouse who wants to leave a marriage to stay. Even the sanction of community disapproval, which might have given moral judgments force, has largely dissipated. If we listen closely to what interviewees say, most do not argue that people should do whatever will give them the most pleasure. What they declare instead is that it is not meaningful to talk about obligation or sacrifice in a world where the commitments those words imply could not be enforced. Instead they talk about personal moral choice. People will in the end do what they want, and all one can do is avoid entanglements with people whose character would lead them not to want to do what is right.

The view that people must do only what they freely choose to do appears most strikingly in interviewees' responses to vignettes about hard choices created by misfortune or intractable circumstance. As these interviewees see the world, no external obstacle, however obdurate, can negate individuals' freedom to determine their own destinies. Neither resignation to one's fate, nor loyalty to kin or community, nor submission to God's will, for example, seems to these middle-class Americans adequate justification for action. Only the self's free choices make action legitimate.

I used two vignettes about sacrifice (see the appendix) in which people had to choose between their own happiness and their obligations to others. In the first story, one spouse was faced with a difficult choice when the other fell into an incurable depression; in the second, a couple had to resolve a conflict between one's job and the other's "once in a lifetime opportunity" for graduate study. Responding to the career-conflict vignette, a twenty-six-year-old dance teacher, married only a year, said, "I think if they love each other one will sacrifice. . . . They will want to sacrifice. It may be very hard, but they will want to do that for the other person." Thus love can make people voluntarily choose sacrifice, and "wanting to" makes sacrifice acceptable. But because sacrifice must be voluntary, it is limited by what people really want. In the crunch, the fate of the relationship hangs on people's inner selves, what they really feel. Asked how the couple should decide who will move, she says, "[If] she feels school is more important than her love for him, then she should go to school. If he feels—you know, it's a gut feeling thing. What they feel in the heart is right." Wanting to sacrifice turns out to mean sacrificing only if you want to.

In a fully voluntarist understanding, the concept of sacrifice evaporates altogether. A person who knows what he wants and acts on that knowledge cannot sacrifice, since anything he truly wants to do is not a sacrifice. Art Townsend, the self-actualized minister whom we met in chapter 4, articulated this clearly: "What is a sacrifice? . . . If something is really in my own best interest, is that a sacrifice?" Asked whether a wife sacrificed by staying with her badly disabled husband, he argued, "How about . . . that the greatest love is the love that sees beyond the apparent, to what in fact is real. And tell me, on that level, what was the young woman sacrificing, really?" In his view, the very idea of sacrifice is simply a symptom of inadequate self-understanding. Only a person who denied her own power to choose could imagine that she was "sacrificing" for another.

This widespread moral vision holds that people should know what they really want, and that when a person is clear about his or her own priorities, nothing is really a sacrifice. In this spirit, a thirty-five-year-old divorced photographer considers whether she is "sacrificing to some extent" by neglecting her work to spend time with her children. "No," she says, "making priorities—what is really important. I don't want to sacrifice, because if I sacrifice then I'll be resentful." Her children are most important right now. "There are things I would love to be doing, but there will be time. It will resurface. There's a lifetime." Here the optimism that says "there's a lifetime" seems a way for this single mother to shore up her strength so she can continue to make the sacrifices she must make by denying the costs to herself. She rejects the language of "sacrifice" because in a world where your only obligation is to do what you really want to do, to admit that one is sacrificing would be to invite the suggestion that one should simply stop and pursue what one really wants. People seem to fear that with nothing but their individual psychological commitments to back up their sacrifices, if they start counting the costs, they will bankrupt the system. Therefore one can have priorities and make choices, but no options are really closed. Seeing one's choices as a sacrifice would mean being somehow false to oneself.

For some respondents, denial of sacrifice requires a tenacious optimism. No one need sacrifice, because everything will work out for the best. But this optimism in turn rests on the solipsistic view that apparent obstacles originate within the self and can be dissolved by a change in attitude.[8] For Cindy Davis, an unmarried student in her early twenties, the question of whether the man in the career-conflict vignette should sacrifice his job for his long-term girlfriend's education "depends on how flexible he is" or "if he sees himself as—'how dare she even suggest that I make the move.'" Value-laden psychological diagnosis substitutes here for a language of purely moral evaluation. If the man is psychologically together, if he is flexible rather than rigid, secure rather than defensive, then he will be willing to move.

The work world, Cindy presumes, creates few real constraints: "Most jobs nowadays are flexible. Normally when you do leave a job you end up getting a better advancement. Even if he had to start over, it may be a good and exciting thing for him." The right attitude could turn potential sacrifice into "an exciting new start" for both members of the couple, and the boyfriend's attitude largely determines whether his job is too good to give up: "He shouldn't give up if he really feels his job is really too good," but "sometimes some of your statements are made out of fear—'I'm afraid to leave my job.' Does he really want to stay because he loves his job?" Resolving conflict between the two individuals' interests then is not a matter of discovering what is objectively fair or evaluating competing moral claims. Rather the two individuals must examine their own psyches to find the internal psychological obstacles that are preventing agreement. The boyfriend should "try," "look into possibilities," to show he cares. Even if he has to compromise, "It shouldn't be really a sacrifice on his part. He should feel that he cares enough to say 'I'll do it.'" Thus the individual is free to choose, in a world so benign that sacrifice is unnecessary for one with the right attitudes, as it is impossible for one who is only doing what he really wants to do.

Where stubborn realities force real choices, the mandate to choose what one really wants can become an insistence on putting the self first. Asked about the wife whose husband is incapacitated by depression, Cindy Davis sees the wife's guilt as the problem to be overcome. "I think she probably should leave. Staying just for guilt. If he ever found that out it would make things worse. . . . You want them to be with you because they love you and want to stay." Indeed, the optimism that denies sacrifice easily turns into a pessimism that discourages it—since it would not work anyway. It would only "make things worse" for the husband if he knew his wife had stayed out of guilt. And, as many other interviewees also noted, self-sacrificing behavior would backfire because the person making the sacrifice would, in the end, be unable to endure violating her real wants or needs. The very concept of sacrifice, then, raises insoluble problems for a voluntarist ethic in which only the self's free choices should determine action.

Choosing Commitment

These interviewees did not, however, favor selfishness or reject commitment.[9] Their attitudes toward sacrifice stemmed rather from an assumption that the self and its free choices are the source of all effective legitimate social bonds (see Varenne 1977). This assumption appears especially clearly when they talk about obligation. "Owing" seems to them not fully voluntary and thus incompatible with authentic moral action. Cindy Davis responded impatiently to a question about whether a married woman in love with another man "owes" her husband anything after their years together: "It's that type of thing of guilt and owe that I don't like. If she still loves him and is a caring person and a strong person, she should stay." The kind of self one has determines how one should act.

For an occasional respondent, aversion to the idea of "owing" reflects a me-first ideology—like that of the divorced photographer who, asked what the wife tempted to leave her husband for another man should do, said "go for it," since "if something comes along and you have these opportunities . . . and it feels right, one ought to do that." In general, however, those who reject owing hold a more complex view. Married ten years, with one child, Jemina Pearson, a thirty-four-year-old travel agent, agrees with Cindy Davis that the wife who has fallen in love owes her husband nothing: "You don't marry and then take on a huge debt. . . . Certainly you end up with guilt feelings for various and sundry reasons, but that's something you set up yourself." Indeed, she insists, the woman "can't make her decision based on what it's going to do to him. She has to make it based on what she needs and what she wants out of life."

Jemina Pearson is very committed to her own marriage, although she doesn't believe that marriage as an institution is "important." She says that her husband is the most important thing in her life. Her moral rule is not that the self should come first; it is rather that the self should choose its commitments.[10] Asked whether a wife is right to leave a husband who refuses demands for greater communication, she replies, "If she thought that was what she had to do, then she was right." If the woman forced herself to stay, "She would have to compromise herself and her ideals. If she was able to live with that, fine." But whatever the reasons for her choices, in the end, she should do whatever she really wants to do. If, for example, she wants to leave because "she's just tired of" her husband, "then she should get out of the marriage. It's not doing either one of them any good." If the wife loves another man? "I don't know. [laughing] If she feels that strongly about it, then she should go for the second man, I suppose."

This real-politik-of-the-self makes it unrealistic to ask whether people *should* do what they do not want to do.

Underlying this position is a demand for authenticity. Only commitments freely made, by selves who take responsibility for their actions, can endure. Thus people must know what they want in order to form ties to others. Sacrifice and obligation are wrong because they imply a falseness to the self—wanting one thing while forcing oneself to do another (or pretending to want one thing, while choosing another). Since only an authentic self can form valid social ties, rejecting sacrifice becomes a way of affirming connection. Considering the couple for whom career and schooling conflict, the travel agent, Jemina Pearson, says, "I don't think you have to sacrifice. I think you have to decide what's most important to you. If the most important thing is being together . . . " Even for those who accept the term "sacrifice," it is still what people want that really matters. As the dance teacher quoted above says, "they will want to sacrifice. It may be very hard, but they will want to do that for the other person." For both these women, despite their different views of "sacrifice," people can freely choose to put their relationships first.

Resistance to the idea of "owing" can sound quite old-fashioned, harkening back to the traditional American ideal of self-reliance. A woman in her fifties, married more than twenty-five years, says, "I don't like the feeling that I owe anything to anybody. I like to do it because I want to, and because I care enough." Fred Rowan, the teacher and devoted family man in his early thirties, "chose very carefully" when he married because marriage was "forever." He willingly acknowledges "some kind of duty to each other, especially in relation to kids." Nevertheless, he insists, "I don't look at it as owing. I never liked the idea of owing anything to anybody, so I don't think I would look at it that way." These people oppose owing not because they object to enduring commitments or want to be free to pursue "self-actualization." Rather they want the sense of autonomy that comes with possessing oneself free and clear, thus being able to dispose one's commitments voluntarily.[11]

To Thine Own Self Be True

These ways of thinking about obligation and sacrifice reflect a shared moral understanding of action, even when they justify quite different life commitments. Free choice by an autonomous self makes action valid. Assumptions about such selves—how they are developed, on what bases they choose, and how they can form social bonds—frame moral discourse.

Within this framework social and moral principles can be debated, but such debates take the form of disagreements about the character, motives, and choices of independent selves.

When Cindy Davis, the student quoted above, rejected "that type of thing of guilt and owe," she was not advocating that a wife cavalierly leave her husband. But her moral view came packaged as a theory about individual character rather than as a claim about what is generally right. "If she still loves him and is a caring person and a strong person, she should stay." What someone "should" do depends on the kind of person she is. Indeed, in her view, whether the woman has a "right" to leave her husband depends on her own strength or weakness. "It depends on how strong a person she is—if she can live leaving a man who loves her. . . . if she is really that self-centered." She then continued, "If she's like that then it would be very hard for her to find real love. . . . You can't always think just about yourself." Cindy Davis thus insists that answers to moral dilemmas depend fundamentally on personal qualities. Or rather, it is pointless to debate moral obligations when psychological capacities are the real determinants of individual action.

Even those who put commitment, tradition, or family first share similar underlying premises about social life. Almost all my respondents understood their own moral commitments—however various—as a consequence of the unique individuality that defines who they are. Both the sober engineer and the successful lawyer of chapter 2 justified their stable marriages in terms of their personal preferences, offering versions of the argument that "that's just the kind of person I am."

Maryellen Palmer, the recently remarried, forty-two-year-old wife of the business executive, Brian Palmer, embraces the idea of sacrifice, but justifies it by appealing to her idiosyncratic preferences. A "practicing Christian" (in her husband's admiring words), she enjoys taking care of others, particularly in her roles as wife and mother. Asked what makes a relationship "work," she responds, "a lot of being able to give. A lot of sacrificing." As "really a pretty subservient-type person," she says, "I like giving. I'm a very giving person." Yet even this giving Christian sees sacrifice primarily as an expression of her individual personality. While "giving" has religious meaning ("I feel that we're really here to help each other"), she stresses its satisfactions for her. "I feel very empty when I can't give to somebody"—"empty" because "not fulfilled, I think. I really get a lot of pleasure out of it." Thus, for her, self-sacrifice is a form of self-fulfillment, good because she freely chooses it and because it expresses her own deepest self. Asked if there is a danger of sacrificing too much, she says, "I think when you sacrifice so much that you're not your own person anymore."

Sacrifice makes sense only in terms of an autonomous self. In her first marriage, to an alcoholic, "I was sacrificing so much that pretty soon I felt really totally just empty. And I didn't like myself the way I was." Sacrifice that undermines the self undermines the very source of valued action.

Despite her deep sense of religious conviction, Maryellen Palmer talks as if "values" were purely individual matters. Friends with different values were "never a threat, because I had to live with me. That's the only person I have to live with is myself, and they had to live with themselves. It was O.K. for them. I didn't care what they did." Jemina Pearson, the travel agent, irreligious and involved mainly with her family, offers a similar observation about the vignette of the wife who left her uncommunicative husband: "If she thought that was what she had to do, then she was right." For her, as for Maryellen Palmer, the operative rule is that one must obey one's own, internal standard. If the wife forced herself to stay, then "she would have to compromise herself and her ideals. If she was able to live with that, fine." [12]

What is this core self that cannot be violated? It is defined less by its content than by its function as the seat of the capacity to choose. In order to choose, the self must have criteria for judging the world. Those criteria are a person's "values." Nan Pfautz, the fortyish divorced administrator (from chapter 5) who is also a committed social and religious activist, says that in serving others one must not sacrifice one's own "well-being"—for example, doing "something that was against your conscience." Conscience consists of one's personal "values"; and values in turn define the self: "Your values are very important to you, and if you sacrifice your values . . . then you're losing a lot of yourself." But values are important not because they are religiously validated or because they express the nature of human existence. Rather, one's values are right because one has chosen them: "For some people it's a value as to how they eat, whether they eat only natural foods, but for me that's not a value. But if that were my value and he wanted refined sugar and I did it and it was going against one of my values, then I would be losing part of myself." Thus in a kind of circular logic, the self becomes both the source and the end of its own existence.

Do You Love Me?

In the American musical *Fiddler on the Roof,* Tevye asks his wife of twenty-five years, the mother of his three daughters, "Do you love me?" The song evokes poignant laughter in audiences because it speaks to a profound sociological issue. In a world where marriages were secure, where the bond could be taken for granted, the question "Do you love me?" would not arise. American audiences long for that security, yet they embrace the voluntarism that makes it "nice to know" that the answer is "yes."

I argued in chapter 6 that the mythic culture of love reproduces the institutional features of marriage—all-or-nothing, exclusive, status-transforming, enduring—as if they were characteristics of the feelings partners in a relationship inspired in each other. People use mythic love to formulate choices—whether to enter into or remain in a marriage. In this chapter, I have explored the prosaic-realistic culture of love. This culture describes ways to stay married by managing relationships and working on the selves who create those relationships. People use the diverse wisdom of the prosaic love culture to think about ongoing relationships.

Even people who think about love very differently (or who draw simultaneously on a hodgepodge of various understandings of love), I have argued, address a common problem—how love relationships can last even though they rest on the free choices of the individuals who create them. The culture of love flourishes in the gap between the expectation of enduring relationships and the free, individual choice upon which marriage depends.

There is an institutional correlate to this voluntarist understanding of love. The institution of marriage is less and less institutionally distinctive (see Cherlin 1992:71) and the legal obligations it creates are more fragile and less onerous (see Weitzman 1985; Prager 1982). Even the informal but once powerful sanctions that supported marriage as a set of enforceable social obligations have largely dissolved. Now if it is "wrong" for someone to leave her spouse, the person herself must feel that it is wrong, or the moral judgment is empty. Love relationships are increasingly matters of individual choice, and no authoritative power—kin group, community, or law—forces individuals to do what is "right." Therefore, what is right in love relationships becomes a matter of the character and motives of individual selves who, after all, make the crucial choices love involves.

A more general case can be made that there is a powerful but paradoxical relationship between moral claims and institutional sanctions. It is difficult, if not impossible, to assert a moral claim that could not conceivably be enforced. In a brilliant study, *Medieval French Literature and Law* (1977), R. Howard Bloch has shown that new conceptions of personal moral responsibility emerged in Europe as feudal courts developed the power to impose a settlement on contending nobles. Autonomous political authority gave reality to an autonomous moral standard. Jorge Arditi (1998), in an even more ambitious analysis, has shown how in the succeeding centuries new configurations of political authority altered patterns of social relationships among the European nobility. The social moralities of *courtoisie, courtesy,* and eventually *civility* and *etiquette* both reflected and made possible transformed "infrastructures of social relations."[13] Increasingly autonomous, internally disciplined selves could meet and form ties in a collectively fashioned civil society.

In a similar way, today's notion of universal "human rights" is made plausible by international organizations, such as the United Nations and Amnesty International, which can define and monitor such rights (see Boli and Thomas 1997; McNeely 1995), and by the possibility demonstrated at Nuremberg that standards superior to the sovereignty of national states are enforceable.[14] In the case of human rights, of course, the idea is grand and enforcement is puny. But the growing credibility of this idea in the last decade suggests that changes in international institutions have made the concept of morally authoritative human rights increasingly real.[15]

While institutions, or the capacity for action that institutions create, may help make ideas real, people elaborate culture where institutions are incomplete. Contemporary marriage inspires culture creation precisely because it is institutionally incomplete. The effort to hold a valued social arrangement in place, to restore the solid outline to an increasingly sketchy, uncertain shape, has generated energetic cultural activity. These efforts take a wide variety of forms, from the turn to fundamentalist religion among those seeking stable families (Stacey 1990; Kaufman 1991), to the anti-abortion movement (Luker 1984), to the elaborated theories of the self I discuss here.

Without expectations of (or hope for) stable relationships, there would be no need for a culture of love. People would come together or drift apart as friends do in our culture, arousing feelings we might frequently describe as "loving," but without the need for a special cultural category of "love"—neither the mythic love that makes one person uniquely right, nor the prosaic love that makes relationships last.

Without voluntarism—cultural practices that make social relationships matters of choice—there would also be no need for a culture of love. Like Tevye's wife, people could be married without continually examining whether or not they loved their partners enough to stay in the relationship, or in the right way to make the relationship last.

"Love," like other powerful cultural concepts, embodies a contradiction central to the society in which it flourishes (Hewitt 1989).[16] The ideal of love describes a relationship so right that it can be simultaneously perfectly free and perfectly binding. A purely voluntary commitment, love is a contradiction in terms. The power of the concept of love is continually renewed by the contradiction it bridges. Only if there really is something like love can our relationships be both voluntary and enduring.[17]

Here again we see that culture is elaborated where there is active work to be done. Problems of action generate meaning. Insoluble problems of action generate intense, powerful, relatively coherent meanings. But because love and marriage create multiple problems of action, and because people devise a variety of strategies for negotiating these dilemmas, people frame their understandings of love in multiple ways and they shift frequently among differing conceptions of love. The unsettling issues that love raises stimulate the production of multiple—sometimes overlapping, sometimes coherent—theories to meet the irresolvable contradictions of institutional incompleteness.

Hewitt (1989) explains vacillations between individualism and community in American life by arguing that American individualism orients participation in large, impersonal contexts like the market and the state, while people seek community in smaller, more intimate primary groups. While Hewitt is right to recognize the contradictoriness of this culture, he cannot be right about its sources. It is precisely in the intimate "community" of marriage and family life that I found voluntarist individualism so elaborated. People also had other, more "communitarian" ways to talk about love and marriage, but the story of how individual selves choose was central for real love. Thus the contradiction is not between impersonal and personal domains but between the premises and the promises of marriage.[18]

When marriage was a firmer institution, the mythic culture of romantic love helped bridge the gap between the voluntary choices of individuals to marry (the uninstitutionalized part of the institution of marriage) and the institution of marriage itself. In the current period, when divorce has radically altered marriage, a new culture of prosaic love attempts to bridge the gap between the persisting expectation that marriages should last and the increasingly insecure character of the marriage bond. Where institutions have begun to unravel, men and women do active cultural work to patch together rents in the institutional fabric.

It is necessary to note, of course, that the remedies for marital instability proposed by the utilitarian, Christian, and therapeutic cultures of love do not succeed in the sense that they do not prevent the breakup of relationships. But, as I argued in chapter 6, the cultural worldviews that sustain strategies of action do not describe an objective, external reality. Instead they outline the structure of a strategy of action itself. The culture of love would die out, lose its plausibility, not if marriages did not last (they don't) but if people stopped trying to form and sustain lasting marriages. The prosaic love culture I have explored in this chapter does not describe how marriages actually work, nor does it provide practical recipes that keep marriages together. But it does describe the efforts people make to treat marriage as an enduring institution.

This chapter and the last, focusing on institutions, have offered one answer to the question of why culture might develop coherent patterns even though individuals operate quite happily with diffuse, often incomplete and internally contradictory cultural resources. This cultural structuring by institutions might be thought of as operating from the outside in, organizing dispersed cultural materials the way the field surrounding a magnet links iron filings or the way the gravity of the sun orients the planets. That is, as persons orient themselves to institutional demands and institutional dilemmas, they continually reproduce structured cultural understandings, even when those structured pieces do not add up to an internally coherent whole. In the next chapter, I suggest two other ways culture may be structured by social processes in the larger public arena, even when the thoughts and feelings of individuals are quite unsystematic.

CHAPTER 8

CODES, CONTEXTS,

AND INSTITUTIONS

*T*his book has explored how culture works by asking two interrelated questions: first, how do people use culture? and second, how does culture influence action? I have argued that because answers to the first question turn out to be so complex, sociological answers to the second question need rethinking. Because people hold multiple, sometimes ambiguous, sometimes competing cultural understandings, and because they know much more culture than they use at any given time, we must examine why people mobilize the culture they do and how they adapt or rework it before we can analyze how culture shapes experience and action.

Our usual metaphors for thinking about culture's influence involve "depth." Some culture is deeper, more embedded, closer to the core of a society or a self. And the metaphor implies that the deeper the culture—either deeply internalized in the self or deeply embedded in society—the more powerfully it will affect action. But this equation between cultural depth and cultural power needs to be reexamined. Here I want to look at what gives force to cultural meanings without assuming that deeper cultural meanings inevitably have more powerful effects on action.

In exploring what actually gives cultural meanings the power to shape action, we must look not only at what goes on inside individual psyches but at the larger contexts that govern action (see Wuthnow 1989). We must move beyond the question of whether people believe or practice culture with greater or less intensity, depth, or devotion to ask what gives a cultural formulation the power to affect action. We will see that cultural elements can have enormous power, even when they are very lightly, ambivalently, or insincerely held. And even very deep cultural beliefs and practices may constrain action intermittently or not at all.

In analyzing where and when culture actually affects action, I concentrate on forces that focus, organize, and enforce cultural meanings: codes, contexts, and institutions. These operate "from the outside in," as, for example, when cultural codes define what an individual's action means, independently of what the person intends it to mean. This differs from our earlier exploration of when culture becomes meaningful for particular people or when and how they apply culture to their life experience. In this chapter I develop the argument that culture can have powerful influence on action even when individuals do not deeply internalize its meanings, when it remains a matter of indifference or antipathy, or even when they are ambivalent or confused about its meanings. Codes, contexts, and institutions provide crucial links between culture and action. They do so by structuring the external environment of meanings that surround actors, giving those meanings coherence and direct implications for action that they often lack in the thoughts and feelings of individuals.

Because of the kind of argument I develop in this chapter, I make very little use of my interview materials here. Interviews inevitably focus on the ways culture and experience are organized (or as I argue, not very organized) within the experience of particular individuals.[1] Instead I draw examples from a wide range of sources, from studies of social revolutions to practices of gift-giving in an American community. This is because I am trying to illustrate a variety of possible ways in which cultural meanings are structured—and sometimes brought to bear on action—by processes that lie outside direct individual experience. This is not a matter of drawing some sharp boundary between the inside and the outside of what I somewhat inelegantly think of as "people's heads" (and would necessarily include their bodies and their emotional repertoires as well). Rather, it is a matter of analyzing how culture operates simultaneously—but with different organization—at different levels. Culture is, of course, inside people's heads. But culture often has powerful causal influence on action when it is structured and given force by other processes—such as codes, contexts, and institutions—that organize cultural meanings and bring them to bear.

CODES

In a study of Christmas gift-giving in "Middletown," Caplow (1982, 1984) offers a wonderful example of how culture can influence action from the "outside," whether or not people deeply believe it. Caplow notes that Christmas gift-giving occupies an important place in Middletown's culture. People spend a great deal of time and money buying gifts; they fret about finding the right gift; many plan all year to complete their gift-giving responsibilities by Christmas. But when Caplow and his associates interviewed people about giving Christmas gifts, they found great ambivalence. Many people felt that Christmas had become too commercialized, that gift-giving violated the real meaning of Christmas, and that retailers promoted Christmas giving only to stimulate sales. They found the process of both buying and receiving gifts unsatisfying, feeling that most of the things they gave and received were useless. In short, Middletowners were highly critical of Christmas gift-giving. Then why, Caplow asks, did they continue this ritual despite their disenchantment?

Caplow found the answer in an examination of actual gift-giving practices. Looking closely at what people gave, he found that a simple "semiotic code" was at work. The more important someone was to the giver, the more valuable the gift. Thus not to give a gift was to send a message: no gift would signal that the (non)recipient was not valued. Caplow argues that this system of meanings enforced conformity to gift-giving practices without "normative consent." By this he means that people gave gifts not because they themselves believed in the practice, found it meaningful, or even acted from unthinking habit. Rather people were constrained by their knowledge of *what their actions would mean to others.*[2]

In recent years, terms like "semiotic code" and "discourse" have infiltrated the social sciences from the humanities. Such terms relocate culture in the public domain, focusing on publicly available systems of meaning, on the codes that define what it is possible to say, rather than on the particular thoughts or utterances of individual speakers.[3] But following Caplow, I think of a semiotic code in a more limited way than many contemporary culture analysts. A semiotic code is a self-referential system of meanings in which each element in the system takes its meaning not from its inherent properties or from some external referent, but from the meanings created by the code itself. Thus if a school divides its students into two competing sports teams, the "Blues" and the "Golds," the meanings of Blue and Gold within that school are defined by the system of competing teams, the assignment of students to teams, and the rule that each student must be either a "Blue" or a "Gold." The system of Christmas gift-giving is a semiotic code in the sense that the "meaning" of a gift is defined in relative terms: the more valuable the gift, the more valued the recipient. Gifts are markers in a system of meanings, and thus whatever the "private" meanings individual givers and recipients hold, knowledge of the code defines the public meaning of the gift.

Semiotic codes are often thought of as the "deep structure" of a culture, by analogy with the deep structures of language, the general set of invisible but necessary rules that make it possible for people to generate and understand particular utterances. I argue, however, that semiotic codes can be culturally powerful even when they are of recent origin, lightly held, or even widely mistrusted. Extending Caplow's example of Christmas gift-giving, which might after all be regarded as a deeply embedded traditional practice despite recent cavils, we might consider the public pressure by florists and greeting-card companies to celebrate Mother's Day. The publicly promoted code is that if you love your mother you will remember her with a card, a gift, or flowers on Mother's Day. Whatever their cynicism about the holiday, many people, realizing that their mothers and their mothers' friends have probably seen the same deluge of advertising they have, conclude that, however much both they and their mothers know that a child's real love for a parent is expressed in other ways, it is prudent to send at least a token of that love on Mother's Day. For some, of course, Mother's Day may have special sentimental meanings; some families make it the occasion for a celebratory outing or breakfast-in-bed for Mom. But all know the public code, and if they do not follow it, they may need to negotiate a way around it.

Even Mother's Day may seem culturally deep, if only because, founded between 1907 and 1912, it celebrates the nation's special valuing of mothers.[4] But take the recent introduction of National Secretaries Week, which appears designed to tide florists over the spring hiatus between Easter and Mother's Day. Here a semiotic code has been established simply by saturation advertising: bosses who value their secretaries will give them flowers and take them to lunch during Secretaries Week. And the difficulty is that even the most skeptical, who recognize the trumped up, commercial origins of the occasion, may find themselves trapped by the wide publicity of the code. If one's boss won't even spend a few dollars, does that signal that he or she doesn't care? Both bosses and secretaries, however distasteful they may find the holiday, may nonetheless worry about the signal their actions will send. Indeed, that is the key to semiotic constraints on action. One is constrained not by internal motives but by knowledge of how one's actions may be interpreted by others.

Semiotic codes like the one promulgated by National Secretaries

Week are not deep, integral parts of the wider culture. But they *are* eminently political. A national secretaries union, publicizing a "Bread, Not Roses" campaign, might shift the code, pressing bosses to enter labor negotiations during National Secretaries Week and making flowers without a raise a sign of contempt. Politics very frequently consists in such struggles over meanings. Culture and power interact directly as groups struggle to define the meanings of their own and others' actions.

Gender politics in recent decades have been dominated by just such battles over semiotic codes. While quite rightly pointing to women's very limited gains in the workplace and a "backlash" among some opinion leaders, feminists have succeeded in producing a remarkable shift in the basic cultural codes that organize gender understandings.[5] The clearest example is the emergence of the term "macho," which defines a hypermasculinity that is automatically suspect. It relabels some traditionally masculine behaviors—such as acting tough and domineering, getting into fights, or swaggering—as symptoms of an exaggerated need to assert masculinity, a need that may be a cover for masculine inadequacy. And while there is no exact converse term denoting excessively passive, foolish femininity, we can clearly see the emergence of such an image, recoding what were formerly valued feminine traits. The antiheroines of such pop-culture films as *An Officer and a Gentleman, Working Girl,* or *Erin Brockovich* suggest that real women are forthright, tough, and sexually open, while women who act traditionally feminine—dependent, helpless, vulnerable—are manipulative, selfish schemers.

The reorganization of gender codes can be seen both in didactic works and less self-conscious genres. A movie like *Aliens,* with its tough, machine-gun-toting heroine and its all-devouring, egg-producing-mother monster seems a meditation on the basic ways we encode femaleness. Disney's fairy-tale *Beauty and the Beast* intentionally plays with gender expectations. Gaston's "perfect" masculinity is shown to be ridiculous and then evil. The Beast earns Beauty's love by his gentle vulnerability; and Beauty proves herself by being literary and adventurous rather than simply beautiful.

Such movie efforts need not work directly on hearts and minds to influence action. By reworking existing codes, they can alter the meanings of gender attitudes and behaviors. Rather than making men believe, for example, that they ought to be more nurturant or making women feel that they ought to be more assertive, such gender recodings recast what it is to be a real man or a real woman. Gender recodings sway people not by persuading them to want to be different but by suggesting that old styles and behaviors will be read in new ways. What formerly signaled maleness now signals insecurity about one's masculinity; what formerly were feminine virtues have been recoded as signs of a selfish manipulator.

Semiotic codes thus provide one answer to the question of how the welter of competing cultural meanings is actually brought to bear on action. Codes influence action by ordering the profusion of cultural information into a few simple categories and defining the signs of membership in each category. Actors are then constrained by their knowledge, often implicit, of how their action will be read by others. People may be especially constrained by cultural codes in impersonal, public contexts, and somewhat less constrained in intimate situations where they can more directly influence the ways their behavior will be read by others.

Of course, all social action involves awareness of the actions and responses of others. Indeed, Max Weber (1968:4–12) defined social action as action that is meaningfully oriented toward the action of others; and symbolic interactionists, such as George Herbert Mead (1967), see the internalization of a "generalized other," the ability to understand how our action will seem to others, as a fundamental capacity of all normal social actors. But this capacity differs from what I emphasize here. The way culture shapes our selves as we internalize knowledge of how others will perceive our actions is not the same as the more direct influence publicly enunciated codes can have on action, whether individuals internalize those codes or not.[6]

One of the places I could see effects of cultural codes on action was in interviews with evangelical Christians (see chapter 3). Such interviewees (from several different churches) made a fundamental distinction between "Christian" and worldly activities. Much in the spirit of Max Weber's Calvinists, they drew a line between Christians, those who had found Christ, and those who had not. While in evangelical tradition salvation is potentially available to everyone, there is a sharp division between those who have accepted Jesus and those who have not (see Sikkink 1998; Smith 1998).

Like other Christians, these evangelicals varied in how much their religious beliefs pervaded their lives. But they were distinctive in attaching great significance to behavioral markers that for them defined the boundary dividing "Christians" from others. One set of such markers had to do with family life. As other researchers have noted (Hunter 1983; Ammerman 1987; Smith 1998), one of the distinctions on which today's conservative Christians place great emphasis is their commitment to the traditional family. More even than the Catholic Church, with its direct prohibition of divorce and abortion and its moral condemnation of homosexuality, the evangelical and fundamentalist Protestant churches see themselves as upholding traditional family values. For a Christian, they say, family comes first; the roles of husbands and wives are clear; divorce is wrong. They pride themselves on these family values as what Christians have that those enmeshed in "the world" do not. The Christian campaign against abortion and, more recently, Christian organizing against homosexual rights reflect a similar search for a bright line separating Christian from worldly politics.

Conservative Christian interviewees also demarcated themselves from others on more minor matters. Several said that they could tell the difference between Christians and those who had not accepted Jesus by the latter's use of profanity, by the way someone lost his temper, or by other matters of personal decorum. Evangelical Christians mobilized particular elements of their moral repertoires and gave them special consistency and force by making them decisive markers separating Christians from others. This deployment of a semiotic code distinguishing two types of people made these behaviors into critical emblems of a core identity.[7]

A semiotic code creates a problem for everyone who hears the message (and knows that others have heard it), not just for those who believe it.[8] To the degree that the categories define total identities like "homosexual" or "mad" (Foucault 1965; 1978), "saved" or "damned," the code's categories transcend the importance of any particular act.

A semiotic code affects not only how one sees oneself, but the meanings assigned to one's conduct by others. One's own intentions do not count for much when a public code shapes others' attributions (see Collier 1997). The fear that a wrong move could leave one categorized in ways one cannot control gives extra intensity to normative systems governed by semiotic codes.[9]

In research on Indian men's attitudes toward love and marriage, the sociologist Steve Derné (1992, 1995) has developed the idea that cultures vary in their commonsense "frameworks for understanding action." He thus locates the power of culture to shape action in the frameworks people use to interpret the meanings of others' action. For the Hindu men Derné interviewed, it was normal that people be guided by external social pressures. These men insisted that arranged marriage was necessary, even though cheerfully acknowledging, as one interviewee put it, that "To marry for love is a marriage in the true sense, and to marry according to one's parents' wishes is not successful in the true sense. . . . The arranged marriage is like some hackneyed thing that is unable to achieve its end" (1992:273). Several men said that love marriages made people happier or that their own arranged marriages were unhappy. Many men also spoke of the necessity of joint-family living (brothers and their wives living with

the man's parents) and of norms that forbid open affection between husbands and wives, even when they were critical of such practices as overly
restrictive or harsh. As Derné notes, "[b]ecause most Hindu men see themselves as rightly driven by social pressures, they often are not upset when
inner desires and external demands conflict" (p. 273). For these Hindu
men, it is important to know of others (and to have known of themselves)
that their behavior is under the control of a social community. Thus men
should live with their parents and be subject to them; wives should obey
their mothers-in-law; and children should accept arranged marriages. All
these kinds of conformity ensure "honor," and in so doing assure others
that the person is a well-regulated individual. A man may be highly critical of many or all of these social practices, and may even be affectionate to
his wife in private, as long as he signals his social regulatedness.

That people are subject to others' control is the dominant "framework for understanding action" among the Hindu men Derné studied,
while in our own culture the dominant framework for understanding action is that persons are governed by internalized controls. Throughout
this book we have heard people insisting that they must make their own
choices, that only a person who knows and accepts herself can really love
others, that dependence is a sign of personal inadequacy, that helping
someone you love should not be a matter of sacrifice or obligation but of
personal choice.

Voluntarism has cultural power not because everyone believes in it,
but because it has attained public status as the dominant code. One demonstrates one's value before others by showing that one is an autonomous
person. Many people do not feel autonomous. Indeed, women (and some
men) in these interviews worry again and again about being too dependent. People recognize their dependence on and their obligations to others.
But they also understand that in the dominant code, acting autonomously
signals reliability as a social actor. In such a code, action governed by others—action that is conformist, done to please others, done to fulfill a
role—is inauthentic and unreliable. Actors who can be counted on are
those whose actions are freely chosen. People understand that their own
action will not be properly assessed if it is not presented as the result of
free choice by an autonomous individual actor. It is this complex semiotic
web that then governs both the ways Americans talk about their actions
and the ways they actually try to behave.

Some semiotic codes are narrow and specialized in their application
(sending a Mother's Day card as a signal of filial loyalty); others seem deep
and pervasive, like the code that makes autonomous choice the sign of authentic, reliable action. But I would caution against the assumption that

deeper, more pervasive, more invisible culture is more powerful. For example, the code that signals reliable, consistent action through proclaiming autonomous choice is cross-cut by other codes, such as those through which people signal their friendly intentions (which may involve conveying an eager willingness to please), their loyalty, their social status (DiMaggio 1987), their honesty (see Lamont 1992), or their social power (Collins 1977, 1988).

On the other hand, even newly invented codes, when fully publicized, can exert surprising force. For example, only relatively recently has a code emerged defining ethnic or racial identity as central to one's membership in American society (Omi and Winant 1986). Modeled originally on black racial identity, the code that makes each person White, Latino, Asian American, Native American, or African American has rapidly acquired authority. The code itself is subject to continual change and elaboration—"Asian American" becomes "Asian-Pacific Islander"; Black evolves into African American. Gender and sexuality cross-cut and overlap categories of ethnicity and race. Whites have only partially embraced European ancestry as an identity category. But "multiculturalism" and the code that assigns people identities based on these categories have become remarkably powerful.

When such a code defines oneself, then individuals may also need to develop an interior to go with their identity, to learn more about their culture or their sexuality; while other identities, such as those of family status, region, wealth, or even religion, which may have been more deeply internalized in childhood, fade in salience.

The power of semiotic codes comes from the actor's often implicit knowledge of how his conduct will be read by others. This is shared culture in the sense that the actor is influenced by his knowledge that particular codes are widely disseminated. But the shared culture need not be consensual in the sense that actors believe the code is "right" in some evaluative sense, or even that it is true in a cognitive sense. As with recent accounts of ethnic identity, categories may quickly become naturalized so that people really do seem to exist only in the varieties the code designates.

Codes can be powerful, however, even when they do not seem so inevitable or so important. Their sharedness is not a matter of common, consensual belief but of widespread publicity.

An admittedly trivial example can perhaps suggest the power of codes, even lighthearted ones. When I was in college, an enterprising reporter for the campus newspaper wrote an article about the "three flavors" categorizing campus women—as I remember them, vanilla, chocolate, and lime—describing middle-class public-schoolers, arty bohemian types, and upper-class socialites. The morning the article appeared, my friends and I faced a crisis: what to wear. As we stood half-paralyzed before our mirrors, we were responding to the fact that a new code had been unleashed in our community. What one wore would now convey something new, and perhaps something one never intended.

CONTEXTS

The debate over whether or how much culture influences action obscures a crucial insight: that culture's influence varies by context. Max Weber is known as an "idealist" who stressed the influence of ideas on action. But Weber emphasized that the influence of ideas varies, and he sought in his substantive work to delineate the contexts that enhance the influence of ideas, such as an autonomous priesthood in an organizationally independent church (Weber 1993).

Few sociologists of culture have seriously explored the path opened by Weber, however (Wuthnow 1989 is an important exception). There is remarkably little analysis of the contexts in which culture is brought to bear on action. And the analysis of extreme contexts like cults, communes, and total institutions is rarely considered to have anything to do with the sociology of culture (Lifton 1989; Goffman 1961; Zablocki 1971; Kanter 1972).

I have maintained throughout this book that culture is omnipresent, but that it is often too multiplex, ambiguous, and contradictory to have the effects culture theorists assume it has. Social contexts make a difference because some contexts systematize and unify culture, magnifying its influence. Culture's effects are strongest where the context demands and enforces public cultural coherence.

Our usual stereotype is that public contexts—group meetings, for example—produce *in*coherence, because individual views, which may make perfect sense on their own, have to be trimmed, modified, or gutted to produce something like a group consensus. But some public settings clarify and organize cultural meanings.

One dramatic example is political polarization during revolutions. As revolutionary situations intensify conflict, actors face increasingly clearly opposed alternatives. Cultural styles and worldviews that had easily commingled become sharply differentiated. Everyday cultural activity may muddle the inner logic of ideas, but political conflict makes that logic manifest.[10]

In revolutionary situations, what had been complexly intermingled cultural positions crystallize into clearly opposed cultural systems. In early seventeenth-century England, for example, many who supported Parliament in its conflicts with the Crown had aristocratic titles, Anglican religious sympathies, and were loyal to the king. But as the political crisis intensified in the decade preceding the outbreak of civil war, politics became increasingly polarized between Court and Country parties (C. Hill 1961). Royalist loyalties, a pleasure-seeking, urban way of life, and anti-Puritan religious views increasingly coincided in opposition to an austere, Puritan, anti-Royalist, "Country" stance (C. Hill 1961; W. Hunt 1983). Religious views, politics, and style of life became culturally aligned, however reluctant or ambivalent particular individuals may have been.

What about such political situations clarifies and unifies cultural meanings? What creates consistent implications for action, even when cultural understandings remain confused? We can see how a revolutionary context produces cultural consistencies in the case of the French Revolution. Many historians (L. Hunt 1984, 1992; Furet 1981; Sewell 1985; Ozouf 1988) argue that during the French Revolution, ideas (or rather an entire cultural complex that included ideas, attitudes, dress, behavior, and public rituals) took on a life of their own. The Revolution became a much more radical event, both culturally and politically, than its instigators intended or could have imagined. But the revolution that "ate its children" is not so atypical. Rather it exemplifies general social processes that intensify culture's influence on action.

First, the French political crisis of the late eighteenth century produced great uncertainty, especially after the calling of the Estates General in 1788. Conflict between the Third Estate and the nobility paralyzed government and created a situation of great danger. Lives and political fortunes were at stake in a chaotic, unpredictable conflict. (If contemporary scholars are still unable to draw clear lines among social groups that took different sides in the revolution, if no unified theory seems to explain the social forces and personal motives at play, how much more precarious it must have seemed to people at the time, trying to negotiate a perilous game in which a wrong move could prove fatal.) In such an uncertain situation people may not be more logical than in more settled times, but they are certainly more alert, actively "reading" their environments for cues about how to act. They are also acutely aware of codes that may determine how their behavior will be read by others.

In unstable, high-risk situations, people may seize on coherent ideologies, not because they deeply believe them but because they need some way to organize action when settled habit no longer suffices. This is especially true when people must mobilize and unify their allies, both among the general populace and, perhaps more important, within the core group of political actors (Palmer 1989). While in settled times the search for allies may lead people to soften their political disagreements, during dangerous crises people need to tighten their alliances, to know who is really with them.

One way of defining friends and enemies is to generate clear ideological disagreements that force people to choose sides. Leaders attempt to consolidate control over allies and keep opponents off balance by pushing ideological extremes, eliminating compromise positions, forcing allies to burn their bridges, and keeping opponents on the defensive.[11]

During the course of the French Revolution, the revolutionaries developed increasingly radical interpretations of their ideas. What Sewell (1985) has called the "discourse of rights" became increasingly dominant and ever more clearly opposed to the repudiated "discourse of privilege."[12] More and more positions came to define one as an enemy of the revolution. But this polarization, which intensified and clarified ideological divisions, was produced by the particular political context, not by the ideas themselves.

The third critical element of the French revolutionary context, one that is often forgotten, is that much of the political activity, and a great deal of the ideological discourse, occurred in public meetings—meetings that generated intense public interest and excitement. From the moment when the Third Estate declared itself a National Assembly, through the Legislative Assembly and the National Convention, the Revolution carried out its political theater in open public forums. Jacobin clubs met in the cities and towns of France, debating and carrying out the business of the Revolution. Even secret meetings of the Committee of Public Safety, created in 1793 to centralize control of the Revolution, fostered intense mutual scrutiny among the inner circle of the revolutionary leadership (Palmer 1989). And the twelve Committee members, in turn, could carry out their work only by bringing their demands into public forums.

Face-to-face settings like meetings intensify all the processes described above. In a situation of conflict, danger, and uncertainty, cultural matters from personal adornment (wearing the Cockaigne or revolutionary hat) to personal style (whether contemporary feminists wear makeup or perfume) to expressions of political ideology become signs in a powerful if constantly shifting semiotic system. Attempting to differentiate friends and enemies, to portray one's enemies as traitors to the cause, and to intimidate wavering allies drives leaders of the revolutionary faction to more and more extreme denunciations of others and more pointed enunciations of their own views. Whether or not most individuals hold consistent, unified cultural views, they rapidly understand the contextual meaning of taking one side versus another, and the potential meanings of expressing doubts, attempting to qualify their opinions, or objecting to aspects of what has become defined as a unitary position.[13]

Even in less politically charged times, many of us know the experience of participating in a polarized meeting. Our personal views on the issues at stake may be confused, ambivalent, or even at odds with those of our allies. But when the issue becomes framed as a conflict between opposed factions, then that public arena and the semiotic code generated within it define the meaning of various positions, independent of their manifest content. To be feminist versus antifeminist, to support the union position or not, to be pro- or anti- the dominant faction, comes to be defined with respect to a coherent political "line." Whether participants start out with clearly defined views, whether they stretch their views to accommodate the evolving ideology, or whether they simply suppress qualms because they know which side they are on, the effect is to bring cultural meanings into public alignment, whatever private confusions remain.

Striking parallels to the ways political contexts affect cultural coherence come from a study of the ways members of divorcing couples transform uncertainty and ambivalence into coherent but opposed accounts in the polarizing context of a divorce. Joseph Hopper (1993) notes that divorcing couples develop roles as either the initiator of the divorce or the noninitiating partner. Once these identities emerge, they structure the ways people reconstruct their motives in the divorce.

> [T]he motives that divorcing people attributed to their actions cohered around their identities as either initiators or noninitiating partners: They described what led them to seek a divorce or, conversely, they described why they opposed a divorce. However, nothing prior to a divorce seemed to predict who would become the initiator and who the partner. (p. 805)

Hopper (p. 811) finds that before a divorce, the feelings of both partners are characterized by uncertainty, ambivalence, and confusion. There are plenty of "events, feelings, facts, and 'motives'" to explain any line of conduct. "But just as many events feelings, facts, and motives that would explain numerous other possible outcomes were there as well." In fact, Hopper (p. 810) argues, "the motives by which divorcing people interpret their behaviors have less to do with actual events leading up to divorce and more to do with an emergent symbolic order structured around the initiator and noninitiator identities."

The ways contexts organize and give force to cultural meanings can be shown in several other ways. One may observe that after revolutionary crises have passed the revolutionary ideas, which had seemed to have a dynamic of their own and to have penetrated every aspect of daily life, recede with astonishing rapidity. After the counterrevolution was defeated in France and the revolutionary leadership deposed, the Directory was no longer subject to the new "discourses" that had seemed overwhelmingly powerful during the Revolution itself.[14]

It is not that the revolutionary culture lacked influence. But since it operated through a publicly enforced code, that new culture lacked force once the context was gone. Of course the new terms it made plausible—the notion of "rights," the perception of the Revolution as a heroic liberation from feudal conditions, or the ideals of liberty, equality, and fraternity—remained culturally available. But now they circulated alongside many other ideas—old views of privilege, new understandings of status, loyalties to family, region, class, market, and so forth. Only the public context of revolutionary polarization, the need to consolidate alliances in the midst of a social struggle, and the specific contexts of highly charged public meetings could make these discourses into dominant influences on action.[15]

Similar observations could be made of the relaxation of semiotic codes in other postconflict situations. In England after the Puritan regime ended in 1660, in America after the Revolution, or now in post-Maoist China, the context that made a unified political "line" powerful has disappeared. The new political ideas may endure, or they may be discredited, but in either case, without a context that makes "Which side are you on?" the critical question, the ideas lose force.

The threat of sanctions also enhances the ability of codes and contexts to shape action. But the direct power of sanctions is enormously magnified by contexts that make culture cohere. Michel Foucault's concept of "power/knowledge" conveys his argument that various "human sciences" defined people in new ways, inventing new semiotic codes through which human beings could be measured, evaluated, and labeled. These new disciplines, especially psychiatry and psychology, made their categorizing schemes real and socially effective through their power in specific contexts—the power of mental hospitals to confine those who fit psychiatry's diagnostic categories, the power of courts to mete out punishment corresponding to new theories of human nature, the power of psychology to label and treat deviant psyches. Thus presumed personal traits were effectively turned into defining characteristics of persons as those persons' fates were subjected to powerful sanctions like psychiatric labeling and treatment, imprisonment, or hospitalization.

Foucault shows how a social context can give coherence and force to a cultural code so that it affects not only action but the very nature of personhood. The controlled context of a court, a prison, or a mental hospital gives semiotic codes, amplified by the authority to sanction, a powerful reality. The coercion used on mental patients, prisoners, or other deviants then energizes a larger cultural code affecting a much wider range of persons than the sanctions themselves ever directly touch.

Particular contexts can make semiotic codes powerful even when these codes never become institutional common sense. The series of campaigns the Chinese Communists mounted from 1949 onward as they tacked back and forth from economic growth to political rectification (Schurmann 1970; Hinton 1966; Madsen, Chen, and Unger 1984; Madsen 1984) provide a dramatic example. During each campaign powerful new codes were promulgated—categorizing people by class background, defining enemies of the regime versus progressive elements, and so forth. Public meetings "criticizing" class enemies or, during the Cultural Revolution, "criticism-self-criticism" sessions directed against party leaders and officials, forced participants publicly to embrace these new terminologies. Such events made the slogans and categories real. Even those who remained privately skeptical had to learn to manipulate the new codes in order to survive. The power of the new codes rested on ideological mobilization in public contexts backed by threats of dire sanctions.

Neither the succession of ideological campaigns in China nor the periodic shifts of categories and slogans when interests at the center changed prevented these ideologies from exercising coherent cultural power. If individuals became more and more cynical with each succeeding wave of government sponsored enthusiasm, the cultural codes, as long as they were mobilized in public settings and backed by sanctions, powerfully influenced action. Each succeeding code organized a field of social meanings that defined the statuses and vulnerabilities of social actors. Each code was authoritative as long as it lasted; each disappeared when the context changed.

In a study such as this one that relies on interviews, the context does not vary, so it is hard to observe the effects of context directly. As a context, the interview is neither very dangerous nor very consequential for participants, but it does have its own structure and assumptions (C. Briggs 1986). Because I asked people to give an account of themselves, my interviews probably invoked an implicit distinction between good, ethical, worthwhile people and others. But the interview also invoked many other contexts, those life situations interviewees were asked to imagine or report on. What appears as cultural confusion or inconsistency in my interviews might better be seen as the residue of many different contexts that are intermittently suggested or remembered, shaping particular fragments of discourse, while the interviewee simultaneously strives to fit another contextual framing: that individuals have a coherent life narrative that makes sense, from which they can draw consistent lessons over time (see Shore 1996:284–306).

If cultural logics are firmed up and brought to bear on action in particular contexts, then cultural coherence may be real, but that coherence may be internal to situations rather than to persons. Walter Mischel and his colleagues (Mischel and Shoda 1995) have argued something similar for the coherence of individual personalities (see also Fiske and Taylor [1984:370–79]). In a study of children at summer camp, they found no consistency of individual personalities across different situations. They did find, however, that individual children tended to behave in the same way in the same kinds of situations—when being teased by other children, when being praised by an adult, when learning a skill, and so on. What consistency in personality individual children displayed was due to their tendency repeatedly to get into certain kinds of situations.

If some situations turn inchoate cultural images into clearly delineated public facts, we still understand very little about how the ordinary range of contexts might affect the power, coherence, or inescapability of cultural meanings. It is not even clear along what dimensions we might want to analyze contexts. I have suggested that situations of extreme polarization and acute uncertainty produce cultural coherence and that public meetings can make ideological loyalties highly visible. Weber (1993) suggested that where priests have an autonomous institutional base they are more likely to focus on logical problems in their doctrines. But we do not know whether small, recurrent gatherings are likely to produce less ideological consistency because meanings can continually be renegotiated in the meandering conversations of close intimates; or whether irregular, more anonymous situations might produce greater inconsistencies since what one says or does has few consequences (like confiding to a stranger on a plane). But without an analysis of contexts, we cannot understand why cultural logics sometimes matter, and why they matter more in some times and places than others.

INSTITUTIONS

Institutions also structure cultural meanings, giving them a coherent logic despite ambivalence or skepticism on the part of individuals. Indeed, chapters 6 and 7 focused on just such structuring, arguing that the institution of marriage organizes middle-class Americans' understandings of love, even when people find their experience in conflict with these understandings.

Institutional demands create cultural consistencies in two different ways. First, institutional constraints can give coherence to individuals' life strategies and thus to the cultural narratives, practices, or capacities they make use of. Thus individuals for whom marriage is central monitor their experience for (and soak up popular culture that describes) feelings that would sustain an enduring, exclusive, all-or-nothing, socially defining commitment like that of marriage. And they may suppress or rationalize away experiences that do not fit that institutionally anchored life strategy (see Quinn 1996:418).

Individuals participate in many such cultural complexes, because they participate in many institutional arenas. The culturally mediated strategies they develop to make their way through each institution, along with the relevant cultured capacities for action, may add up to a quite incoherent-seeming sum. But each set of cultural capacities may turn out to have its own logic, if only we can understand the institutional challenges that anchor its meaning. What sounded like inconsistent understandings of love in my interviews turned out to be ways of dealing with two different institutional aspects of marriage—the choice that commits people to a marriage and the negotiations that sustain ongoing relationships. (The culture that putatively helps sustain relationships is especially incoherent, with its never-ending flow of varied recommendations and recipes for happier, more fulfilling, or more exciting and challenging relationships.) There are, thus, powerful cultural consistencies, but they are less a consistent set of internalized beliefs than coherent orientations to the demands of institutions.

Institutions also create cultural consistencies in a second way—by providing the basis for a shared culture. It is because so many Americans deal with the institution of marriage that there is a shared culture of love. Consistencies across individuals come less from common inculcation by cultural authorities than from the common dilemmas institutional life poses in a given society.[16] Not shared indoctrination but shared life-structuring institutions create the basis for a common culture. The myth of romantic love appears again and again, tailored for a new audience or with a twist to keep it fresh. It retains its vitality because it speaks to dilemmas created by the institutional structure of marriage.

Even when individuals consciously disbelieve dominant myths, they find themselves engaged with the very myths whose truths they reject—because the institutional dilemmas those myths capture are their dilemmas as well.[17] The myths that sustain beliefs in American individualism are precisely of this sort. Survey and interview studies find that Americans do not really believe, for example, that their country provides equal opportunity for all or that ability and hard work account for success, especially when people think about concrete cases (see Mann 1970; Huber and Form 1973; Kluegel and Smith 1986; Swidler 1992). Yet these beliefs appear again and again, especially as general platitudes, even among the poor and disprivileged (see Lane 1962; Rainwater 1974; Reinarman 1987).

We may reconcile these puzzling findings by seeing that even when people know that the social deck is unfairly stacked, the major institutions they have to deal with are those of a market society (see Collier 1997). And a market society requires personal effort—a willingness to promote one's own virtues or to offer one's labor—while it repeatedly creates the experience that one's own "traits" (grades, test scores, or credentials, for example) determine one's options. Even a rich boy whose family pays for college and law school has the experience of putting forth his grades, test scores, recommendations, and essays as "reasons" why he should be admitted to a particular college or law school. And even the poor child, whose family and school experience have left her with few options, will be led to feel that her poor grades and lack of motivation in school account for her poor opportunities (see Clark 1960; Brint and Karabel 1989). If she wants a job, she will have to go out and look for one, making the best case for herself that she can. Thus the experience of living as a market actor continually reproduces the ethic of self-reliance, making it seem realistic even for those who know that it is a poor description of their own life chances or of the general distribution of opportunities and rewards among their fellows.

It may be, indeed, that a good deal of what we normally mean by culture is not an internalized set of beliefs or values, easily transportable from one institutional setting to another. Precisely the opposite: most culture sustains the symbolic capacities people develop to deal with institutions. The sense of cultural disjointedness one feels in moving to or through a foreign culture is primarily a sense of the misfit between one's cultural expectations and an alien set of institutions.[18] Young Americans who consider themselves alienated from their own society may not realize how truly American they are until they go abroad—when they try to get routine paperwork done at a foreign airport, or when they discover that they lack the cultural skills to negotiate successfully (or at least, without feeling suspicious and resentful) in a market without fixed prices.

Even the deeper parts of a culture—how people conceive the nature of personhood, the sense in which one is an individual, or the ways one feels obligated to collectivities, personal or impersonal—all of these may be much more directly tied to institutional forms than we normally acknowledge. Take two very different comparative cases: Michèle Lamont's (1992) study of American versus French senses of honor, prestige, and individuality; and Dorinne Kondo's (1990) work on the "crafting" of Japanese selves. Both suggest indirectly that the specific components of a cultural repertoire, and the parts of that repertoire that are invoked in any particular setting, are linked to distinctive institutional structures. For example, the fact that the French educational system decisively separates members of the elite from those who do not pass examinations for university admission makes evident to French men and women that some people are superior to others in a general cultural way, and that such superiority is important. And the fact that inheritance and employment security in Japan are both tied to family or familylike arrangements with employers and fellow workers contributes to the vitality of the notion of the household as the core definer of social commitments. In contrast, the American belief in a universalistic, impersonal sphere within which each individual has a right to claim dignity and respect is surely in part a correlate of real aspects of our institutional life.[19] In America the market supplies more of our wants, and with less need for personal contacts and support than in any other modern market society, while the educational system remains formally open to talent and effort throughout life, and public bureaucracies dispense benefits without respect to rank or particularistic connections to all who mobilize the requisite middle-class bureaucratic skills.

Institutions structure culture, then, by creating the dilemmas in response to which individuals develop culturally mediated life strategies and by creating the situations in which people invoke one or another part of their cultural repertoires. In this sense, then, institutions both shape culture and structure the situations in which particular cultural elements will be brought to bear. The resources the Western culture of love provides are influential in organizing how people think about their life commitments, in people's assessments of particular relationships, and in the aspirations they bring to relationships. But it is the possibility (or the specter) of marriage that invokes those cultural images, making them central shapers of action at some points, misleading fantasies or irrelevant platitudes at others.

Throughout this chapter I have attempted to distinguish two important issues that are usually confounded: one is how deeply, coherently, or fully culture is internalized; the other is how powerfully culture influences action. Sometimes culture may affect action, as Weber argued, because individuals hold systematic, unified, consistent worldviews and apply them directly to action. But it is just as likely, and indeed more common, for culture to influence action from the "outside in," because culture shapes what action can mean.

This formulation of how culture influences action calls for an approach different from those that prevail in much of the sociology and anthropology of culture. First, it suggests that rather than looking at cultural meanings in the abstract, it is crucial to attend to the contexts in which they are actually used.[20] Ideas that are incoherent or inconsistent in the minds of individuals may acquire coherence and direction when they are mobilized in a particular context. Second, while ideas and cultural meanings come in many forms—evoking ethos and feeling tone, specifying modes of interaction, articulating values and norms for guiding daily life—I contend that "semiotic codes," systems of meaning that define what our actions will signify to others, have a special status. These meaning systems shape our action by becoming known, not necessarily by converting us. They derive their effectiveness from publicity and the power of public scrutiny. Deployed in public settings and backed by sanctions, they solidify the cultural control of action.

Cultural meanings can be systematized and given coherence from the outside in, as well as through their inner logic. In polarized political contexts, from gang wars to revolutions, what one wears or how one walks, as well as what ideas one espouses, can become linked to one faction or side in a conflict. And through such polarization, matters of style and substance may become increasingly part of a coherent cultural package, unified by the conflicts in which they are invoked (Hebdige 1979). Thus the tight integration of a cultural system may come as much from cultural differentiation from enemies or competitors as from the unified inner logic of a system of ideas (Schneider 1976; LeVine 1984).

Finally, institutions can provide templates for the organization of particular cultural packages. To the degree that institutions structure major life strategies, the cultured capacities for action that individuals develop will be coherent not within an individual self but within a particular institutionally organized arena of action.

All this suggests that sociologists of culture might profit from much more systematic investigation of the contexts in which cultural meanings are brought to bear and the systems for encoding meanings that are made available in a given context. Sociology has a rich tradition of research investigating individual attitudes and beliefs, both in the structured form of the social survey and in the more intimate, flexible format of the in-depth interview. Anthropologists have extensive experience investigating ritual practices, symbol systems, and the larger semiotic codes that structure a group's collective products—their myths, tales, folklore, and so forth. But neither approach really gets at the place where semiotic code, cultural context, and institutions meet.

Individuals in interviews often seem to know very well what they think, even when what they think seems quite inconsistent. One reason is that they are often responding not to an abstract question about some general set of principles or beliefs (or even some fund of common sense or popular wisdom) but to their sense of what answer would make sense in the particular situation the interviewer's question suggests. Thus the vignettes I used often generated strong responses as interviewees imagined particular situations. They attributed various meanings to the actions described in the vignettes, seeing particular behaviors as indicators of larger complexes, such as psychological dependency or being "a person who could do that" (leave a sick spouse, for example). These interview responses seem incomplete or incoherent only because we are still too wedded to the view that what we are seeing when we observe culture is an internalized complex of meanings and practices, rather than people's knowledge of how a set of publicly available codes and situations operate.

It is this publicly available (indeed sometimes unavoidable) configuration of codes, contexts, and institutions that actually structures our cultural usage. Exploration of this complex set of interactions can allow some of the sophisticated new ways we have of thinking about culture to be incorporated into more powerful theories linking culture and action.

TOWARD BETTER QUESTIONS

O ver the past two decades sociologists have developed increasingly complex, theoretically sophisticated conceptions of culture. Despite these advances, however, we still rely on remarkably one-dimensional images of how culture works, how it affects experience and action. One purpose of this book has been to develop conceptions of culture's effects that match the sophistication of our analyses of culture itself.

Simply posing more pointed questions, which might form the basis for future research and theorizing, constitutes progress in a field as inchoate as the study of culture. Therefore I want to return to some central themes of this book to see what questions remain unanswered. I hope in this way to take stock of where we are, to focus future theoretical debate on questions that can be explored empirically, and thus to encourage cumulative development in the sociology of culture.

IS CULTURE COHERENT OR INCOHERENT?

When we talk with ordinary people, even (or especially) about so fundamental a matter as love, their responses are often disjointed, self-contradictory, or fragmentary. But how does this square with the image of culture as a "system"? Robert LeVine (1984:72) has noted that "[n]othing is more characteristic of contemporary anthropologists than the conviction that the customs they study are connected and comprehensible only as parts of a larger organization—of beliefs, norms, values, or social action." This view is shared by sociologists as well. Jeffrey Alexander (Alexander and Smith 1993) has argued for the continuity and coherence of American culture, while Richard Biernacki (1995:12–13) sees coherence as the very criterion of distinctively cultural explanation: the "line of reasoning specific to cultural analysis" is that practices form "a meaningful constellation" such that a distinctly cultural argument is "configurational, attached to an overarching pattern of techniques rather than to a simple outcome."

Yet anthropologists and sociologists also repeatedly report incoherence along two dimensions—whether cultural meanings are internally consistent and whether they are shared. Roy D'Andrade (1984:90), the anthropologist, notes that "[a]lthough the conception of culture as consisting of the shared knowledge of individual minds marked a clear advance over earlier theories of culture . . . many things one would want to call cultural are not completely or even generally shared." Those who attend to how ordinary people talk and think note, as Michael Billig (1987) does, that commonsense understandings develop in a continual process of argument that constantly doubles back on itself, crossing and recrossing its own tracks. People generalize from a few cases, formulate something like an all-purpose rule, attend to exceptions to the rule, and then form new generalizations, in a process that never reaches closure. In *Talking of the Royal Family* (1992), Billig notes that people routinely take both sides of the arguments they have with themselves and others, insisting, for example, that "the Royals" are no better than anyone else, while repeatedly presuming that it is precisely because the Royals are so superior that to be just like them is to be superior oneself. Like my interviewees when they discuss their marriages, British commoners offer not an axiomatic system of first principles and logical consequences, but a "kaleidoscope of common sense" (p. 48)—a swirling pattern of shifting justifications.

If we no longer build into our assumptions and our methods the notion that culture is by definition a "system," then we can focus on the unanswered questions that evidence of both cultural coherence and incoherence raises. The issue is not whether the glass is half-empty or half-full, but what creates cultural coherence and in what places, and what accounts for the extent and shape of cultural incoherence.

Keeping One's Options Open

I want to begin with the sources of cultural incoherence. It is important to note that while cultural contradictions, confusions, and inconsistencies may worry researchers, they do not seem to bother ordinary people in the course of their everyday lives. Indeed, as I have argued, people are better equipped for life if they have available multiple approaches to situations, if they can shift justifications for their actions, and if they can mobilize different meanings to organize different lines of action.

The anthropologist Lawrence Rosen (1984), in a classic study of Moroccan kinship, points out that for Moroccans, statements about the world—in particular claims of kin relationship—are not statements about a fixed, external reality so much as positions to be negotiated. Since kinship groups are themselves flexible, indeterminately bounded "personally-centered action groups" (p. 163), a kinship claim is neither true nor false until it is realized. In negotiations over correct terminology, the "practical question is how to convert mere utterances into truth-bearing propositions and how to do this most advantageously" (p. 122). Rosen points out that since life is uncertain, Moroccans employ strategies of network diversification, seeking not to keep all their eggs in one basket, but hoping to have an alternative if their preferred strategy fails. But this uncertainty is not a feature only of life in Morocco. It might be said of middle-class suburbanites' understandings of love, as much as of Moroccan kin terminology, that "[at] their very heart the terms that imply some form of obligation or reciprocation . . . remain incompletely defined, open textured, until, by a process of mutual negotiation, an actual relationship comes to be conceptualized under them" (p. 118).

Cultural meanings, then, often remain fluid, waiting to be filled and made real by the relationships they help to create.[1] And because life is uncertain, people keep multiple cultural meanings on tap. In this sense, what appears as cultural incoherence is also adaptability, flexibility, keeping options open. And this is as much a cognitive as a relational reality. A worldview that could be shattered by a single setback or contradiction would be a very fragile one (see Padgett and Ansell 1993; Leifer 1991).[2]

How Meanings Mean

Many researchers assume that cultures must be coherent because coherence is an essential property of the semiotic systems through which meanings can be conveyed. William Sewell Jr. (1999:39–40) explicitly argues that while individual cultures may be incoherent and disorderly, "culture" as an analytic aspect of human societies is necessarily coherent because it is only through structures of relationally defined meanings that meaning can be communicated. But this picture of how meanings systems work is misleading.

If culture is a communicative system, its meanings are neither fixed as the structuralist image of a semiotic code might suggest, nor loosely related like the set of overlapping associations that Wittgenstein described. Rather, culture conveys meanings through adherence to and deviations from locally established expectations or conventions. There are three aspects to this incoherent coherence: First, cultures communicate by ringing (usually small) changes on established expectations, so meaning systems are necessarily more innovative and unstable than we usually imagine. Second, partly because of this innovativeness, semiotic systems often have intense local variations, so that a small subculture, or even a subgroup within a subculture, may experiment with new variations on established meaning systems. Third, this local variation means that while particular semiotic codes have systemic qualities, people necessarily keep multiple ones on tap. Thus the problem of meaning and of cultural coherence cannot be solved without some way of understanding how people switch from one code to another, what contextual cues signal which code is in effect, and how people keep multiple interpretations of action available simultaneously, crystallizing situations and meanings only occasionally.

To take the first point, cultures communicate as much by violating as by adhering to established meanings and expectations.[3] The rebellious British punks Dick Hebdige (1979) describes created a powerful subculture that systematically violated conventions of middle-class respectability to convey contempt for bourgeois taste and values. Through exaggerated stylization punk youth communicated that they defied convention intentionally, that it was members of the conventional middle class who did not really understand what was going on. (Middle-class observers presumably felt befuddled, perhaps a more common experience than theories of meaning usually allow [see Rosaldo 1989:91–126].)

If codes "communicate" when people violate expectations, cumulative violations make the codes themselves dynamic. Of course, expectations must exist in order for violations to be experienced as meaningful (L. Meyer 1956; Alter 1981). And meaning systems can be stripped of their expressiveness by overuse. It is hard to write a stellar recommendation when everyone uses superlatives; intentionally torn or "ugly" clothing conveys contempt for the status order only until it becomes a fashion statement. As violations accumulate (as did the use of "vibrato" to emphasize important musical passages), what is conventional is itself changed (vibrato became standard, so that passages are highlighted now when played without vibrato [L. Meyer 1956]). Many social processes appear to work this way, from the status distinctions established by having a certain kind of taste or lifestyle (Weber 1968:926–40; Fallers 1966; Bonfenbrenner 1966; Bourdieu 1984) to the codes that define in-group and out-group membership (Frith 1981; DiMaggio 1982; Lamont and Fournier 1992).

This dynamism of meaning systems then leads to the second point— that codes often are local, both in the sense that they may be shared by a local subgroup (and indeed, the more intensively organized the subgroup, the more dynamic its transformations of the meanings of a semiotic code may be—as any student of the meanings conveyed by teen subculture dress-styles, for example, can attest),[4] and in the sense that a semiotic code may organize a single domain of action—gang turf claims or faculty teas—and be largely unknown or incomprehensible outside that domain.

If cultures are made up of many semiotic codes and these vary locally, then—and this is my third point—any given individual can read or communicate in several different codes. People participate in multiple spheres of action and interact with different social groups, and thus they usually communicate in and move among many different semiotic codes.[5]

Each of these semiotic codes may be orderly and rule-like in its own terms (even if, as Bourdieu [1977] emphasizes, the "rules" exist because there is the possibility of breaking them); but because the "rules" are a moving frontier, and because people vary in terms of where they are in relation to multiple frontiers, it is highly unlikely that their knowledge of or participation in a variety of semiotic systems will amount to a coherent culture. At any given time particular people may be able to maneuver quite well in relation to the codes that currently apply to them or that they can "read" in the behavior of those to whom they are oriented socially, but this capacity to construct, renovate, and navigate within semiotic systems would be unlikely to produce coherence. Indeed, what something "meant" would depend very much on the context in which it was offered and understood. This is not just a matter of confounding the problem of the coherence of concrete "cultures" with the coherence of "culture" as an analytic aspect of human experience, as Sewell (1999) suggests. The nature of semiotic systems themselves, precisely as communicative systems, necessarily generates multiple, overlapping, if locally systematic, meanings.

Unanswered Questions about Coherence

This way of thinking about the numerous and perhaps shifting codes that constitute any meaning system raises a number of difficult questions. First, if the meaning of a particular action, or the overall scheme of interpretation that is to govern a particular encounter, depends on the context, how do people establish or negotiate the context that is operative in a situation?

Bourdieu (Bourdieu and Wacquant 1992:94–115) writes about "fields" as arenas in which particular criteria of valuation become established (see also Boltanski and Thévenot 1991); and Goffman (1974) analyzes the "frames" that govern particular interactions. Sewell (1999:56–57) suggests that the state may play a central role in organizing and making coherent what could otherwise be disconnected arenas of discourse. But we still understand far too little about how people know what situation they are in and what codes apply.

Of course, "mistakes" may occur—from the police officer stumbling upon a movie filming of a robbery to a misunderstanding about when a business lunch has become a date. But what is more remarkable are the relatively smooth ways people navigate transitions from one situation to another and from one semiotic code to another. Even when multiple potential framings are available simultaneously—as they are when people talk about "love"—people easily assume one frame and operate within it and then switch frames when the implicit situation seems to shift. Remember, for example, that how interviewees reacted to a vignette depended on how they framed it, and often they could offer multiple readings as they thought through one framing after another. When discussing their own life experiences, people first anchored themselves in a context—a real or imagined situation—and then derived beliefs or arguments from that situation. Imagining a lasting marriage, for example, they were able to adduce a range of sometimes contradictory arguments about why one would want to stay married. But when some question provoked a shift in the imagined context that anchored their thinking, their entire orientation could shift.

Just what structures such framing processes, and how people keep multiple potential frames on hold, seem central questions for cultural analysis.[6] By assuming that symbolic activities have a single meaning, we compromise our ability to understand what skilled interactors do. The challenge is to accept that cultures are multiplex, fluid, and contradictory, and then to rethink models of when and how culture constrains action and experience.

Given the importance of contexts, we have few clues about what are the defining features of social contexts or situations, or about how people "read" the crucial features of situations and how they invoke one situation and its codes versus another. Despite the enormous attention cognitive psychologists have given to scripts and schemas, which define situations, they have focused on their cognitive-processing aspects without trying to understand the basic structure of the situations those scripts and schemas describe.

Sociologists who want to understand what mediates between cultural meanings and action, or, indeed, what variations in cultural meanings signify, will need a richer, more systematic way to analyze contexts. Whether there is some fundamental set of situations out of which particular situations get constructed as social psychologists tend to imply, or whether situations are culturally constructed in the same fluid and sometimes contradictory ways as other cultural elements, sociologists of culture would benefit enormously from a more systematic analysis of contexts as they structure meaning and action.

What Is a Cultural "Logic"?

Almost all of those who work on culture assume that cultures have "logics." Even if we do not subscribe to the notion that each culture is a unified whole with a single overarching logic, we assume that each subpart of the culture, each semiotic code or institutional arena, has its own logic. Indeed, here even (or especially) the very cultural-studies analysts who promote the notion that cultures are fragmented and fluid specialize in finding the deep logics that link up consumption and capital, gender and patriarchy, love and individualism (see, e.g., Butler 1990, 1993; Haraway 1983, 1991; Baudrillard 1975, 1983; Illouz 1997). But the key unanswered question is what a cultural "logic" is—or rather, by what kinds of logics different kinds of cultural elements are integrated.

To think about this question, we need to consider what people do with culture, what different kinds of culture are "used for." In chapter 4 and subsequent chapters, I argue that cultural meanings operate less as logical structures that integrate ends and means, and more as tools or resources that cultivate skills and capacities that people integrate into larger, more stable "strategies of action." But that kind of integration is different from the logic that sociologists and anthropologists have traditionally assumed.

The Logic of Deductive Inference

For Max Weber, interpretive analysis (*verstehen*) linked ideas and action through deductive logic. The analyst entered imaginatively into the ideas and motives of those whose action he or she was trying to understand. Beginning with the logical and psychological premises of action, the analyst could arrive at an understanding of how those starting presuppositions led to particular kinds of action in the world. While such cultural logics might rest on irrational premises, and while many factors besides a cultural logic could influence concrete historical outcomes, the power of sociological analysis was its ability to tease out the logic of the ideas and presuppositions fundamental to a cultural system.

In analyzing the basic forms of social action, Weber (1968:5–6) argued that "rational action" was the baseline for cultural analysis.[7] Given a set of ends and the facts about the world as understood by the actor, the analyst could understand the action that would flow from those premises.

What, then, was the "logic" of Weber's logic? At bottom, it was straightforward deductive logic (see Weber 1968:6). If one believes in an all-powerful creator and judge who will send one to heaven or hell, then one will try to earn salvation by living up to that God's commandments; if one believes that human suffering is caused by alienation from the divine, then one will seek to unite the self with the divine through mystical contemplation. Even Weber's recognition of the power of nonrational motives testified to the power of the logic of ideas. In a famous footnote to *The Protestant Ethic* (1958a [1904–5]: 232), Weber notes that:

> The Calvinistic faith is one of the many examples in the history of religions of the relation between the logical and the psychological consequences for the practical religious attitude to be derived from certain religious ideas. Fatalism is, of course, the only logical consequence of predestination. But on account of the idea of proof the psychological result was precisely the opposite. . . . The *electi* are, on account of their election, proof against fatalism because in their rejection of it they prove themselves. . . . The practical interests cut off the fatalistic consequences of logic (which, however, in spite of everything occasionally did break through).

One candidate for cultural logic, then, is deductive logic; and implicitly or explicitly, many cultural analysts see the way a culture "hangs together" in such terms. But there is ambiguity about where such logics are located. Weber clearly saw logic—even when its presuppositions were irrational and its implications thwarted by practical constraints—as residing in individual thought. Weber recognized, of course, that socially influential ideas were the product of the collective life experiences of carrier groups. Nonetheless, Weber thought about the logic even of large social formations such as authority systems as if they were exchanges between parties to a debate, and he analyzed such phenomena as the relationship between class and status claims by exploring the deductions individual or collective actors would draw from their ideas.

I have argued that such constraint by logical deduction rarely influences social action directly. While people vary in how thoroughly they articulate their understandings of their experience and how coherently they present these understandings, throughout this book I have shown that people are little constrained by logic. Other researchers, studying a variety of problems, report very similar results (see DiMaggio 1997). Especially in settled situations and in the realm of common sense, logical consistency is a scarce commodity. Indeed, deductive logic is not the place to look for the most important links between culture and action.

Looser Logics

Even if full-blown deductive logic is not central to the organization of cultural systems, nor a primary link between culture and action for individuals, in recent social theory other more limited logics have been seen as central to the way cultural systems are organized. The issue of the kind of logic is often confounded with the question of where the logic is located socially (in the consciousness of individuals, in collective discourses, in embedded social practices, or in institutions) and with the question of what substantively the logic organizes (discourse, semiotic codes, practices, interests, lines of action, institutions, etc.). But here I want to look at alternative candidates for cultural logics themselves—logics that may be less determinate in their constraint over outcomes than rational-deductive logic, but that may offer better models of how cultural elements are actually organized.

Binary Oppositions

Since Lévi-Strauss and Jakobson (and indeed since Durkheim) analysts have seen cultural logics as organized around binary oppositions. In part, as Kenneth Burke (1970) emphasized, symbols themselves create the possibility of imagining (or articulating) oppositions. Lévi-Strauss (1963) located the role of binary oppositions in organizing symbolic systems (totemic organization, kinship, and myth, for example) in fundamental properties of the human mind, but others have seen such oppositions as fundamental to the nature of symbol systems and to the capacity of symbols or discourses to convey meanings (see Leach 1976). If semiotic systems define meanings relationally, then opposition is at least the elementary operation by which meaning can be defined.

Narratives

Another logic that appears to organize many social processes is narrative. While the temporal form of narrative may sometimes trace causal connections that could be described under formal logics, narrative is less rigidly structured. Nevertheless, narrative forms are fundamental devices for ordering understandings of the social and natural worlds.

There is an enormously rich literature on narrative and narrative forms (Propp 1968; White 1973; Chatman 1978; Todorov 1969, 1977). Anthropologists and sociologists have noted that a culture's logic can be carried by its dominant narratives, either recounted or enacted. Victor Turner (1974), for example, describes how societies continually reenact certain dramatic narratives, whether in the form of repeated ritual enactments like pilgrimages or processions, or that of typical social dramas.

Sherry Ortner (1989), analyzing the founding of the first celibate Buddhist monasteries among the Sherpas of Nepal, offers an example of the way narratives (what she calls "schemas" or "scenarios") order social transformations. Drawing on Sahlins (1981) and Geertz (1980), she describes "cultural dramas or scenarios, that reappear over time and that seem to order the ways in which people play out both conventional and historically novel social encounters" (Ortner 1989:60). The monasteries' founders, she argues, reenacted traditional Sherpa narratives in which a hero fights for supremacy, is driven into exile, acquires powerful divine and/or human protectors, and then returns to triumph over his rivals and establish a new order.

Homologies, Resemblances, Resonances

If "cultural logic" ultimately means cultural ordering, then there are other forms that cultural logics might take. One of the simplest is associating like with like, generalizing a pattern of resemblances. Of course, these resemblances may be organized in a wide variety of ways. Huizinga (1954) pointed out long ago that medieval European culture saw "sympathies" or what we would call analogies operating everywhere. Plants could be linked with diseases because of some physical resemblance between the plant's flower and the organ it was thought to cure; the twelve apostles were connected to the twelve months by their number; and the four-petaled dogwood blossom represented the cross.

While such resemblances seem too fuzzy to constitute a "logic," many claims of cultural ordering depend upon precisely such metaphoric linkages. Even Geertz's (1973b) attempt to identify "ethos" (typical "moods and motivations") as central to cultural "systems" suggests that resemblance in emotional tone or mood is basic to cultural logics. The difficulty of course is that if cultural logics can move along such varied paths, with such diverse outcomes, it is hard to know when a cultural logic is at work.

The Logic of Practice

The term "practice" in contemporary cultural sociology has acquired a range of meanings. Ortner (1984) emphasizes practice theorists' focus on agency (itself a highly fraught term)—on the ways active, strategic agents reproduce, resist, or change social structures and rules. This focus on agency, reproduction, and power is confounded with another set of issues—"practice" as unconscious, embodied, or habitual action, contrasted with articulated, conscious ideas (S. Turner 1994; Biernacki 1999: 75–78). This meaning of practice at least overlaps with the notion that cultural organization is located less in conscious ideas or shared cultural symbols than in the routines of institutions and actors, routines that, to return to our theme, have a logic of their own.

Michel Foucault (1978, 1983) has attempted to uncover the logic of practices that define categories of human beings, or that redefine human properties, pathologies, or potentials. He usually (at least in his more "structuralist" phase [see Dreyfus and Rabinow 1983]) has identified a Lévi-Straussian binary logic as the core feature of practices that "divide," "confine," or categorize human beings. But the source of these logics is not some universal feature of minds, or even of symbol systems. The division of human beings into different "kinds" of persons—separating the normal from the pathological, or the criminal from the mad, for example—depends not on universal human mental organization but on the organization of institutional practices themselves. Thus, in *Madness and Civilization* (1965), it is the existence of practices of exclusion—setting apart a group to be isolated in a distinctive physical space—that creates the framework for such categorization. Foucault writes hauntingly of the leper houses, which set the pattern of confinement that would, centuries later, undergird the categories of the mad and the sane:

> Leprosy disappeared, the leper vanished, or almost, from memory; these structures remained. Often, in these same places, the formulas of exclusion would be repeated, strangely similar two or three centuries later. Poor vagabonds, criminals, and "deranged minds" would take the part played by the leper, and we shall see what salvation was expected from this exclusion, for them and for those who excluded them as well. With an altogether new meaning and in a very different culture, the forms would remain—essentially that major form of a rigorous division which is social exclusion but spiritual reintegration. (p. 18)

Other sorts of practices—the pastoral practice of the modern welfare state or the probing practice of the confessional, re-created in psychoanalysis and therapeutic self-scrutiny—have very different structures and thus generate logics with very different ordering principles (Foucault 1978). These forms can be generalized or transposed to new arenas, but the shape of each logic cannot be deduced from any universal mental structure.

Institutional practices may anchor a semiotic system, given plausibility by that set of practices. But the "logic" derives from the practices themselves. So, for example, in a system that differentiates the deserving from the undeserving poor, a line is drawn between those who can work and those who cannot—with women, children, and the insane categorized together and separated from the criminal and the vagrant. But it is the existence of confinement—the workhouse, and later the prison and the asylum—that gives the categorization of the poor versus the criminal versus the mad its plausibility. The pathbreaking work of Mohr and Duquenne (1997) demonstrates how a system of categories and a set of practices can mutually constitute one another. Welfare clients form categories based on kinds of services they receive (ranging from the monetary to the minatory), while welfare services are categorized by the kinds of clients to whom the services are available. Thus a set of practices and a system of categories mutually constitute one another.

Despite the apparent logic in the linkage of practices and categories in Foucault's work, it is not clear what kind of logic this is. The image of power as a kind of self-multiplying practice, probing and penetrating wherever it finds an opening, continually constituting new realities, does not suggest logic in the usual sense. While some practices of power may penetrate further when they are more systematic (like the Enlightenment legal regulations that made punishment proportional to the severity of crimes [Foucault 1977]), other practices may resist systematization. The perpetual proliferation of new practices of power and resistance is not really compatible with the notion of an overarching logic.

In *The Logic of Practice* (1990:86), Pierre Bourdieu adduces an array of reasons why "practice has a logic which is not that of the logician." For Bourdieu, "practice" refers to action that is oriented to practical outcomes, is strategic, and is largely organized by unconscious schemas, so that it operates as an intuitive skill or tact. Practice cannot follow "logical logic" first because of its relation to time. In arguments familiar from *Outline of a Theory of Practice* (1977), Bourdieu stresses that for practice, unlike logic, "[i]ts temporal structure, that is, its rhythm, its tempo, and above all its directionality, is constitutive of its meaning" (p. 81). Practice requires instantaneous judgments anticipating future actions, as when "a player who is involved and caught up in the game adjusts not to what he sees but to what he fore-sees . . . in response to an overall, instantaneous assessment of the whole set of his opponents and the whole set of his team-mates, seen not as they are but in their impending positions." He does so under conditions of "urgency" that "exclude distance, perspective, detachment, and reflection" (pp. 81–82).

Practice, Bourdieu (1990) insists, has a "practical logic": it "is able to organize all thoughts, perceptions and actions by means of a few generative principles, which are closely interrelated and constitute a practically integrated whole." But it can achieve coherence precisely because it ignores the niceties of formal logic. It sacrifices "rigour for the sake of simplicity and generality." To fulfill its "practical functions" the logic of everyday life requires "unity and regularities" and also "'fuzziness' and . . . irregularities and even incoherences" (p. 86). This is an "economical logic" in which "no more logic is mobilized than is required by the needs of practice." The same term may be used in contradictory ways in different situations because "it is very unlikely that two contradictory applications of the same schemes will be brought face to face" (p. 87). Its schemes are simple and since they operate "without conscious reflection or conscious control . . . [t]he most characteristic operations of its 'logic'—inverting, transferring, uniting, separating, etc.—take the form of bodily movements, turning to the right or left, putting upside down, going in or coming out, tying or cutting, etc." (p. 92).

Finally, and most crucially for Bourdieu, practical action is driven by urgent necessities. Cultural analysts may divide the world into sets of oppositions, but the most important life activities—for the Algerian Kabyle, "marriage, ploughing or harvesting"—require rituals "to overcome in practice the specifically ritual contradiction which the ritual taxonomy sets up by dividing the world into contrary principles and by causing the acts most indispensable to the survival of the group to appear as acts of sacrilegious violence" (p. 97 and pp. 210–70 ff.). Examining the contradictory interpretations that have been offered of Kabyle rain-making rites, in which key ritual objects can be seen as sometimes male and sometimes female, sometimes the source of rain, sometimes in need of rain, Bourdieu notes that "this distinction, which has worried the best of interpreters, is of no importance . . . the two perspectives being equally valid by definition when it is a matter of reuniting contraries" (p. 264). This is not a matter of an elegant ritual logic that creates and then resolves contradictions. Rather "practical logic," driven by urgency, "never ceases to sacrifice the concern for coherence to the pursuit of efficiency, making maximum possible use of the *double entendres* and dual purposes that the indeterminacy of practices and symbols allows" (p. 262). Especially in desperate "situations like drought . . . the threshold of logical requirements [is] lowered even further so as to exploit all the available resources" (p. 264).

Bourdieu's Kabyle are in this respect not very different from the middle-class suburbanites I interviewed who used all the sometimes mutually contradictory arguments and understandings at their disposal when they shored up the hope that their marriages would last or explained having married the "right" person for them. But understanding the partial, overlapping, indeterminate logics of practical action still leaves unclear what organizes the practical agendas around which practical logics swarm.

The Logic of Existential "Fit"

What makes accounts of cultural logics persuasive is the apparent "fit" among different aspects of a culture. To see how an account of such a cultural "fit" is constructed, let us consider the problem, which Geertz among others has repeatedly dealt with, of what kinds of selves are constituted in different social worlds. In an early essay, "Person, Time, and Conduct in Bali" (1973h), Geertz links Balinese naming practices, the Balinese sense of time, and Balinese rules about conduct. To oversimplify, the dominant naming practices are relational, so that a given person's name changes over the lifecycle (as our terms "Mom," "Grandma," and so on do), and cyclical, so that the same generationally specific names recur (as if the term for "Grandma" and "great-granddaughter" were the same). Geertz argues that these practices tend to deny historical change, so that change becomes simply the recurrence of things that have already been. It is not persons' uniqueness, their "special, never-to-be-repeated, impact upon the stream of historical events—which are culturally played up, symbolically emphasized: it is their social placement, their particular location within a persisting, indeed an eternal metaphysical order. The illuminating paradox of Balinese formulations of personhood is that they are—in our terms anyway—depersonalizing" (p. 390).

The "depersonalizing" Balinese "conception of personhood" is in turn "linked" to a "detemporalizing (again from our point of view) conception of time" (p. 391). The Balinese calendar defines the ritual significance of each day (determined by the ways multiple day-naming cycles overlap), categorizing time rather than measuring its passage. The calendrical "cycles and supercycles . . . don't tell you what time it is; they tell you what kind of time it is" (p. 393).

Balinese time and personhood join with a third factor, "the ceremonialization of social intercourse," to form "a triangle of mutually reinforcing cultural forces" that eliminate, so far as possible, the "consequential" relations among human beings (Geertz 1973h:399): "To maintain the (relative) anonymization of individuals with whom one is in daily contact, to dampen the intimacy implicit in face-to-face relationships . . . it is necessary to formalize relations with them to a fairly high degree. . . ." Balinese "ceremoniousness" is "*a logical correlate* of a thoroughgoing attempt to block the more creatural aspects of the human condition—individuality, spontaneity, perishability, emotionality, vulnerability—from sight" (p. 399, emphasis added).

Geertz (1973h) sees these Balinese cultural practices as linked by a distinctive kind of "logic" that I term "existential." He begins: " 'logic' is a treacherous word; and nowhere more so than in the analysis of culture. When one deals with meaningful forms, the temptation to see the relationship among them as immanent, as consisting of some sort of intrinsic affinity (or disaffinity) they bear for one another, is virtually overwhelming" (1973h:404). But "meaning is not intrinsic in the objects, acts, processes, and so on which bear it." Rather the nature of "cultural integration"—what makes cultural patterns fit together, or come into conflict, or change—must be sought in "the experiences of individuals and groups of individuals as, under the guidance of symbols, they perceive, feel, reason, judge, and act" (p. 405).

Cultural logic, for Geertz, turns out to be an existential matter of how "experiential impacts play into and reinforce one another."

> A penchant for "contemporizing" fellowmen blunts the sense of biological aging; a blunted sense of biological aging removes one of the main sources of a sense of temporal flow; a reduced sense of temporal flow gives to interpersonal events an episodic quality. Ceremonialized interaction supports standardized perceptions of others; standardized perceptions of others support a "steady-state" conception of society; a steady-state conception of society supports a taxonomic perception of time. And so on. . . . (1973h:406)

In the end Geertz comes back, as he often did in the essays of this period, to universal features of the existential human situation:

> The close and immediate interdependency between conceptions of person, time and conduct which has been proposed in this essay is, so I would argue, a general phenomenon . . . because such an interdependency is inherent in the way in which human experience is

organized, a necessary effect of the conditions under which human life is led. But it is only one of a vast and unknown number of such general interdependencies. . . . (p. 408)

The universal "conditions under which human life is led" to which Geertz refers here are presumably those of the succession of generations, the balance between individual personhood and social interdependence, and, as we shall see below, human similarity and difference, among others. This existential argument makes cultural logic a matter of the basic psychological way human beings solve universal problems of human experience across different domains of social life.

The existential logic Geertz articulates operates at an abstract, psychologized, almost aesthetic level quite apart from the practical problems people normally use their cultural resources to solve.[8] How people find allies, arrange marriages, inherit land, or feed their families is never visible. The logic Geertz finds is real, but the source of its coherence is misspecified by ignoring the role of institutions.

Institutional Logic

To see how a more institutionally grounded analysis might push the same questions further, let us turn briefly to Geertz's later treatment (in "From the Native's Point of View" 1983b) of conceptions of personhood in Morocco, Bali, and Java—this time comparing his analysis of Moroccan personhood to Lawrence Rosen's description of the same Moroccan city Geertz studied, Sefrou. Geertz observes of the Moroccan use of the *nisba*, a kind of additional surname or tag that locates a person in some geographic or group identity that differentiates him in his immediate local context, that

> the nisba way of looking at persons—as though they were outlines waiting to be filled in—is not an isolated custom but part of a total pattern of social life. This pattern is, like the others, difficult to characterize succinctly, but surely one of its outstanding features is a promiscuous tumbling in public settings of varieties of men kept carefully segregated in private ones—all out cosmopolitanism in the streets, strict communalism (of which the famous secluded woman is only the most striking index) in the home. (pp. 132–33)

The logic here is manifestly functional, in the experiential sense:

> Moroccan society does not cope with its diversity by sealing it into castes, isolating it into tribes, dividing it into ethnic groups, or cover-

ing it over with some common-denominator concept of nationality, though, fitfully, all have now and then been tried. It copes with it by distinguishing, with elaborate precision, the contexts—marriage, worship, and to an extent diet, law, and education—within which men are separated by their dissimilitudes, and those—work, friendship, politics, trade—where, however warily and however conditionally, they are connected by them.

To such a social pattern, a concept of selfhood which marks public identity contextually and relativistically . . . would seem particularly appropriate. Indeed, the social pattern would seem virtually to create this concept of selfhood, for it produces a situation where people interact with one another in terms of categories whose meaning is almost purely positional, location in the general mosaic, leaving the substantive content of the categories, what they mean subjectively as experienced forms of life, aside as something properly concealed in apartments, temples, and tents. (p. 133)

In contrast to Geertz's existential account, one can begin to see how the practices of naming and identity, and ways of defining contexts as public or private, might "go together" in Morocco if one adds to the analysis institutions and their effects on practical action (which Geertz seems almost calculatedly to ignore). Lawrence Rosen (1984), Geertz's sometime coauthor (Geertz, Geertz, and Rosen 1979), also describes the Moroccan use of the *nisba* to highlight context-based social identities. But he adds the additional pragmatic element that makes the culture's patternedness make sense.

Because Moroccans are continually trying to establish relationships for trade, exchange, and marriage alliances, information that locates others socially is acutely important:

For to know another's origins, in this broadly geo-social sense, is to know what kinds of personal characteristics a person does or is most likely to display or acquire, what kinds of ties he or she may already possess, according to what customs one is most used to forming relationships with others, and—perhaps most importantly—what bases exist for the establishment of a personal bond between another and oneself. (Rosen 1984:24)

Thus Rosen also identifies a fit between social practices and cultural understandings. But it is not "fit" in the sense of experientially compatible solutions to universal dilemmas. Rather, specific institutional features of Moroccan society—the importance of alliance and exchange networks;

the use of social identities to establish ties of mutual obligation—provide the pragmatic basis for cultural practices such as the *nisba*. When one Moroccan hears another identified by a *nisba*, "that information itself begins to clarify some of the contexts through which the other, and potentially oneself, can be conjoined and known" (p. 24). This complex of belief, behavior, and symbolic action fits together because it is oriented to the same institutional order—one in which allies are a key social resource. In such an order, it makes sense to think of the self as having identities that create similarities with and differences from others, to "bargain" for social ties, and to name oneself and others in a way that highlights bases for making claims and forming alliances while leaving open precisely what kind of relationship will be established.

This kind of logic is not deductive nor is it in any strict sense "semiotic."[9] The fit among cultural practices is due to their common link to practical problems generated within an institutional order. The institutional order is itself, of course, culturally constructed (Scott 1994; J. Meyer et al. 1997). And the existing repertoire of cultured capacities (Moroccans' verbal facility [Geertz 1976], their flexible opportunism, and what Rosen [1984:28] describes as the extraordinary ability to absorb information about diverse social groups, customs, and particular others that might someday be useful in "forming networks and assessing others") constrains the kind of institutional order that is possible. But the continuing plausibility or reality of the meanings an institutional order generates, the eagerness people have to master the skills it requires, and the strategies individuals form in relation to its possibilities are linked by the institutional pattern itself.

Such a pragmatic logic may be conveyed through cultural symbols and stories; it is reproduced through unanalyzed social practices (like naming people with a *nisba*); but it is taught and enforced through the pragmatic structure of life-problems.

An important recent study (Collier 1997) traces a dramatic transformation in such institutionally grounded cultural logics. By following the impact of market logic as it shifts the ground of cultural meaning, Collier demonstrates that such logics are not anchored in some self-reinforcing circle of experience but in institutional orders that, when they change, rapidly alter understandings of personhood, time, and conduct as well.

In the rural Spanish village of Los Olivos in the 1960s, a family's wealth and social standing depended on the land or other property it owned. In such a world, families thought of their "honor" (the purity of their women and thus the integrity of their claims to inheritance) as the key to their family's well-being (Collier 1997). The practical "logic" of such a system was reproduced because a family's honor affected its children's marriage chances; and an advantageous marriage (and the habits of thrift and diligence that preserved the family estate) was the way families acquired or retained property. With the collapse of the agrarian economy in the post-Franco era, land became essentially worthless. In less than a generation, from the 1960s to the 1980s, the logic of market work supplanted that of agrarian inheritance.

In the earlier period women spent their adult lives promoting their family's honor by suppressing any sign of their own sexuality, advertising their "obligations" to others, and working to build up the stock of home furnishings that would make their children good marriage prospects (Collier 1997). In the market world, however, such "self-sacrifice" no longer made sense. Each person now had (market) value based on her talents and abilities. Rather than dressing in black and becoming matronly upon marriage, women dieted, wore makeup, and dyed their hair. Rather than valuing sacrifice for others, people sought to increase their own value by improving themselves. Sacrifice on behalf of others came to be seen as hypocrisy, a failure to act on one's true feelings. In short, the logic of family honor was replaced by the logic of market individualism.

This shift in pragmatic logic altered what Geertz would think of as understandings of the self, along with the public vocabularies in which people justified their behavior to themselves and to others. Collier (1997: 183–87) describes, for example, the heavy black mourning clothes worn by the women of Los Olivos (woolen stockings and layers of heavy wool clothing even in summer) to show "respect for the dead." Younger women rejected mourning dress as a "stupid custom" because what one wore could not express one's true feelings. It was not simply that older and younger women disagreed about mourning customs. It was that they no longer communicated in the same cultural language: for the younger women, what behavior meant had to do with one's motives and wishes; for the older women, behavior signaled willingness to perform social obligations and to maintain family honor. Even when younger women wore black dresses (usually stylish ones) to please their mothers, they explained that what really mattered was what you felt. In their mothers' world, however, following one's own feelings or wishes was a sign of self-indulgence, putting distractions ahead of obligations. Social signals that the daughters saw as guarantees of good conduct—sincere feelings, loving one's family, wanting to make them happy—only distressed the mothers who longed to hear that their daughters would sacrifice their own wishes to meet their obligations to others (Collier 1997:192–94).

In Los Olivos, mourning dress did operate as a semiotic code. The language of "showing respect" for the dead made sense, and wearing heavy black mourning for years asserted status, when one's prospects in life were determined by inherited property. Collier notes that "[i]n the early 1960s, villagers argued endlessly over exactly which items of mourning dress a woman who was 'touched' [by a death] had to wear, and for how long. But they all agreed on the basic principle that a woman's mourning dress should reflect her genealogical relationship to the person who died" (p. 188). The extent of mourning also conveyed information about inheritance: "[b]y observing which women put on which items of clothing in the days following a death, villagers could assess, with fair accuracy, not only the genealogical relationships through which inheritances were supposed to pass, but also the quality of relationships among living family members . . . [as well as] a woman's possibilities for inheriting from distant kin" (pp. 190–91). Furthermore, being known as a person who maintained appropriate mourning customs, despite discomfort and inconvenience, may have "attracted inheritances" (p. 191). A woman who demonstrated willingness to sacrifice for her obligations signaled childless elders that she might make a good caretaker and heir.

Younger women, oriented to market and marriage, demonstrated their ability, sincerity, talent, and drive by their appearance and attitude and by the testimonies they offered to the sincerity and depth of their feelings.[10] They sought to demonstrate that they did things not because they were obligated to, but because they wanted to. Love became the best predictor of whether a couple would marry, rather than "the properties and reputations of their respective families and . . . the couple's respect for social conventions" (p. 103). Women sometimes succumbed to passion, in part because withholding sex until marriage came to seem calculating in a world that valued sincere feeling and rejected conformity to social conventions. Younger women no longer sought to "subjugate" their children (as their parents had to keep them from risking family honor and the chance of an advantageous marriage). Rather they sought to foster their children's talents and to teach them independence.

In the contrast of these two cultural patterns, we can identify a kind of cultural logic. But in what does this logic consist? It is not the resonance of a unified ethos across various spheres of life (in fact, as Collier notes, in modern Spain calculation in the market sphere has been accompanied by the expectation that family life will be emotional, intimate, and free of mercenary motives [see pp. 108–10; 132–35]). Nor does a cultural logic link one sphere to the next through the experiential interdependencies Geertz would see among solutions to existential human dilemmas. And these cultural logics are not abstract deductive systems. The logic, including the logic of the associated semiotic code, hangs together to the degree that its various elements derive from (and help constitute) the same institutional order. When dominant institutions create similar dilemmas of action, there will be what looks like a unified cultural logic. To the extent that institutions develop divergent patterns (as, I have argued, the state, the family, and the market do in contemporary societies), there will be multiple, sometimes non-overlapping cultural patterns (see Friedland and Alford 1991; Friedland and Hecht 1996). And even a single institution creates dilemmas and uncertainties that elicit multiple, sometimes contradictory strategies of action.

In contemporary America, I have argued, two different ways of understanding love are rooted in different aspects of the institution of marriage. The contemporary structure of marriage as an institution—exclusive, voluntary, life-transforming, and enduring—generates no single logic. Rather, it poses tasks or practical difficulties of action, to which the wider culture generates many different, sometimes competing, and always only partially satisfactory solutions.[11] The culture of "prosaic-realistic love" addresses the problem of how to make a relationship last. "Mythic" or "romantic" love focuses on the problem of deciding: whether to commit oneself to a relationship and how to choose whether or not to stay in a relationship. The culture of romantic love reproduces the institutional features of marriage as psychological states, honing the capacity to identify one other person as *the* person whom one loves and to know that this relationship is "it."

While basic institutional contradictions—in this case the contradiction between the voluntariness and the permanence of marriage—generate dilemmas for actors, the cultural solutions to those dilemmas are not simple reflexes of the institutional order itself. The solutions share a logic, not in the sense that they share similar ideas but because they provide alternative routes to the same destination. There are wide variations and sometimes dramatic shifts in theories and techniques for solving these dilemmas, even while those varied solutions share a common orientation to the institution itself. The prosaic-realistic love culture, for example, may teach patience, the value of affection over infatuation, and how to discount strong emotions in favor of more constant thoughts and feelings, as well as such skills as "communication," "sharing," sexual intimacy, and managing conflict. These are skills that many contemporary Americans believe make the difference between relationships that last and those that fail. But shared religious commitment and the quest for personal fulfillment may also at one time or another, for one group or another, be envisioned as ways of making relationships last.

Alternative strategies of action not structured by the model of lasting marriage are also possible, although I found only scattered hints of this among the middle-class married and/or divorced suburbanites I interviewed. As I mention in chapter 6, older, divorced women who had largely given up on marriage occasionally used a different logic in talking about love, one in which friendship, mutual support, and fair exchange were the criteria of a good relationship, and the word "love" no longer made sense. Some research on gay relationships suggests alternative strategies of action in which life is organized not around finding a single, lasting relationship but around friendships in which love and sex mingle, without "love" implying a lasting, exclusive relationship (see Popovitch 1989; Nardi 1999:74–101).

The culture of romantic love has a stricter logic, presumably because it is more tightly bound to the key institutional features of marriage. Nonetheless, romantic love may enshrine sudden passion, a gradually growing inner certainty, or careful weighing of pros and cons as ways to know whether a relationship is worthy of commitment. These cultural solutions are not united by their inner logic, nor by pervasive schemas that are transposed from one arena to another. Rather, however internally diverse, fluid, or incoherent they are, these cultural patterns are given unity by the institutional dilemmas to which they are addressed.

Institutions

The concept of an institution plays a large role in this book, yet I have not explored it directly. The best definition of an institution is probably that of Ronald Jepperson (1991:145), who treats institutionalization as a matter of the degree to which a practice or structure is stable and self-reproducing:

> An institution is then a social pattern that reveals a particular repro-
> duction process. When departures from the pattern are counteracted
> in a regulated fashion, by repetitively activated, socially constructed,
> controls—that is by some set of rewards and sanctions—we refer to
> a pattern as institutionalized.

Others (Bellah et al. 1991:10–12, 39–41; Scott 1994; Selznick 1957, 1992; Friedland and Alford 1991) have emphasized that institutions are stable, patterned systems based around culturally defined purposes.[12] In this view, some stable social practices (what aisle holds fresh produce versus meats at the supermarket) may still not be "institutions." And similarly the university, or baseball, is an institution because it has a set of core meanings that define its purposes—even when particular universities or baseball teams, or perhaps even the whole academy or all of American baseball, fail to live up to those ideals. That is, the "institution" is defined by the existence of a set of rules or purposes that transcend any particular organizational or social embodiment.

The "new institutionalism" of John Meyer and others (see DiMaggio and Powell 1991; Fligstein 1990) emphasizes how institutions import fundamental elements of their purposes and structures from outside themselves. John Meyer (1983, 1987; J. Meyer et al. 1997) has postulated a kind of floating environment of institutionalized rules about what features and associated purposes constitute a nation-state, a corporation, a school, or a marriage, and he sees the instantiation of a relatively stable set of externally available rules as the defining feature of institutions. For Meyer, environments become more "institutionalized" as the comprehensiveness and elaboration of the rules that define entities and the kinds of entities that can exist expand. But this alerts us to a central feature of institutions—that they are patterns of "constitutive rules."

One of the most helpful discussions of the nature of institutions as culturally constituted entities comes from the cognitive anthropologist Roy D'Andrade (1984). D'Andrade (1984:90), paraphrasing Geertz (1973c:11–12), notes that "[m]arriage is part of American culture, but marriage is not the same thing as knowing how to marry people or knowing how to get married or understanding what it is to be married. Most Americans have an understanding of what banishment is and how to banish someone (were they Richard II), yet these understandings do not make banishment a possibility in American culture." He quotes John Searle, the philosopher, on the special quality of certain statements (such as saying "I do" in a legal marriage ceremony) that, within the constitutive rules of an institution, create a certain state of affairs:

> It is only given the institution of marriage that certain forms of behavior constitute Mr. Smith marrying Miss Jones. Similarly, it is only given the institution of baseball that certain movements by certain men constitute the Dodgers beating the Cubs 3 to 2 in eleven innings.
>
> These "institutions" are systems of constitutive rules. Every institutional fact is underlain by a (system of) rule(s) of the form "X counts as Y in context C." (Searle 1969:52, quoted in D'Andrade 1984:91)

An institution, as D'Andrade (1984:94) points out, depends on "social agreement that something counts as" something, and on adherence to (or enforcement of) that rule and the "entailments incurred by application of the rule." As D'Andrade conceives them, these "entailments" are linkages between the rules that constitute an institution and norms (regulations of action) that flow directly from the constitutive rules. As he emphasizes, these norms "are not a matter of logic, but rather consist of the assumption that such linkages exist." Thus, he argues, "wearing a tie" is "linked to constitutive rules by which formality is defined and created," just as, we might note, wearing heavy mourning was linked to the rules that constituted kinship and inheritance in Los Olivos in the 1960s.

Thinking of such behavioral entailments as "norms" is probably not as useful as thinking of them as semiotic codes: a tie signals the formality of an occasion while mourning dress signals (and enacts) the closeness of a kin relationship. All institutions have signaling systems that permit monitoring and enforcement of the basic structures of the institution. The institution of family inheritance in Los Olivos entailed an elaborate system of codes by which people demonstrated their willingness to sacrifice for their family obligations, including the mourning dress that showed "respect for" the dead. Indeed, Bourdieu (1977) rejects the idea of normlike rules for behavior precisely because he recognizes that any institutional order creates corresponding "games" through which individuals manipulate what the codes that define institutional positions allow them to "say" (see also Crozier and Friedberg 1980).

Unanswered Questions

Wide variation in kinds of cultural "logics" suggests that social analysts need to consider carefully what kind of account they are offering when they claim to have uncovered a cultural logic or to have observed a logic being played out. Part of what we mean by cultural explanation is that some logic internal to culture itself drives social processes. Yet we understand all too little what we mean by various claims that particular cultural processes have a logic, and we know less about how much those logics are constraining.

I have suggested that the notion of a "logic" as some form of rational, deductive logic (albeit with "nonrational" premises) does not really capture what analysts in concrete cases understand as "logical" about the cultural logics they analyze. But it is still an open question how far deductive logics (or other kinds of formal logics, like the binary logic of Lévi-Straussian structuralism) play an independent role in structuring cultural processes. There are, for example, hints in some cultural analyses that cultural oppositions are linked, so that a change in one impels change in others (for example, Wright's [1975] study of the changing plot structures of cowboy movies), but we have little notion of how general such processes might be.

Second, while I have argued that cultural logics are anchored in institutions, we do not really know to what degree similar ways of solving problems transfer from one institutional sphere to another—or to what degree there is strain toward consistency across institutional arenas. This might be understood as a question about the limits to human beings' cognitive and social capacities, although DiMaggio's (1997) recent review of cognitive psychology suggests that human beings keep multiple scripts and schemas on tap simultaneously. On the other hand, researchers like Dobbin (1994) argue that at the societal level, "solutions" to at least some problems of social organization tend to be stable over time and consistent across different domains of social activity (though Ziegler [1997] finds domain-specific solutions to similar problems).

We need more explicit attention to the question of how different logics interconnect (and disconnect) and why. If human beings can function in multiple modalities—impersonality at work, intimacy at home, and hedonism away from home, for example—then questions about whether or not there are necessary linkages among spheres may require analysis at another level. John Meyer's work might suggest consistency in cultural logics across spheres, not because there is some functional need for coordination but because institutions draw on a common world-level reservoir of institutionalized rules to establish nation-states, school systems, corporations, and even selves (Thomas, Meyer, Ramirez, and Boli 1987; J. Meyer et al. 1997). But the reservoir of constitutive rules may not be consistent across institutions or cases. And as in other cultural arenas, pressures for innovativeness and organizational distinction may lead to the transformation of constitutive rules themselves. If chiefdoms, territories, tribes, and empires have all given way to the institutional form of the nation-state, are not the number of things that can be squeezed under the nation-state umbrella constantly expanding, even as the notion of the nation-state as the highest organizational unit in the world polity is itself under challenge (Soysal 1994, 1997)?

A third unanswered question about cultural logics concerns the relationship between institutional orders and the semiotic codes through which they are enacted. To go back to Collier's (1997) case of Los Olivos, if showing that one would make sacrifices for family honor was important for marriage alliances and "attracting inheritances," then wearing cumbersome mourning dress, while not directly preserving property, may have seemed a logical correlate of being a successful or high status family. Such claims themselves are of course socially constructed rather than purely "logical"—in one place self-sacrificingness might be signaled by intensity and duration of mourning, while in another by the burdensomeness and expense of funerary rituals or by willingness to go hungry to feed one's children. As I suggested in chapter 8, there can be social debates about the codes that signal various traits or properties (such as current debates over what traits are masculine or feminine) so that the content of a semiotic system can shift, while its underlying "point"—what it seeks to convey—remains pretty much constant. But we know relatively little about how tightly linked semiotic codes and institutional orders are. In some cases institutional orders may remain stable while the semiotic codes in terms of which they operate shift.[13] In other cases, a semiotic code may be adapted to convey new meanings, linking it to a different institutional order than the one in which it originally made sense.

Finally, we need to understand the contexts in which "logical logic" does make a difference in social life. To the extent that individuals use cultural resources not only to organize strategies of action but also to justify their actions to themselves and others, those accounts may have logical entailments. This is certainly the burden of Weber's (1968) analyses of legitimations of authority, of the symbolic content of status claims, and of the independent effects of religious worldviews. Without trying to revisit Weber's arguments about rationality and rationalization (see Swidler 1973), or to judge how far some inherent propensity toward logical consistency plays a role in social life, I want to suggest that once we stop assuming that "cultural logics" are transparent and that how the logic generates implications is obvious, we may develop more powerful ways of analyzing cultural logics—even if those logics turn out to be multiple, overlapping, and varied in their structure.

Do Some Cultural Elements Control Others?

The biggest unanswered question in the sociology of culture is whether and how some cultural elements control, anchor, or organize others. Indeed, this partially subsumes other questions of cultural integration or cultural logic.

If we have finally won the Weberian battle to demonstrate that cultural factors influence human action, we are nonetheless in great danger of losing the war. For if everything is culture—from the structure of organizations, actors, and nation-states (Thomas, Meyer, Ramirez, and Boli 1987), to the fundamental constituents of economic life such as markets (Reddy 1984) and labor (Biernacki 1995), to the dynamics of revolutions and social movements (Sewell 1980, 1985; Tarrow 1998; Johnston and

Klandermans 1995)—we need to differentiate the culture concept to explore which kinds of cultural elements organize others, and which control particular kinds of social processes (see Jepperson and Swidler 1994).

We can see the difficulty by turning to William Sewell Jr.'s important essay, "A Theory of Structure" (1992). Sewell recasts the perennial problem of the relationship of culture and social structure by redefining structure itself, as "composed simultaneously of schemas, which are virtual, and of resources, which are actual" (p. 13). In a brilliant inversion of the older view of culture as the unexplained residuum left over when material factors have had their causal impact, Sewell argues that structures themselves can be "read" for the schemas they contain, and that reproduction of a structure is the reenactment of a schema using human and material resources. Because of the "multiplicity of structures" and the "polysemy of resources," structures can be reinterpreted to generate schemas different from those that originally produced them. Thus human agency is possible (indeed ubiquitous) in "the capacity to reinterpret or mobilize an array of resources in terms of schemas other than those that constituted the array" (p. 20).

Sewell (1992:22) directly confronts the major difficulty this new conceptualization raises. If everything from "structures that shape and constrain the development of world military power to those that shape and constrain the joking practices of a group of Sunday fishing buddies or the erotic practices of a single couple" is a structure organized by schemas, then it is essential to differentiate among kinds of structures—to analyze, in my terms, whether and how some structures organize or constrain others.

Sewell (1992:22) suggests a categorization of structures by "depth, which refers to the schema dimension of structure, and power, which refers to the resource dimension." These dimensions provide a way of analyzing which structures organize and control others: "deep structures are those schemas that can be shown to underlie ordinary or 'surface' structures, in the sense that the surface structures are a set of transformations of the deep structures." Deep structures are also "pervasive" and "relatively unconscious." A structure's power, on the other hand, is its ability to mobilize resources. So language is a structure that is deep but not powerful, while nation-states are powerful but not deep. "[R]elatively near the surface of social life . . . [s]tate and political structures are consciously established, maintained, fought over, and argued about rather than taken for granted as if they were unchangeable features of the social world" (p. 24).

Sewell's formulation is a great advance in rethinking the distinction between culture and social structure. But the attempt to specify why some schemas are more influential than others is less satisfactory. As I argue in chapter 8, "deeper" cultural meanings do not always have greater capacities to organize other social patterns. The uncontested, taken-for-granted meanings that pervade much of ordinary social life may be so loosely organized and so internally contradictory that they have little influence on social action (see Swidler 1986; also Billig 1987, 1992). At the same time, sometimes apparently superficial cultural practices, like gift-giving on Mother's Day, can constrain action by defining the meaning of social gestures, while being neither deep nor powerful.

There is a question as to whether "depth" and "power" are the right conceptual tools at all. Labeling a structure "deep" (having the broad capacity to organize other domains of social life) or "powerful" (able to mobilize extensive human action) simply describes the outcome we are interested in, without really accounting for it. Indeed, these metaphors may mislead us about what kinds of cultural schemas (or structures in Sewell's terms) have these effects.

Richard Biernacki's *Fabrication of Labor* (1995) suggests why depth and power may be the wrong metaphors for thinking about what makes culture influential. Biernacki traces the effects of the different schemas that constituted labor as a commodity in England versus Germany. These schemas were certainly deep in the sense that they were unconscious and taken for granted. British owners and textile workers "defined the factory employment relation as the appropriation of workers' labor concretized in products" (that is, cloth), while "German employers and workers . . . acted as if the employment relation comprised the purchase of labor effort and of the disposition over workers' labor activity" (p. 43). These differing schemas had widely pervasive effects, according to Biernacki, structuring everything from mill architecture, to the timing and shape of strikes, to the fundamental intellectual differences between British political economy and Marxian analyses of "labor power."

Despite being unconscious and taken for granted, however, the core schemas, what Biernacki calls "silent practices" for negotiating labor arrangements, were not "deep" in the sense of lying "underneath" everything else. They were anchored in and reproduced by specific, everyday practices, not deep conceptual assumptions, and when these practices were changed, the different understandings of labor disappeared with them. It was the negotiation of piece-rate wage scales—reproducing shared assumptions about what there was to negotiate over—that kept the contrasting British and German patterns intact. "The German piece-rate system centered its comparisons of different ways of weaving on the motion of inserting a pick [weft thread], without respect to the visible length of the finished product. The British pattern compared the picks [weft threads] in different kinds of finished products rather than in motions" (p. 50). When the ways laborers and owners negotiated wage rates changed, German-British differences in the constitution of labor as a commodity vanished—essentially overnight (Biernacki 1995:495–97). During World War I, governments in both countries began setting wage rates directly. This interruption in the practices of negotiating piece rates eliminated the British-German difference in how labor was constituted as a commodity.

Thus what look like relatively unimportant surface practices—such as how wages are negotiated—can organize (indeed define) important characteristics of the physical and conceptual universe. But it is not clear that "depth" is what gives these practices their pervasive influence. The intellectual challenge for students of culture is to think more broadly about why some cultural schemas dominate or organize wide areas of social life. It is an open question, I think, whether such pervasively influential schemas are also the most enduring—although logically it might seem the two should go together.[14]

Sewell argues that "deep" structures affect broad domains of life because their basic schemas underlie many "surface" structures that are transpositions of them. But very influential structures do not necessarily work by generating homologous versions of themselves. I have argued instead that social institutions shape action because they define problems actors must solve. The various solutions then share common schemas (or common cultural logics) because they are solutions to the same institutionally structured problem. Thus the mechanism Sewell proposes to explain why some structures are broadly influential (and why some schemas are widely reproduced) may be wrong. It is not self-propagation of schemas through homologous transposition that is at work, but active agents constrained by the same institutional logic who seek out cultural resources to solve similarly shaped problems.

Cultural styles, skills, and habits of the sort I discuss in chapter 4 (and certainly the *habitus* as Bourdieu describes it) may indeed be propagated by the replication of analogous schemas in the way Sewell describes for "deep" structures. I have argued that culture in the sense of "cultured capacities" for action, feeling, and perception influences action because it is easier for people to use skills they already have and to apply them to new situations than to develop new ones. (People may also develop new cultural capacities by modifying ones they already possess, or by prolonged contact with models whose styles and habits they can imitate.) Homology rather than complementarity is the rule here. But while such cultural styles have some of the attributes Sewell would identify with "depth"— they may be unconscious and ingrained and, as I have argued, they may be difficult to learn or unlearn—there are usually many such skills and habits, and they may be brought together in diverse arrays rather than by some unifying structural logic.

Of course features of institutions themselves may be generated by cultural schemas transposed from one arena to another—as, perhaps, the logic of free choice and contract structures Americans' thinking about government and marriage, as well as about market transactions. But as both government and marriage illustrate, actual institutional structures do not necessarily approximate the schemas people attach to them. Thus Americans cannot decline the contract government offers, while marriage involves vows that people are not required to honor.

John Meyer and his collaborators might adduce the "rules" that define institutions as examples of "deep" structures. And indeed the cognitive frames—in D'Andrade's terms the "constitutive rules"—that make some structures universities and others nation-states might be candidates for such deep structuring principles. But as the Meyer group has demonstrated in their empirical work, such structures are themselves in a process of constant evolution—sometimes according to quite superficial, faddish principles—so that the "recipe" for making a nation-state, for example, increasingly requires more form (an elaborated constitution, a large number of cabinet departments, and data-gathering capacities, all validated by recognition by the United Nations [Boli-Bennett 1979; McNeely 1995]) and less by way of effective content (a military able to assert sovereignty, effective rule over territory, long continuity of rule).

If "depth" is not the right metaphor for suggesting which structures or schemas will be widely influential, "power" does not solve the problem either. Of course in an obvious way powerful social structures that mobilize vast resources will be widely influential. But thinking about their direct "power," their capacity to mobilize things or people, does not answer the question of whether the patterns they create are central in anchoring or shaping other structures and schemas. Sewell seems to be thinking primarily of the state as the paradigmatic example of a structure that is "powerful" but not "deep." But it is not clear that the state's influence comes directly from its power over resources, so much as from its ability to set the limits or constraints within which other institutions operate. Theorists such as Fligstein (1990, 1996) have increasingly pointed to the state's crucial role in setting constraints that define the limits of rational action for other actors. Thus Fligstein (1990) shows that the American state's legal and regulatory environment—laws against cartels, trusts, and restraints of trade—directly affected the form corporations adopted and the "conceptions of control" their managers embraced. In a similar way, the legal order created by the state anchors the institution of marriage and ultimately affects the way that institution itself is defined. But this role of state action does not quite fit Sewell's notion of "power" as the capacity to mobilize resources. The activities that embody state "power"—say, drafting a large army, collecting taxes, and imposing criminal sanctions—may not shape other structures and schemas in a way at all proportional to the "power" these activities involve. At the least, more analysis is necessary to determine what elements of a state's effects on society are widely influential in structuring other patterns and which have less influence on the shape of other structures and schemas.

If depth and power are not what make some cultural patterns especially influential, recent research offers other suggestions. Biernacki's (1995) analysis of how labor was constituted in England versus Germany suggests that social formulas that mediate ongoing negotiations of antagonistic interests may be particularly enduring. Each side in a dispute, in formulating and pursuing its interests, continually reproduces the schema in whose terms it seeks advantage. Such structured antagonisms may also account for why German versus British schemas for constituting labor had such wide influence. Biernacki emphasizes that these were "silent practices" rather than consciously articulated ideas. The ways people actually defined what they were doing while they worked (producing a length of cloth of a certain value, or sending the shuttle across a certain number of times) and how much they deserved to be remunerated were influential because they were "unobtrusive." But we could make the same point slightly differently by saying that these unobtrusive practices operated as "constitutive rules," defining what it was that employers purchased from workers, and that the other arenas in which this schema was also influential—structuring the ways labor was withheld during strikes, or what factory architecture attempted to regulate, or how employers fined or penalized tardy or absent workers—were all sites where conflicts between workers and employers played out. So rules that constitute something that becomes the ground for repeated conflict may have particularly wide and lasting influence.

Constitutive rules may also be anchored by public practices. Elizabeth Armstrong (forthcoming) has traced the crystallization of a "gay and lesbian community" in San Francisco in the early 1970s. This community was defined by the diverse groups that it comprised—and its constitutive rule was embodied (and annually enacted) in the Lesbian-Gay Freedom Day Parade, which displayed those diverse identities. This new rule—congealed in a relatively short period of time but almost immediately widely influential—spawned the rapid formation of hundreds of identity-expressive organizations in a population that earlier had supported only a small number of political groups, each of which had tried to represent gay or lesbian interests in general. This example suggests how a key symbolic or ritual practice may instantiate the constitutive rule that defines a social entity, making real, for example, what "membership" in the "community" consists in.

Sewell (1996; see also 1990) has brilliantly analyzed how emblematic public action—such as ritual displays during a revolution—can encode new constitutive rules (that "the nation" now equals "the people"), model new forms of collective action, and enact new understandings of public order and social progress. In the key case he analyzes, that of the fall of the Bastille in the summer of 1789, a new constitutive rule crystallized very quickly and came to organize broad domains of public action. Of course, not every new form of collective action is "successful." The question of why new constitutive rules sometimes take root is precisely what further research along the lines Sewell has laid out would explore.

What is fascinating about the kinds of constitutive rules Armstrong and Sewell analyze is how quickly they can establish themselves, becoming the accepted reality not through long usage but through their capacity to establish a public model of collective life. But even when a schema is neither taken for granted nor unconscious, it may be enduring and pervasive, I have argued, if it is the shared "default option" for collective action in periods of uncertainty. Thus Americans, while they can constitute and navigate formal organizations, contractual exchanges, and governments that require obedience, nonetheless tend to fall back on the notion that action is coordinated by the voluntary choices of individuals (Swidler 1992). It is true that sectors of American social life are organized this way—from Bible study groups, to churches, to fraternal organizations. But the schema is not "transposed" everywhere. Rather, it is the fallback position—that form of coordination people assume that others will turn to when the bureaucratic, corporate, familial, or state system isn't there. There is a great deal of conscious cultural elaboration of such a schema, perhaps precisely because it is less institutionalized. Voluntarist social action survives in the cultural repertoire as a focus of story and myth as well as occasional enactment. People want to know "how to" do it, and they want to see examples of how such action is performed successfully. In other cultures, family loyalty, or sacrifice for the group, or revolutionary exaltation is the "default option" that people assume will solve collective problems.

The difficulty in developing cumulative theory and research about which cultural practices anchor or organize others is exacerbated by confusion about levels of analysis in social theorizing. In contemporary theorizing about culture there is a kind of unspoken assumption that societal-level cultural factors—"discourses"—are impersonal, pervasive, and enduring, while individual-level beliefs and attitudes are particular, concrete, and variable. But it may be instead that there really are public cultures—not simply generalized discourses or semiotic codes (in whose terms many things can be said, but which don't directly say something in particular) but quite particular beliefs—that are, so to speak, the authorized beliefs of a society about itself (see Jepperson 1992; also Nicolopoulou and Weintraub forthcoming). These might be quite long lasting but nonetheless subject to change in the light of publicly authorized or validated historical experience. In *Forging Industrial Policy* (1994), for example, Frank Dobbin analyzes continuities in French, British, and American patterns of economic regulation. Dobbin argues that each nation has pervasive schemas that are publicly defined as answering the collective question of how it can maintain social order and produce progress. Those implicit theories, he argues, are established by authoritative interpretations of early successes, particularly in establishing political order. Such modes of problem solving persist until there is publicly defined catastrophic failure and repudiation of specific elements of the available theory of public coordination (as there was in the United States after political corruption seemed to damn the capacity of local government to assure economic progress). Such a perspective would hark back to Bendix's analysis in *Work and Authority in Industry* (1974) of how dominant ideologies are constructed. But it would not assume that powerful ideologies operate as deep, largely hidden structures of discourse. Rather it would accept that there are public ideologies that are not reducible to shared private opinions but are instead public realities that directly confront (and sometimes conflict with) individual views.

These are only tentative suggestions about where we might look for distinctions among types of culture that would let us answer the question of what makes some cultural elements able to organize others. At this point, we should take persuasive empirical studies of how culture operates and think inductively about what aspects of a particular cultural schema make it dominating, pervasive, or enduring (or weak, narrow in application, or fleeting). Our empirical studies will make much more substantial contributions if we can begin, however uncertainly, to formulate general theoretical questions about culture that can guide research into the roles that it plays. This book is intended as a contribution to that endeavor.

Methodological Appendix

This study is based on eighty-eight interviews conducted by myself and three research assistants in 1980 and 1981. I shall discuss three issues here: whom we interviewed and why; the nature of the interviews; and the status of the interviews as evidence. Following this discussion I provide the Basic Interview Guide, the Professional Interview Guide, and the Vignette Interview Guide.

THE INTERVIEWEES

I sought to interview a fairly homogeneous group of middle-class Americans, since I was interested in understanding how people made different uses of a common cultural repertoire. I also wanted to understand the sources of the ideas that influenced these middle-class adults' conceptions of love and marriage, so I interviewed a number of ministers, therapists, and marriage counselors about their own understandings of love as well as about what they saw as important for their clients.

I tried to find a middle-class sample, uncontaminated, as I thought, by the specialized culture of Stanford University where I taught then, or by the notoriously liberal culture of San Francisco, to the north. Thus I interviewed primarily in San Jose and its suburbs. San Jose is a diverse city surrounded by vast suburban sprawl. While its suburbs are middle class in atmosphere and in their distance from a cosmopolitan center, it is upper-middle class in income. With the rise of Silicon Valley, whose electronics industry was in full flower in the early 1980s, real estate prices were high and poor and moderate-income housing extremely limited. While only a few of my interviewees were engineers or others employed directly in high-tech industries, almost all were professionals or white-collar service workers—secretaries, schoolteachers, or accountants, for example.

Because I was interested in how people's understandings of love are shaped by experience, I sought to interview people who had been married and also those who had gone through the disruptive, and sometimes disillusioning, experience of divorce. I also interviewed a few younger single persons to see whether romantic understandings were more central for those with less experience and to see whether and how these young singles anticipated the issues that concerned the married and divorced.

To find interviewees, I used a snowball sampling method. My initial contacts varied widely. I began with therapists and marriage counselors listed in local directories and with ministers of churches listed in the phone book or mentioned in the San Jose suburban newspapers. I then asked ministers to suggest members of their congregations and counselors to contact current or former clients who might be willing to be interviewed. I also asked for volunteers to be interviewed from a night class for adults taught at a local junior college. A research assistant also found a half-dozen interviewees through her family contacts in a local lower-middle-class community. Eighteen interviews with professionals constituted our initial contacts—seven with ministers and eleven with therapists or marriage counselors. But these interviews cannot be easily divided from the other interviews, since some professional interviewees talked quite openly about their own experience while others talked about issues that arose for their clients or parishioners.

Starting with these initial contacts, my research assistants and I asked interviewees for the names of a neighbor, a coworker, and a friend, in the expectation that contacts drawn from these three sources would differ in the ways they were similar to the original contact. Some people were, however, more willing to give the names of friends than of neighbors and coworkers, so my sample is biased toward friends. I also tried to use no more than three or four interviewees in a chain stretching from one original contact, and I tried, where I could, to interview a neighbor or coworker rather than a friend, because I reasoned that friends were more likely to share a common background and worldview.

In addition to the overwhelmingly middle-class bias of the sample, it had some other peculiarities due, in part, to the fact that we were asking people to talk about love. Since all the interviewers were women, in the case of married men it seemed best to interview both members of the couple, to reassure the wife (and perhaps the husband as well) about such a potentially intimate conversation. (Husbands and wives were interviewed separately except on one occasion, when there was a misunderstanding and the couple assumed they would do the interview together.) It was also harder to find men to interview than women, so the sample is disproportionately female. It was more difficult to find divorced men than women who had not remarried, partly because it is less likely for women over thirty to remarry than for men.

The following table lists basic demographic characteristics of the sample. I do not claim that this sample is representative—certainly not of the American population, but not necessarily even of the suburban, white, middle class. It is wealthier, and it is disproportionately clustered around age thirty-five, containing very few people under twenty-five or over fifty-five. However, it is also not biased in the direction of much of the popular literature on love. Unlike the self-selected samples who volunteer for sex surveys or couples studies, these are ordinary middle- and upper-middle-class men and women. While the interviewees represent a range of views—from feminists disillusioned with love and marriage to fundamentalist Christians who regard marriage as God's will—they are on the whole conventional members of what they regard as the American mainstream. Even though some of my initial contacts were through ministers, only thirty-four of the interviewees made religious understandings central to the ways they discussed their lives (eleven Evangelical Christians, nineteen mainstream Protestants, four Catholics, and three with mystical, Buddhist, or occult interests); three interviewees were Jewish, all nonpracticing; fourteen had an active therapeutic worldview that shaped the way they understood themselves and others; and the rest, while some were occasional churchgoers or were still affiliated with the religion in which they had been raised, no longer saw it as an important part of their lives. About half the women were working outside the home, but there was strong representation of more traditional, but no longer typical, families with nonworking mothers. These were, on the whole, people to whom love and family mattered.

Representativeness of the sample is also not an issue for this research in certain respects. I make no assertions about the distribution of views of love within the wider American population or within the population from which my interviewees were drawn. I do use the interviews as evidence in other specific ways that do not depend on their representativeness. For example, I claim that the people I interviewed employed multiple, sometimes contradictory, cultural understandings of love simultaneously. I would, and do, argue that this is a general process, in part because I can see no reason why my sample is biased in ways that should make it unusually culturally complex. I acknowledge that in very different kinds of societies, or perhaps in very different parts of this society, people may not *have* so many opinions, may not be so readily able to talk about their lives in general terms, and thus may make different uses of culture than the ones I describe

Gender	Marital Status	Age	Education	Number of Children
Men (39)	Married (48)	20–29 (23)	High school (2)	None (31)
Women (49)	Divorced (14)	30–39 (42)	Some college (25)	One (7)
	Remarried (8)	40–49 (17)	B.A. or B.S. (15)	Two (28)
	Single (13)	50+ (5)	B.A.+ (16)[a]	Three+ (8)
	Unknown (5)[b]	Unknown (1)	Advanced degree (26)[c]	Unknown (14)
			Unknown (4)	

here. (Daniel Lerner, in *The Passing of Traditional Society* [1958], addressed this issue when he argued that people from traditional societies did not think in hypothetical terms. One of my research assistants, herself from India, noted that Indians "would not have so many opinions.")

The subset of people we interviewed is, however, probably biased in some important ways relevant to the nature of the research itself. The most important is nonetheless hard to demonstrate. Because we relied on a chain of personal recommendations for interviewees, I believe we encountered an unusually psychologically healthy, and perhaps happy, subset of the population. While like other researchers (Rubin 1973; Komarovsky 1964) we found that a number of our interviewees had had difficult childhoods (an alcoholic parent, for example), I was struck by how rare were the kinds of psychological difficulties that might have made interviewees incoherent, terribly anxious, or particularly defensive in talking about their lives and their beliefs. Although we encouraged those who gave us contacts not to recommend only their "most wonderful" or "happiest" friends but to suggest people who were "just average" or "ordinary," I think our contacts still disproportionately selected people whom they were not worried about contacting on our behalf, and people with whom they thought we would find it interesting or satisfying to talk. To put it in the colloquial terms that best describe it: I was struck by how "together" and how "straight" our interviewees seemed.

I also suspect that the people we interviewed were unusually articulate and thoughtful. For the same reasons that people may have avoided

[a] Includes teaching credential.

[b] In interviews with professionals, interviewers did not press for personal information, although interviewees often volunteered it.

[c] M.A., Ph.D., or other professional degree (for example, social work, engineering, or divinity).

contacting acquaintances with serious emotional difficulties, they may have also favored those who they knew would enjoy, or be good at, talking about themselves. Thus, while I have tried to describe a range of ways people make use of culture, and in chapter 3 I have focused special attention on those who give very little abstract thought to their experience, a study of this sort is necessarily biased by its reliance on talk, and its reliance on those able and willing to talk about their experience. This problem is compounded by the reliance on middle-class interviewees. Researchers such as Mirra Komarovsky (1964) and Basil Bernstein (1975) in England argue that members of the working class think in much more concrete, "restricted" terms about personal relationships, often without a vocabulary to describe abstract emotional states (see especially Komarovsky 1964; Rainwater, Coleman, and Handel 1962; and the Hollingshead studies of class and mental illness, especially Meyers and Roberts 1959). More recent studies, for example those of Veroff, Douvan, and Kulka (1981), may indicate that an interest in and ways of talking about personal relationships have become more widespread since the 1950s. But nonetheless, these interviews draw on a culture where conversation about feelings, about relationships, and about "love," is not only possible but regarded as normal. On the other hand, this is precisely my point. The culture of love and analysis of personal relationships is a central one for those I interviewed and so provides a good place to look at how culture works for those to whom it matters.

People evidently enjoyed the interviews, liked talking about themselves and their beliefs, and cared about the issues we discussed. But despite our efforts to establish rapport, and our general sense that we succeeded (after all, we ourselves liked hearing our interviewees' life stories and talking with them about love), there were almost certainly variations in rapport and in the comfort and ease with which our interviewees discussed their understandings of love and marriage. Because this book tries to analyze how people use their culture as well as to describe something of the content of the cultural meanings associated with love and marriage, there are special problems regarding the quality of the interactions in the interview. For example, when, in chapter 3, I analyze variations in how fully people integrate their culture with their life experience, or in how much of their cultural repertoire people actually mobilize, what is the evidence for these judgments? How can we tell a "superficial" versus a "deeper" engagement with culture? Sincere versus cynical attitudes? Or even more and less coherent cultural patterns? And perhaps most troubling, how can we tell the difference between a particular interviewee's way of using culture and the quality of the interview—the tact or tactlessness of the interviewer, the rapport between interviewer and interviewee, or even whether the interviewee (or the interviewer) is having a bad day?

The answer, in the most general terms, is that we can't. Nonetheless, rather than characterizing particular persons as "deep," "superficial," "confused," or "coherent," I tried to analyze the range of patterns in the ways people link culture and experience—to demonstrate that there are very different ways of making such links. I of course think that there are consistencies in the ways people use culture that constitute aspects of the "style" that makes a person what he or she is.[1] Conversation and self-disclosure are skills, learned with more or less facility like any other, and conversation is one of the key sites where experience is integrated and given meaning in relation to wider cultural understandings. As a skill or habit, someone's way of talking about himself or herself is likely to characterize many of that person's interactions.

On the other hand, people's modes of using culture vary by subject and context. An inarticulate engineer may wax lyrical at work when discussing bits and bytes. A person who actively uses cultural understandings of love to explore personal experience may rely almost exclusively on platitudes and clichés in talking about politics. It is not necessary to my argument that any given person always use culture in the same way, or even that I have correctly characterized a particular person at a particular moment.

THE INTERVIEWS

Interviews ranged in length from ninety minutes to about three hours and were tape-recorded. We used two different interview formats, sometimes together and sometimes separately. The basic interview (below) was an extended discussion of the respondent's life history, his or her understanding of love, ideals about relationships, and experiences that had affected his or her views. We also used a vignette interview (also below) consisting of seven vignettes about difficult decisions faced by people in love relationships, using these dilemmas to probe interviewees' views of love. In those vignettes we used protagonists whose gender matched that of the interviewee, hoping to maximize identification with the stories, although in a few interviews we tried using vignettes with protagonists whose gender differed from that of the interviewee to see how much gender ideologies affected people's views about what spouses or lovers should do in difficult situations. About two thirds of the interviews (sixty-three of eighty-eight) involved only the basic interview; about a fourth (nineteen) used the basic interview followed by the vignette interview; and six used only the vignette interview, supplementing it with a few basic questions about the respondent's own life.

The basic interview, and to some extent the follow-up questions in the vignette interview, had a somewhat unusual character, related to the kinds of issues that concerned me. Rather than assuming, as many surveys do, that people have a "true" idea or opinion about an issue, which the survey tries to tap, I was interested in the entire range of ideas, understandings, and even inarticulate assumptions people might bring to bear on a problem.

I was less interested in *what* people thought than in what resources they had available to *think with,* and how they mobilized those resources. Thus the interview was open-ended, both in the sense that the questions were unstructured and that I probed what people told me, following up on what they said, asking about its meaning, and trying to determine its ramifications for other things they thought. Thus, while I always covered the basic questions in the interview, often more than once, I also pursued topics of interest to the interviewee, trying to find out how she or he really mobilized her ideas to address different kinds of issues.

I was especially interested in the ways cultural traditions penetrate and shape experience. Thus I asked people to describe their experience and considered how they organized that experience and what kinds of cultural meanings guided it. To understand more deeply how people used ideas, I often responded to statements of general principles ("Honesty is the most important thing in a marriage") by asking for examples, to clarify what grounded the principle's meaning. When people talked in specifics, I often asked for a generalization, to see how they might extend the construction they made of the concrete case.[2]

I also sought to probe my interviewees' ideas in another sense—to see where the logic of an argument slipped or broke down, and thus to comprehend what kinds of cases had made the argument seem plausible in the first place. I tried to engage my interviewees not by challenging them but as a friend might do, by asking a set of "Yes, but what if . . ." questions. People did not abandon their positions when I suggested complications (e.g., "But can being honest sometimes create problems in a relationship?"). Rather, they sometimes vigorously defended or deepened their original claims, and sometimes offered complementary perspectives or assumptions that provided the context for their ideas. (On the other hand, as I have argued above, at unexpected moments people often articulated views quite at variance with ideas they had expressed earlier in the interview.)

The Status of the Interview as Evidence

There is, of course, an important question about the relationship between what people said in these interviews and what they might normally do or think. Indeed, since I am interested in the ways people *use* culture, how does the way people used culture in the interview setting relate to the ways they apply it in their regular lives?[3]

I would begin with the minimal claim that any ideas people put forth and the uses they made of culture were at least possibilities in their repertoire before. In addition, I think there is a good deal of internal evidence in the interviews that (1) people had thought about many of these issues before, in similar terms; and (2) people who were not attuned to a given cultural perspective on their experience (the therapeutic fascination with honest communication, for example) would continue to "miss the point" even of quite heavy-handed questions designed to tap the issue.

Nonetheless, the pragmatics of the interview situation are important, for good and ill, to the kind of evidence I obtained. The most obvious issue is that an interview asks people to think of themselves as a coherent whole and of their lives as having some sort of narrative continuity (see Linde 1993; Reissman 1990). An interview asks in one way or another for an account. Of course a social-science interview is not the only context in which people try to give coherence to the self and narrative continuity to their lives. Sometimes meeting a person for the first time, or reencountering someone at a high school reunion (Ortner 1993, 1998; Vinitzky-Seroussi 1998), or even stopping for a moment to think about one's life can evoke similar narratives. And certainly psychotherapy (Fingarette 1963) and religious conversion (Stromberg 1993) create similar opportunities for the narrative structuring of a life. Indeed, these frameworks sometimes structured how interviewees told me about themselves. Interview talk may be somewhat more coherent than the talk elicited in focus groups (Gamson 1992), for example, or informal family or friendship groups (Billig 1992; Liebes and Katz 1990), because in general people need to construct a narrative about themselves that makes sense during the interview itself. (On the other hand, to the degree that the interviewer imposes the order or sequence of topics, she might interfere with other sorts of coherence that order spontaneous talk.)

An additional issue, which began to worry me more as I started to develop the arguments of this book, is that talk—both the ways people talk to interviewers and the ways they may talk to others in "natural" settings or even to themselves—may represent a concatenation of multiple structures of meaning that are shaped largely by factors outside the talking situation itself. This is the burden of chapters 6–8 of this book, and readers' views of this issue will depend on how much they are persuaded by the argument of the book as a whole. One implication of this argument, however, is that interviews in general, however well or carefully done, may have difficulty capturing the institutions, codes, and contexts that in fact account for both the coherences and the apparent incoherences that arise within any particular segment of discourse. While speech can reflect matters outside itself (a report of an interviewee's educational background, salient facts of personal history, or the traces of institutions, identities, or interests that structure the way someone talks), the interviewer or listener may often not know which images, institutions, cultural codes, or imagined situations are in fact structuring particular parts of someone's conversation. The frequency with which people sometimes changed their view of a question when they reframed their assumptions about its context or meaning—and the ease with which they did so—indicates why the multiple institutions, codes, and contexts that leave their traces in talk can be hard to extract from talk itself. The active problem solving for which actors often use their cultural resources also leaves only intermittent marks on the flow of an interview.

The Basic Interview Guide

INTRODUCTION

This is a study of personal relationships, of what people care about and why. We're asking different people to tall us a little about what seems important in personal relationships, what some of the greatest problems are, what things seem to work well, and what are sources of difficulty. It isn't a study where there are right answers or where we are testing some scientific theory. We're actually just interested in what people believe and what they care about.

1. First, can you tell me a little about yourself? Where you are from? Where you work? Are you married or not? How long?

   [Don't actually ask for all this information here. Just ask people to tell a little about themselves, to get them started. Then, at the end of the interview, go back to fill in any information you missed.]

Age	Spouse's Age
Occupation	Spouse's Occupation
Marital Status	Spouse's Education
Education	
Residential History	

   Family Background
Father's Occupation	Mother's Occupation
Father's Education	Mother's Education
Siblings?	
Any other important information	

2. And can you tell me what are the major things you are doing now, at this time of your life? Is there anything especially important or unusual happening in your life now? What? Is there anything special you are trying to do? What? Or is it just a normal time? Normal in what way?

AUTOBIOGRAPHY — CULTURAL HISTORY

1. Can you tell me something about your background?

   Where you grew up?

   What your family was like?

   Where you lived?

   What your childhood was like? (Was childhood happy/secure? less happy?)

224

[Probe here for anything that seems important to the person.]

2. And now I'm particularly interested in what ideas about love, or marriage, or personal relationships you might have had when you were young.

   What ideas about love do you think you might have gotten from your family?

   Were your parents religious? Did that have any influence?

   Other relatives?

   Friends?

3. Thinking back now, say to when you were younger, maybe a teenager, do you remember what you thought love was, or what you expected it to be? [Probe.]

   Do you know where you got those ideas? Family? Friends? Popular songs, books, TV, movies?

   And did you ever think you were in love?

   How did you know?

   What did it feel like?

4. Was there a first time when you would say you were really in love?

   How was that different?

   What made you think it was love?

   Is that an idea of love you still hold?

   [Here some interviewees may start describing their marriage or their most important love relationship. If so, fine. If not, pursue the whole history of their changing beliefs, hopes, and ideas about love through as many steps as they can reconstruct.]

5. Have your ideas about love changed since then? How? Why?

   [The interview will circle around to these questions again, but it is good to have several takes on the same issues.]

History/Meaning of Marriage, or Current or Most Important Relationship

[If the interviewee has been married or had an earlier central relationship, but also has an important current involvement, try to get histories of his or her experience of both—or more if there are more than two major relationships.]

1. Now, you are married? (divorced? separated?)

   How long have you been married?

   If divorced, how long were you married before you divorced? How long divorced?

2. Can you tell me something about your marriage?

How did you meet?

How did you decide that this was the person you wanted to marry?

Did you think (know) you were in love? Was that an important consideration?

How did you recognize it as love? Were you sure or unsure? What questions did you ask yourself? What did it feel like?

Did you love (him, her) right away, or was it something that grew gradually?

Were you sure that this was the right person to marry? Unsure? Why?

Was deciding who to marry hard or easy?

3. And during your marriage, have your ideas about love changed? How?

4. What have been the most important things you've learned about relationships?

What have been the hardest issues to deal with?

Have there been unexpected things? Good? Bad?

5. On the whole would you say it is a good relationship?

Good in what ways?

Bad in what ways?

LOVE AND RELATIONSHIPS

Now I'd like to talk a little about love and relationships in general.

1. What, in your view, is a good relationship?

What makes it good?

2. And what is a bad relationship?

What makes it bad?

3. What is love? (Or what do you mean by it?)

Is love a meaningful idea? [Probe. Is there some better word or idea?]

What is an example of real love?

How can you tell if it's real?

Does it matter in relationships? Why?

Does it matter to you?

4. During your life, have you changed your view of what love is?

How have your ideas changed?

What are the major lessons you've learned about love?

5. Have you had to give up some ideas you once cared about?

Which?

Why?

What were significant changes?

6. Have you learned something more important? What?

7. General ideas about love:

Does love require some sort of intense, ecstatic experience?

If so, what do you do about the danger of that dying out?

If not, do you worry about missing that? [Probe here. Is the expectation of ecstasy the basic problem with love? Can people who work at it rekindle those feelings?]

Does loving imply obligation? What do you owe a person you love? [Again, probe. if the interviewee doesn't like the idea of obligation, why not? Do people not owe each other anything? Will the desire to care for, help the other person be spontaneous if love is real? What if the feeling of love isn't there?]

What responsibilities do people have to each other in relationships?

Do those responsibilities depend on whether or not they love each other?

What about sacrifice? Should people make sacrifices for those they love?

What about permanence? Does love have to be a permanent commitment?

What about fidelity? Is that important?

[For all these questions, probe for the general logic of the interviewee's thinking. Ask for examples.]

And what about communication? Is that important in relationships? Why?

What about honesty? Openness? [Probe here. Are there any limits on honesty in relationships? What if honesty might hurt the other person?]

What about personal growth for you as an individual?

Is growth, personal development an important idea?

Can it be reconciled with the responsibilities you have to a relationship?

What if two people in a relationship grow in different directions?

Should a person be able to give up some opportunities for personal development to preserve his/her relationship?

When there is a conflict, should you do what's best for yourself or best for the other person in a relationship?

Do people who love each other have a special way of treating each other? Special obligations? Or do the same values apply to all relationships?

[For all these questions, try to get at the interviewee's central logic for thinking about personal relationships, and try to probe for the limits of that logic. When you ask for examples, what are the kinds of situations your interviewee sees as "typical" for the kind of moral worldview he or she adopts? What kinds of situations fit less well? And what are the major cultural influences? Has your interviewee joined any social movements, personal growth movements? What about religion? What about books? Movies?]

General Values

1. What is worthwhile in life? What makes a good life?

2. How do you know what you ought to do? (What do you go by?)

   Is it hard or easy to know?

   How do you decide?

   Does doing the right thing come naturally? Or is it hard?

3. What makes an act right?

   Rules?

   Consequences?

   How it feels?

4. Are there any actions that are absolutely wrong in themselves? What? Why? [Probe: examples.]

5. Have your views on right and wrong undergone any important changes? What? Why?

6. Are there some problems about what is right and wrong, or about how you should act that you still find difficult? What? Why?

7. What can you build your life around?

   Other people? (narrow circle—family, relatives, friends—or more general commitment to other people?)

   Only yourself?

   Work, career?

   Church? God?

   Broader goals—community, politics?

8. What is a person?

   Do people stay the same? Change?

   Can you count on other people?

   What about yourself? Do you stay the same? Change?

9. What would you say are the most important influences on the person you are today?

    What is most important to you? (new experiences? being a good person? accomplishing something? etc.)

10. When do you feel most like yourself?

    When do you feel most like the self you would like to be?

11. How big is the world you feel you live in? (Family and friends? Community? Nation? Human world? Natural world?)

12. What kind of community or society would you like to live in?

13. What kind of support does your community give you to have the kind of relationships you want? The kind of society?

14. What would a good society be like?

15. What kind of a world do you hope for your children?

[At the end of the interview, go back and ask about any specific biographical details you may have missed, reviewing the basic age, background, employment information. Then ask if there is anything else that is important to the person you may have missed.

Also fill in information (if it hasn't come up earlier in the interview) about the person's job situation, the way the interviewee functions at work, the kind of work the person does, whether he/she is happy at work or looking for a change. Such information may provide important clues to the way the person defines central issues in personal relationships, but direct questions about work may break the flow of the interview's main focus on love and relationships.]

Professional Interview Guide

(Agency, Church, Therapist, Counselor)

Name of Organization:

Person Interviewed:

Date:

Time:

Place of Interview:

This is a study of contemporary American beliefs and values about love and family life in contemporary society. Since [you] your organization deals with [family counseling, marriage, families, couples, personal relationships, etc.], I was wondering if I could talk with you about what you are doing and what kinds of values and attitudes you see in the people you deal with.

1. Can you tell me briefly about your (practice) organization? How long have you been in operation? What kind of community you serve? Clients you deal with? Issues you focus on?

2. What would you say are some of the major issues concerning marriage, relationships, family life that come up in your work?

3. What are the major problems people bring to you? What is the source of these problems?

4. What would you say are the major values people have for their marriages? Their family relationships?

   Do you think these are changing?[4]

5. How do people see a good relationship? Do people seem to know what they want in their relationships or to be confused?

6. How strong are traditional values about marriage and family? What are these? How much are people attracted to (confused by) new values? [Probe to see whether in the minister/therapist's view people see traditional values as bad, and seek to liberate themselves from them; or good, and people seek to preserve or protect them.]

7. What kind of advice, help, clarification, etc. do you give the people who come to you? [Here get at central language, mode of understanding the service-provider uses to give help to clients—religious or therapeutic, brute realism or supportive encouragement, etc. Is it self-discipline, humility, and trust in God? Comfort? Resignation? The capacity to communicate, to express one's own needs? The ability to hear the other person? Or is it self-realization? The willingness to assert one's self, break from traditional roles, discover one's

self? The goal here is to enter the provider's own language sufficiently to see where it goes, what understanding of love it offers in its own terms.]

[Probe here: What are the most difficult issues? What is the most gratifying part of the work (i.e., what defines success)?]

8. Do the people who come to you talk in terms of "love"? What is the significance of the idea of love for them? What do they mean by the term? How do they think it should be modified? Or why should it be rejected?

9. How do you think about what makes a good, worthwhile, satisfying relationship? [Probe for the interviewee's language. Ask for examples.]

10. What do people who love each other owe each other? Or is it not a matter of obligation, but of something else? What? What about people in a relationship, whether or not they consider it love? What about people who are married? Is that different?

11. What is the right way for people to act? What should they go by? What should they live by? [Try to find a way of asking this that fits with the interviewee's own language for understanding right and wrong.]

12. How can one become a good person, do the right thing in relationships? How can people know what they should do?

13. What tradition do you draw on? What does the church (your profession, training, etc.) say about these issues? How have you had to adjust your beliefs in practice?

14. What kind of community is this? Are there special problems [strengths?] of the people living here? Does it tend to stabilize or pull apart relationships?

[Return to themes of commitment vs. personal development if these haven't been dealt with thoroughly already. Probe to see whether these terms capture the central themes of conflicts interviewees see in the clients they deal with.]

Vignette Interview Guide

(Female Version)

VIGNETTE I

Paul and Marcia were in love when they first married. But after many years of marriage they have drifted apart. They do not talk very much because he is very involved in his work and she is involved with her own family and friends. Marcia has tried to get Paul to discuss things more so that they can share their thoughts and feelings with each other, but each time after a few weeks he gets caught up in his own affairs again and she finds herself lonely. When she says that she is thinking of leaving him, Paul insists that he still loves her and needs her support and understanding. He says there is nothing wrong with their marriage and she is just being selfish. She says he does not understand what real love is all about.

A. Who is right? Why?

B. What does Paul mean when he says he still loves his wife? Is this love?

C. Marcia finally does leave Paul. Was she right? Why?

D. Who is responsible for breaking up the marriage?

E. What might they have done to save their marriage?

F. What would happen if Marcia decided that because Paul still loved her and needed her she would stay with him?

VIGNETTE II

A woman has been involved with two different men. One is kind, trustworthy, and caring. She sees him as her "best friend." The other is exciting and irresistible. She finds herself falling in love with him even though she realizes he is not right for her—he is not dependable and stable. She has tried to get over him, but she cannot. Both men are in love with her and want to marry her.

A. Whom should she marry? Why?

B. Is what she feels for the second man really love? What is love?

C. Is love necessary for a good marriage? For happiness?

D. What would happen if she married the first man, because she knew he would be a good husband, even though she did not really love him?

[Probe: Could she learn to love him in time?]

Vignette III

A couple's happy marriage of many years is disrupted when the husband, John, becomes mentally ill. He is severely depressed and cannot respond at all to Evelyn, his wife. More than a year of treatment does not cure him, and the doctors see little chance of his ever functioning normally. Evelyn is tempted to leave him to try to build a new life for herself, but she feels guilty about leaving her husband.

Should she leave her husband or stay with him? Why?

Probes:

1. Does she owe it to him to stay with him because he was good to her in the past?

2. What if they had not been married very long?

3. What if he had not been a very good husband, had not given her much happiness even before he became ill?

4. What if she made arrangements to have someone care for him while she went off on her own?

5. What if she made herself stay with him to take care of him, but she fell in love with someone else?

6. Would she have the right to the happiness of another relationship if it would not hurt her husband—if he would not know?

7. Does whether she should stay have to do with how much she loves him? What is love?

If she should leave:

8. What if he were not hopelessly ill, and had some chance of recovery?

9. What if she still loves him, even though the relationship is no longer satisfying?

10. What if he were not mentally ill, but she had just gotten tired of him and found the marriage less and less satisfying?

11. Does she owe it to herself to leave? What would happen to her if she tried to make herself stay?

If she should stay:

12. Is it marriage that obligates her to stay? What if they were deeply in love, but were not married?

13. Is it love that obligates her to stay? What if she had never really loved him? What if he had never really loved her?

Vignette iv

Anne and Lawrence married young, and they felt they had a good, satisfying marriage. But then, in her forties, Anne met another man and fell in love with him.

She likes Lawrence. He is affectionate, understanding, and she enjoys his company, but she says she is in love with this new man in a way she had never been with Lawrence. She feels that this relationship has added a whole new dimension to her life. She says that she had never realized that she was capable of caring so intensely or sharing so deeply with anyone.

A.   What should Anne do? Why?

B.   Anne thought she loved Lawrence. She says that she still does love him. Does this make sense? What does love mean?

Anne also says that she did not really know what love could be like before. What is love? How can you tell when love is real? What does it mean to say that you love someone? How do you know?

C.   Does Anne have the right to leave her husband? What does she owe him after their years together? Why? Does it depend on whether they had a good relationship, whether he was a good husband, or only on the fact that they were married? On children? Does Anne have the right to go even if it will hurt Lawrence?

D.   Anne feels that a whole new world has opened up to her because of this relationship. Should she give it up? Can she go back to her marriage?

Vignette v

Linda and George have a very close relationship. They have always preferred to do most things together and they have shared more of their thoughts and feelings with each other than with anyone else. Linda, however, is starting to feel that perhaps they should do more things with other people and develop some separate activities of their own. George says that this might lead them to grow apart and make their love for each other less deep. Linda says it might make their love deeper if they were more independent.

A.   Whose attitude to the relationship is right?

B.   What is Linda's view of love?

C.   What is George's view of love?

D.   Would pursuing Linda's plan for more independent lives be a possible threat to their relationship?

E.   Would pursuing George's plan of sharing their lives mostly with each other be a possible threat to their relationship?

F.   Whom do you think you would like or admire most, George or Linda?

G.   Do you have to be an independent person in your own right to really love each other?

H.   Do you have to have a commitment to sharing your lives together to really love each other?

VIGNETTE VI

A man and a woman have a very close relationship. They have been living together for five years on the West Coast. She is offered a once-in-a-lifetime opportunity for graduate study on the East Coast. They are faced with a dilemma, because the man has a very good job and is unable to leave.

A.   Should he sacrifice his job for her or should she give up her plans to study? Why?

B.   By what criteria do they decide who should move?

C.   Is there a need for sacrifice, or should they allow the relationship to drift apart?

D.   Suppose the couple mutually decide to live apart, but promise to remain faithful to each other. Six months after they separate the man becomes deeply involved with another woman. Was he wrong to become involved with another woman in this case? Why? What if the woman had become involved with another man?

VIGNETTE VII

Jim and Diana have been dating for a long time and are planning to get married. One summer when they were apart Jim had an affair with another woman, but never told Diana about it. When Diana learns of this she breaks off the relationship. Jim says that since he had broken off the affair he did not feel the need to mention it to Diana.

A.   Who is right? Why?

B.   Do you think Diana's reaction to the affair is an indication that she really does not love Jim?

C.   Does Diana have a right to be jealous? To feel betrayed?

D.   What if Jim had told her about the affair? Would that make it all right?

Notes

Introduction

1. I did not exclude members of ethnic and racial minorities from the sample. But such is the segregation of American suburban life by class and race (Massey and Denton 1993) that none of the networks of friends, neighbors, and coworkers we followed from churches, therapists and marriage counselors, or a community college class led to members of ethnic or racial minority groups.

2. There have been many studies of how audiences actually use culture, demonstrating convincingly that people appropriate and rework cultural materials for their own purposes and interpret it to fit their own understandings. See Griswold 1987, Liebes and Katz 1990, Radway 1991, Press 1991, Shively 1992, Lichterman 1992, and Binder 1993.

Chapter 1: Finding Culture

1. A few scholars have asked how and why particular pieces of culture become meaningful for particular individuals (Stromberg 1986, 1993; J. Briggs 1991; Chodorow 1999). Swidler (1986), Schudson (1989), and Sewell (1999) offer varied approaches to the question of why some symbols are more effective than others in particular contexts. Of course Geertz himself has repeatedly asked how a cultural system comes to be meaningful to its members. His analysis of how a people's ethos, worldview, and "sacred symbols" or rituals mutually reinforce one another is central to his approach to culture (Geertz 1973b, 1973d, 1968). But this model of how cultural meanings come to seem "uniquely realistic" (1973b) never addressed the possibility that only some meanings might seem true for particular people or that different meanings within a "cultural system" might be disconnected or conflicting.

2. Tamar Liebes and Elihu Katz (1990; see also Katz and Liebes 1987) explore the varied ways in which viewers of the television program *Dallas* distanced themselves from some aspects of the program while embracing others. Andrea Press (1991) makes a related point about television viewers' expectation that soap operas will be "realistic" in certain respects and not at all in others.

3. David Sikkink (1998:54), in an innovative study of how American Christians define their religious identities, reports very similar findings:

> [M]ost respondents used a variety of different religious images and ideals to situate themselves in religious social space. Their religious

identities had numerous dimensions, rather than cohering around a single frame of reference. . . . Finally, more often than not, our respondents expressed their religious identities in the negative by delineating various practices, ideas, or values with which they did not want to be associated.

4. Probably only in the modern West have cultures appeared to have as much consensus as ours does. In principle, at least, we have authoritative ways of resolving truth. Elizabeth Eisenstein (1969) has argued that printing allowed the preservation of a diverse heritage and, more important, the sorting out and reconciling of competing claims. Bellah (1970) has pointed out how distinctive to Western Christianity is the insistence on "belief" and doctrinal consistency as central aspects of religious participation.

5. Paul Lichterman (1992) comes to a similar conclusion about the ways readers of therapeutic advice literature appropriate particular ideas and techniques while remaining skeptical of the authority of any particular book.

6. The paragraph above is based on field notes from a Presbyterian Marriage Encounter weekend, interviews with encounter-weekend leaders, and issues 2–45 (dated from January 1981-December 1992) of *Spirit*, a Marriage Encounter newsletter produced by the San Francisco Area Presbyterian Community (in the author's possession).

7. There is by now an enormous critical literature on Geertz's work. Important statements include Shankman 1984; Asad 1983; Clifford and Marcus 1986; and Wikan 1992. Some critics fault Geertz for his method or his politics, while failing to assimilate what is most useful from his theoretical contributions (see Swidler 1998). A recent volume, *The Fate of "Culture": Geertz and Beyond* (Ortner 1999), suggests both the breadth of his influence and the importance of his work for advancing current understandings of culture.

8. Mark Schneider (1993), Richard Biernacki (1999), and Stephen Greenblatt (1999) have each commented on Geertz's method of isolating and then interpreting cultural "texts," although with slightly different emphases. Schneider asserts that Geeetz's method leaves it ambiguous whether the meaning of a text resides in the text itself or must be supplied by the interpreter. Biernacki offers a brilliant critique of the trope of "textuality" itself, with its hidden presumption that "reading" a text is somehow a straightforward act. He invokes the historical variability of practices of reading to highlight the inadequacy of this presumption. Greenblatt cleverly notes that Geertz manages to have it many ways at once—characterizing his texts as "not untypical" excerpts that give insight into some wider culture while insisting on each text's unique, ungeneralizable individuality; treating texts as "found" objects that give authentic insight into a strange culture while stressing the shaping role of the anthropologist's interpretive framing; and focusing on isolated texts rather than on global societal analyses while contending that the text makes sense only in its context.

9. Geertz of course pioneered in posing the problem of how people live within multiple cultural realities—how the realities of religion, ideology, art, and common sense intersect. But his analytic technique is still to analyze separately how each reality frames experience, rather than to start with the user of culture and ask how particular cultural meanings are brought to bear on experience. In "Religion as a Cultural System" (1973b), Geertz asks how the "moods and motivations" religious experience engenders "come to seem uniquely realistic" (p. 119). What kind of reality do religions assert, and how does it interact with the realism of ordinary life? Geertz takes as his premise Alfred Schutz's phenomenological argument that human beings regularly slip back and forth between radically incommensurable realities, between "religious belief in the midst of ritual, where it engulfs the total person, transporting him . . . into another mode of existence, and religious belief as the pale, remembered reflection of that experience in the midst of everyday life" (pp. 119–20). Religion places "proximate acts in ultimate contexts," changing the commonsense world, "now seen as but the partial form of a wider reality which corrects and completes it" (p. 122). But if religious reality is a different order of experience than ordinary life, then it is not clear whether or when people caught up in everyday life do place it in the context religion provides. Indeed Geertz himself seems to doubt so strong a claim and instead relies almost exclusively on a kind of aesthetic image, that religious experience affects the feeling tone, the characteristic "attitude toward life" a people holds: "The moods and motivations a religious orientation produces cast a derivative, lunar light over the solid features of a people's secular life" (p. 124).

10. Indeed, Geertz is a brilliant observer of cultural conflict, misunderstanding, and cross-purposes, as his treatment of the brouhaha involving the Jewish trader, Moroccan sheikh, and French captain (1973c) or the debacle of a Hindu funeral reliant on Moslem ritual in a period of political turmoil (1973f) easily show.

11. Geertz himself has repeatedly identified the problem of how to understand variations in cultural intensity or depth—note his brilliant analysis in Islam Observed (1968:61) of "holding" versus being "held by" one's religious beliefs. But his usual method of trying to make an exotic "text" understandable preempts attention to such questions.

CHAPTER 2: REPERTOIRES

1. I want to thank James Fernandez for insisting on this point and providing the phrase.

2. There are, of course, many earlier proponents of this view, among them Geertz (1973g:52): "Becoming human is becoming individual, and we become individual under the guidance of cultural patterns, historically created systems of meaning in terms of which we give form, order, point, and direction to our lives." Mary Douglas (1982:12) makes a similar point: "[T]reat cultural categories as the

cognitive containers in which social interests are defined and classified, argued, negotiated, and fought out. Following this rule, there is no way in which culture and society can part company, nor any way in which one can be said to dominate the other" (quoted in Wuthnow et al. 1984:129–30).

3. There is by now a vast literature in cognitive psychology and in the burgeoning field of cognitive anthropology on the role of scripts, schemas, prototypes, and models in organizing perception and action. For overviews, see Schneider, Hastorf, and Ellsworth 1979, Fiske and Taylor 1984, and D'Andrade 1995. For work that directly tackles the problem of culture and cognition, see Strauss and Quinn 1997 and D'Andrade and Strauss 1992. For an analysis of what the sociology of culture can learn from cognitive psychology, see DiMaggio 1997.

4. Charles Lindholm (1998:248) sees the absence of reasons as an essential characteristic of romantic love, "which is defined and experienced as spontaneous, total and boundless in its devotion to the actual person of the other—to love 'for a reason' is not to love at all. We love because we love, and not because of anything that the beloved other has to offer us beyond themselves." The idealizing love from afar that Lindholm describes is very different from the down to earth attitude of these very domestic, married lovers. But as I argue below, they do *sometimes* use an idea of love that shares this sense of disinterested devotion.

5. Hans Joas (1996:163) uses the process of finding a particular person to love as a prime example of the way in which "we must establish in concrete action-situations what satisfies our aspirations and what accords with our values." He quotes Hubert Dreyfus (1979:277) as follows:

> When a man falls in love, he loves a particular woman, but it is not that particular woman he needed *before* he fell in love. However, after he is in love, that is after he has found that this particular relationship is gratifying, the need becomes specific as the need for this particular woman, and the man has made a creative discovery about himself. He has become the sort of person that needs that particular relationship and must view himself as having lacked and needed this relationship all along. In such creative discovery the world reveals a new order of signification which is neither simply discovered nor arbitrarily chosen.

6. Naomi Quinn (1987:174–76) has described several basic metaphors with which contemporary Americans describe marriage—"marriage is a manufactured product," "marriage is an ongoing journey," "marriage is a durable bond between two people," "a spouse is a fitting part," and "marriage is an investment." These metaphors in turn form part of a cultural model that provides a simplified causal imagery facilitating reasoning about marriage.

7. David Hummon (1990), in a study of popular images of urban, rural, and suburban life, has shown that the common stereotypes are very widespread,

but that people differ greatly in how much they elaborate these images and apply them to their own life experiences.

8. Remember the rock-and-roll classic, "Shop Around."

9. Mark Kelman (1981) has developed what he calls a "topological" model of the logic of American criminal law. He argues that in the legal determination of such issues as criminal responsibility, key background assumptions (for example, the time that may elapse between a criminal act and the duress that lessens criminal responsibility for that act) vary from one arena to another, making legal logic appear consistent from case to case, while, in fact, the underlying parameters that set the "scene" vary. Thus legal reasoning, which prides itself on providing consistent answers to similar problems, relies on such leaps from one set of background assumptions to another to produce different outcomes for different situations while apparently relying on consistent rules.

10. The social-psychological literature on scripts and schemas (Markus 1977; Abelson 1981; Fiske and Taylor 1984; D'Andrade 1995) makes a very similar point.

11. Howard Schuman's (Schuman and Presser 1981) careful studies of structured attitude questions reveal the same phenomenon: small changes in wording sometimes make enormous differences in "attitudes" because, I would argue, the question then taps into a different frame for understanding the issue.

12. This businessman also seemed to have more to say about what was wrong with George's position than with Linda's, even though he made clear that he basically sided with George. It may be that he more fully explored the costs of the independence that was a greater temptation for him. Dependence is bad, but he did not really have to worry about it much, though here too, he had worked out a rationale, based on the golden rule, that "unless you see yourself as an individual and have some regard for yourself, you're not going to have any ability to hold others and give them any love and to treat them as individuals."

13. The anthropologist Bradd Shore (1996) observes that "real life often involves the problematical and often partial resolution of dilemmas proposed by the existence of competing [cultural] models, or models that are incompatible with key experiences" (pp. 302–3). He goes on to summarize his conclusions from a series of anthropological case studies:

> The view that cultural models "construct" reality has dominated cultural anthropology. But a closer look at what happens in the case of conflicting models suggests that the experiences of confusion, ambivalence, and irony, which often accompany serious conflict in models, do not support the strong version of the constructionist view.
>
> Cultural models are better understood as one kind of necessary resource by which people make meaning in their lives. (p. 315)

14. Postmodern approaches to culture of course emphasize incoherence, multivocality, and indeterminacy. But they see this as a recent phenomenon rather than a general feature of cultures and they tend to attribute it to a breakdown of processes of cultural ordering. I view it as a normal aspect of all cultures in which the capacity to move back and forth among cultural meanings and to frame and reframe experience and action is precisely what gives human beings room to maneuver, both individually and socially (for an excellent example, see Maddox 1993).

Chapter 3: Examined and Unexamined Lives

1. See the methodological appendix for further discussion of the interview context and a copy of the interview guide. Charles Briggs (1986) has pointed out how dependent interviews are on the larger context that frames the purposes and meanings of talk—particularly the talk with a stranger about one's own life and opinions that is the "interview" as most middle-class Americans understand it. Nina Eliasoph's (1990) study, for example, may have elicited a particularly high level of cynical, humorous, or evasive responses because she was taping "man-on-the-street" comments for a radio broadcast. Most of my interviewees recognized the social formula that established the meaning and purposes of the interview as "serious" ones, and their answers reflected the desire to give the interviewer a reasonable picture of their own lives, thoughts, experiences, and so forth. Their answers, or at least their tone, might have been quite different had they been engaged in trying to rethink their life direction, regale their friends with an outrageous story, or ruminate about how to solve a particular problem. The shared framing of the interview situation as an earnest attempt to convey to a stranger the central elements of one's life shaped the uses people made of culture and also created occasional moments when people avoided or deflected questions that struck them as wrongheaded.

2. David Hummon (1990) offers fascinating evidence of the variability in the meaningfulness of even widely shared cultural stereotypes. Hummon finds that most Americans are aware of the basic stereotypes about communities—how friendly small towns differ from impersonal big cities, for example. They vary of course in their preferences for small town, city, or suburban living and in the valence they attach to common stereotypes. But most significant for our purposes here, people differ in the salience and symbolic density of their conceptions of place. For most, the characteristics of places are a matter of common cultural knowledge but to which they are basically indifferent. For a minority, however, conceptions of place become important organizers of other sorts of meanings—for example, explaining differences in individual character, biography, or life outcomes. In such cases, ideas about different kinds of places become highly elaborated and are often closely integrated with respondents' interpretations of their own lives or their understandings of the lives of others.

3. These two aspects of the link between culture and experience are reminiscent of Geertz's (1973b) formulation that culture provides "models of" as well as "models for" experience. William Sewell Jr. (1992) has developed another language for talking about this two-sided property of culture, discussing how "schemas" or rules organize the production and reproduction of social structures ("models for") and how cultural objects and social structures may also be "read" for the schemas they embody ("models of").

4. A great deal of recent work analyzes discourse on public issues (Perin 1977; Condit 1990; Dillon 1993; Alexander and Smith 1993; Benson 1996; Ginsburg 1998). As I argue in chapter 8 and the conclusion, public discourse is differently organized and constrained than is individual thinking.

5. While individuals seem to have dominant styles which characterize the interview as a whole, I am describing the way culture is used in a particular interview, rather than characterizing individuals. Because I conducted a single interview with each person, and because I did not usually observe people in other settings, it is impossible for me to separate the quality of a particular interview and the influence of the interview setting from the cultural style of the person interviewed. Peter Stromberg (1993) has argued that the personal style in which people recount aspects of their lives reenacts and reinforces their commitment to the cultural symbols that organize that experience. In this sense, the ways people tell their stories in interviews and elsewhere are a kind of cultural work in which the connection between personal and cultural meanings is fashioned. One implication of the analysis of discourse is that looking for the "real person" who lies behind (or inside) each interactor is a misguided search (see Shweder and Bourne 1984:192). While persons may speak differently at different times, persons also realize themselves in speech, so that talk itself brings culture to bear as a real force in their lives.

6. I also note in the appendix that how articulate people are about their ideas, or how forthcoming, might vary with the rapport between interviewer and interviewee.

7. Note that this argument does not seem to fit Nora's own circumstances very well. She had been willing to have children, even though she allowed her husband's wishes to prevail.

8. Eviatar Zerubavel (1992; 1997:56–65) has shown how consequential it can be whether people are able to revise their mental maps in light of new experience.

9. Another similarity between Paul Manville and Nora Nelson is their detachment from a larger community with which they might share the meanings of their personal experiences. Nora has work colleagues and a close relationship with her husband and her own family, but she has few friends. Paul Manville, absorbed in establishing his own business, avoiding entangling personal relationships, and estranged from his parents, is not grounded in community, marriage, or a close circle of friends.

10. This is precisely the argument Christian Smith (1998) has made about American Evangelicals. He argues (p. 124) that "Evangelicals operate with a very strong sense of boundaries that distinguish themselves from non-Christians and from nonevangelical Christians. Evangelicals know who and what they are and are not. They possess clear symbolic borders that define the frontiers beyond which one is not an [E]vangelical. The implicit distinction between 'us' and 'them' is omnipresent in evangelical thought and speech." At the same time, he argues, Evangelicals are not very different from other Americans in their religious beliefs or their patterns of family life. Rather, Evangelicalism provides a "subcultural identity" that allows its followers to "sustain a religious strategy that maintains both high tension with and high integration into mainstream American society simultaneously" (p. 150). Michèle Lamont (1992) has noted that compared to French men, upper-middle-class American men draw social boundaries disproportionately along moral lines. The case of evangelical Christians also suggests that the intensity of concern with moral boundaries varies among American communities, with morality offering one among several ways of providing a sense of both identity and engagement within a pluralistic society.

11. A good deal of literature on contemporary conservative Christians suggests just this sort of active, boundary-maintaining link between religious belief and action. Conservative Christians demarcate the boundaries of their group and assert their religious identities by insisting on parental authority and disproportionately using corporal punishment (Ellison, Bartkowski, and Segal 1996), opposing pornography (Sherkat and Ellison 1997), and continuing to oppose premarital sex (Petersen and Donnenworth 1997). While some authors highlight the role of specific theological commitments, such as biblical inerrancy (see Ellison and Sherkat 1993; Ellison, Bartkowski, and Segal 1996), there are also strong indications that active participation in conservative religious communities that define themselves by their separation from "the world" sustains a distinctive moral stance on particular issues (Petersen and Donnenwerth 1997).

12. Weber (1993) points out in *The Sociology of Religion* that the forces for rationalization in religious life are continually undermined by the demands of pastoral care—the needs of laities for solace and compromise with the demands of daily life. This is also Weber's point in *The Protestant Ethic and the Spirit of Capitalism* (1958:232, n. 66) where he discusses the tension between the "logical and psychological" influences on religious development.

13. Otherworldly religious cosmologies, which focus religious motives on escape from the world, are, according to Weber (1993), likely to have less influence on the practical conduct of daily life than are "this-worldly" religious traditions that make action in this world the arena for fulfillment of religious obligations. Protestantism, with its rationalized, unified worldview, its commitment to inner-worldly action, and its renunciation of all magical means of assuring salvation, produced the most intense effects on practical action of any of the world religions.

CHAPTER 4: CULTURED CAPACITIES, STRATEGIES OF ACTION

1. This analysis draws heavily on Clifford Geertz's (1973a) understanding of how culture works. I differ from Geertz here mainly in emphasis, since I think of the "moods and motivations" (1973b) a culture teaches not primarily as providing experiential support for the plausibility of its worldview but as cultivating a set of (often diverse) capacities to be a self and to organize self and action.

2. Numerous studies of conversion (Heirich 1977; Stark and Bainbridge 1980) show precisely this pattern. In the preconversion period, those who will eventually convert are actively looking for "something"—that is, for cultural models of selves they would like to become. Often, converts-to-be will try out several religious communities, or expose themselves to associates who are committed to particular traditions, before actually opening themselves to conversion and allowing a cultural tradition to reshape their basic selves.

3. Much of the work in the sociology and anthropology of emotion (A. Hochschild 1983; M. Rosaldo 1980; Lutz 1988; Abu-Lughod 1986; Kondo 1990) concerns the induction of capacities to feel in culturally patterned ways. Such an image of how culture works is also very close to Bourdieu's (1977) notion of the *habitus*. Bourdieu is right to think of such capacities as "transposable dispositions" that can be applied innovatively in varying situations. It is clear that Bourdieu thinks of the *habitus* as involving skills that some actors employ with more dexterity than others. However, this concept of the *habitus* seems to contradict Bourdieu's other image of the *habitus* as a totalized, unitary substratum of experience that locks people into their class position (evident in parts of *Distinction* [1984]). That people feel more comfortable in some settings than others, that they learn habits for using their bodies, talking, and even perceiving, that they develop skills for handling themselves in some situations and not others, still makes the cultural shaping of the self a matter of culturally learned styles, skills, and habits, and not some putatively deeper, unrevisable "inscribing" of environment on the body and soul of the person.

4. Richard Biernacki (1999:75–77) offers three analytically distinguishable ways in which cultural style or practice may be influential independently of what is conveyed culturally by symbols or discourse. He singles out "culture as the corporeal know-how of practice, as the organizing ethos of practice, and as the experienced import of practice" (p. 77). He notes that one may interpret Foucault's *Discipline and Punish* (1977) as showing that "minute disciplinary procedures cohered into an overarching style of practice even when their organizing principles were not articulated discursively. Because they were applied silently, they subverted the clamorous Enlightenment discourses" (Biernacki 1999:76).

5. These are, of course, the kinds of skills Bourdieu (1977) describes among the Kabyle. Norbert Elias (1983:104–6) offers a wonderful example of cultured

capacities for action in his description of the cultivation of "the art of observing people" and "the art of dealing with people" among members of ancien régime court society.

6. In a study of soap-opera watchers, Andrea Press (1991) has found, for example, that viewers rebel when the stories are "implausible"—not when heroes or heroines are trapped in castles, encounter ghosts, suffer amnesia, or turn out to be their own parents' lost siblings, but when the motives of individual characters seem incomprehensible. Thus a good story provides a slight surprise or revelation without misleading cues or an implausible resolution. In bad drama, the clues about character never add up to a comprehensible pattern, and we cannot exercise or refine our skills for interpreting character. Radway (1991) offers evidence of a similar insistence on emotional plausibility among readers of romance novels.

7. As we will see in chapter 5, youth cultures, which generate very distinctive, visible subcultures (Hebdige 1979; Frith 1981; Gaines 1991), also allow young people to experiment with developing new capacities for being varied kinds of selves. Thus these self-consciously self-fashioning cultures should still be seen as creating multiple capacities, rather than as molding a single, unitary self.

8. While a focus on religion leads us to think of worldviews as nonrational cosmologies, we should not forget the important role the cognitive components of a worldview play in the organization of human action. In order to act, people need some confidence that they know what the world is like, and the specific things they think they know—that drugs and doctors cure disease, for example, or that the subway will get you across town—strongly influence their actions. See Warner (1978) for an explication of this point and DiMaggio and Powell (1991) for an analysis of the theoretical shift to cognitive understandings of culture. Cognitive anthropologists (D'Andrade 1995; Shweder 1991; Strauss and Quinn 1997) also emphasize the cognitive components of culture.

9. Riesebrot (1993) offers a different view of Iranian Shiite fundamentalism as a complex attempt to counteract the social consequences of modernity (although see pp. 203–8).

10. These observations suggest revisions in our understanding of Protestantism's effects as well. Contemporary research on the Protestant ethic suggests that it grew out of the consolidation of new social practices and capacities for action which antedated the specific tenets of Calvinist belief. Walzer (1973) suggests that Calvin adapted his doctrine to produce the social discipline he sought. Zaret (1985) shows that English Puritans already practiced disciplined, rational market behavior, which their ministers saw as a good metaphor for their theological concerns. And Gorski (1993) demonstrates that Calvinists developed innovative practices of social discipline which were adopted by nation-building elites in the Dutch Republic and in Prussia. One can thus grant a significant historical role to Protestantism—in teaching, supporting, or consolidating new practices of social discipline—*without* accepting Weber's argument that concern with the ultimate end of salvation was the driving force behind Protestant rationalization.

11. My conception of "strategies of action" is related to but not identical with Bourdieu's notion of the *habitus*. I share Bourdieu's (1977:83) idea that what is important are "transposable dispositions" that make "possible the achievement of infinitely diversified tasks, thanks to analogical transfers of schemes permitting the solution of similarly shaped problems." I very much agree with his emphasis, discussed in note 3 above, on the ways strategies depend on cultured capacities. But I see learning such cultured capacities as a much more active, open, and continuous process than Bourdieu seems to do. I agree with Sewell (1992:15, quoting Bourdieu 1977:95) that there is no reason why the *habitus* should "engender 'all the thoughts, all the perceptions, and all the actions' consistent with existing social conditions 'and no others.'" People certainly do not learn their whole repertoire of styles, skills, and habits in childhood (indeed, adolescence is in many societies a crucial time for developing a new range of styles and skills in contexts outside the family). Furthermore, the ways particular people organize their capacities into specific strategies of action may depend on conjunctures of opportunity, skill, personality, and occasion, as well as on creative efforts to add new cultural skills to the repertoire. This is evident if one considers the active, directed learning of new skills and their assemblage into new strategies that someone like Art Townsend pursues.

12. Of course, where different social institutions and different cultural capacities are involved in forming strategies of action, people would ask other questions (see Derné 1995; Collier 1997): "Who are my allies and who are my enemies? To whom am I obligated and who is obligated to me? What is my family honor?" and so forth. Nonetheless, the central questions are about the capacities, identities, and social resources an actor has to start with, and not necessarily about what she or he "values."

CHAPTER 5: SETTLED AND UNSETTLED LIVES

1. We should not think of young people as trying out cultural styles searching for the *one* style they will ultimately adopt. Rather, as the image of culture as repertoire suggests, people attempt, so far as possible, to "keep their options open." They want a wide enough repertoire to leave them multiple possibilities for constructing life strategies, given the contingencies they may ultimately face. Constructing a strategy of action is not a matter of being passively trained to fit into some adult life course laid out in a culture's dominant scenario. Rather, people attempt to maintain multiple ways of getting along in the world, so that they may use several simultaneously; or they may be prepared to develop alternative life plans, depending on how circumstances develop. (See Gerson 1985 on the contingent ways young women move into their developing life commitments and Mancini 1980 on the "strategic styles" young people develop by adopting cultural models that fit their individual skills and personalities.)

2. Sociologists have long recognized that young adulthood is formative for individuals' social attitudes (Newcomb 1943; Alwin, Cohen, and Newcomb 1991)

and political loyalties (Nie, Verba, and Petrocik 1976). Thus, even fifty years later, young women from the same college cohort are more like one another than they are those of similar life circumstances but different cohorts (Newcomb 1943). The important recent work of Howard Schuman and his colleagues (Schuman and Scott 1989; Schuman and Reiger 1992; Schuman and Corning 2000:916–17) suggests that young adulthood is indeed the critical period when generations come of age, forming long-lasting orientations to the political and social world. Studies of generational shifts in attitudes (Wuthnow 1976; Hoge 1974) also suggest that young adults may adopt more extreme versions of general attitude shifts occurring at the time they enter young adulthood. It is as if they are more culturally receptive than the rest of the population to whatever general shifts are affecting social attitudes. The persistence of those attitudes in muted form results, I would argue, from the fact that each cohort then proceeds to build life strategies using the cultural equipment they acquired when they were young.

3. Other scholars have made distinctions similar to the one drawn here. Skocpol (1985) distinguishes "ideology" from "cultural idioms," and Stromberg (1985) contrasts ideology, tradition, and semiotic code. Geertz, in his writings on religion (1973b), ideology (1973i), art (1976), and common sense (1983a) has noted that different orders of experience operate side by side while people make transitions from one to another.

4. Comaroff and Comaroff (1991) make power central to their analysis, but their approach only muddies the waters. They define "hegemony" as the common sense made dominant by a dominant group. But in fact, much "common sense" is not sponsored or imposed by the dominant group in a society (although certainly the way of life the dominant group imposes—e.g., capitalist labor relations—will determine at least some of common sense)—witness, for example, the prevalence among Americans of the "common wisdom" that the rich always come out ahead, even though this theme is absent in media discourse (W. Gamson 1992). Furthermore, many of the examples the Comaroffs provide in their own work on the colonial encounter are not of items that are ingrained or invisible. Rather, like literacy, or guns, or the grinding of millstones, these objects and practices were highly visible and often objects of awestruck wonder. They were hegemonic not in the sense of being invisible or constitutive of daily life but in seeming to possess special force or power. This perception that some ideas or practices are imbued with greater prestige or authority than others may be closer to Gramsci's understanding of hegemony than is the "dominant ideology thesis" in which ideas are hegemonic by virtue of their invisibility (see Abercrombie, Hill, and Turner 1980).

5. Both Lancaster (1988) and Collier (1997) point out that "tradition" is a way of talking about culture that attempts to establish a certain kind of authority, asserting such matters as shared history or pointing to the distance between a group's conception of itself as "modern" and its (presumed) past traditions.

6. There is an enormous literature on ritual, suggesting a wide variety of functions and meanings. See, for example, Geertz (1973d) on ritual as the symbolic

locale where ethos and worldview come together; Turner (1969) on ritual as providing "limnal" periods that articulate the outlines of social dilemmas; Radcliffe-Brown (1964) on ritual as socially reintegrative; and Bourdieu (1977) and Paige and Paige (1981) on the uses of ritual to establish and cement social alliances. Catherine Bell (1992) and David Kertzer (1988) offer synthetic treatments of ritual that take into account the role of power.

7. Not all traditions are "rituals" in the strict sense. Many practices—like the form of commercial transactions, parliamentary procedure, or the rules of chess—are explicitly articulated and standardized without a social requirement that they be regularly enacted. Traditions also need not claim ancient origins. But traditions in this sense do in general create standardized expectations, expectations that in turn can provide resources for expressing varied meanings through slight alterations of accepted forms.

8. See Philip Slater's (1963) brilliant analysis of how wedding rituals remind couples of their obligations to a wider community.

9. This claim to universal truth is what leads the Comaroffs (1991) to call common sense "hegemony" and Marx and Engels (1970:65–66) to call it "ideology." But the universality common sense claims is actually more modest. Common sense provides the taken-for-granted starting point for face-to-face interactions, and thus it presumes universality (as language use does). But the limited character of that presumption is demonstrated by how quickly people retreat, back and fill, or gloss over gaps when common sense turns out not to be shared after all (Billig 1992).

10. I am indebted to Douglas Roeder for the argument of this paragraph.

11. Another way to think about the long-term causal influence of ideologies is to see ideological systems as experiments in new ways of organizing social action. The long-term effects of particular ideologies then depend on the success of the initial supporters of the ideology in disseminating their beliefs outside their own circle, in dominating others, or both. The new cultural capacities the ideology's adherents develop are likely to have their ultimate influence only in fragmentary, diluted, or paradoxical forms. Thus Protestantism's capacity to support disciplined individual conduct ended up serving ends very different from those the original Puritan saints had sought (Walzer 1973); Protestant capacities for voluntary association became detached from Protestant roots altogether—aiding the formation of English working-class institutions, for example (E. Thompson 1963); and even in the most ardent Calvinist communities, secure social dominance led to a complacent, worldly religiosity in striking contrast with the anxious self-scrutiny of the founding Puritan generation (Miller 1956).

12. The term "loose coupling" comes from Weick (1976). There is a large literature on the weak relationship between attitudes and behavior (Schuman and Johnson 1976; R. Hill 1981). See Cancian (1975) for one interpretation of this gap.

CHAPTER 6: LOVE AND MARRIAGE

1. In the 1950s American psychologists and sociologists identified a "romantic complex" (Waller and Hill 1951) that they believed damaged marriages by creating unrealistic expectations. Later research, however, failed to find that young people believed in romantic love as a basis for marriage. It concluded, instead, that people sought to marry on the basis of companionship, compatibility, and shared values. However, the romantic-love complex does seem to be part of marriage systems under which people arrange their own marriages (Goode 1959). While he finds extreme romantic idealization arising in certain rigidly hierarchical societies, Charles Lindholm (1998:254) identifies "fluid, competitive, insecure and risky social formation[s]" as conducive to Western-style romantic love. There is, by now, an enormous social-psychological literature on love (see Berscheid and Walster 1978; Walster and Walster 1978; Rubin 1973; Rubin, Peplau, and Hill 1981; Kelley 1983; Skolnick 1987; Hazan and Shaver 1987; Beck and Beck-Gernsheim 1995). Most of this work focuses on why couples choose one another and on the attempt to predict marital stability (people like similar backgrounds and values, but perhaps complementary personality types; equality in the resources spouses contribute to a marriage promotes stability), but tells us little about the cultural meanings of love. Eva Illouz's (1997:215–65) innovative study of romance shows how the ideology of "romance" as a utopian sphere separated from practical concerns can operate precisely to select partners who share cultural capital—as when a couple discover that they both love poetry and quiet walks in the woods.

2. Of course internalized schemata "inside" people's heads always interact with external cultural representations, so in this sense it is misleading to counterpose a subjective cultural "interior" against "external" contexts. My point is that both internalized schemata and public cultural representations are too multiple, too disorganized, and too fluid to structure experience and action. Rather, as will become clear below, external contexts of action provide the structuring that both internalized cultural schemata and the teeming world of public culture lack.

3. Watt (1957) also argues that the love story founds the novel as a literary form, so that *Pamela* is the first true novel. See, however, the analysis in McKeon (1987), who traces the origin of elements of the novel form both earlier and later than the novels of Richardson, Fielding, and Defoe that are Watt's focus.

4. The love story works out very differently in France, where love remains tragic and extramarital (think of *Madame Bovary, Nana,* or *The Red and the Black;* such films as *Les Enfants du Paradis;* the many comedies about extramarital "aventure"). One potential explanation for this difference is that for the French bourgeoisie, virtue never supplanted aristocratic prestige, so that tragic lovers signal their true superiority not by winning an ideal spouse but by throwing everything away for love. See Lamont 1992 for continuing resonances of these aristocratic values in French conceptions of individualism, honor, honesty, and love.

5. In love stories with happy endings the individual succeeds in overcoming

opposition; in less happy stories (antibourgeois novels like *Tess of the D'Urbervilles*), society can destroy love. Indeed, society is condemned precisely because it can destroy the ultimate symbol of individual personhood, bourgeois love. In both kinds of stories, individuals preserve (or lose) their selves by loving not in obedience to social convention but in defiance of it.

6. Synthesizing the social-psychological literature on love, Susan Sprecher and her coauthors (Sprecher et al. 1994:352–53) offer a very similar description of the romantic love ideology:

> The belief that love should be a basis for marriage can be considered one component of a larger constellation of beliefs that can be called the romantic ideology. Other beliefs associated with the ideology of romanticism include love at first sight, there is only one true love, true love lasts forever, idealization of the partner and the relationship, and love can overcome any obstacles.

7. Eva Illouz (1997:77) describes the cultural attempt to blend romantic and prosaic understandings of love:

> Paradoxically, at the same time that the distinction between intense but ephemeral romantic experiences and long-term, effortful relationships was being sharpened, the terms of this distinction were becoming less intelligible, because the new ideal of marriage and love prescribed that fleeting and intense pleasures should and could be mixed with domestic models of love based on compatibility and rational self-control.

Illouz emphasizes how understandings of love were reshaped by the marketing of leisure pleasures and new commodities in the early twentieth century. I am struck by the ways the contrasting vocabularies of love are not blended so much as held in awkward tension.

8. Despite a rising age at first marriage, about 90 percent of American women eventually marry (Cherlin 1992:10–11), and even among those who divorce, most eventually remarry (Cherlin 1992:28). And the aspiration to marry remains nearly universal (Goldscheider and Waite 1991:14). Thus most cohabiting couples, even those who reject the legal form of marriage, are seeking the same kind of enduring, all-or-nothing, committed relationship marriage would involve.

9. Like Thomas DaSilva, quoted at length later in this chapter, those who are not thinking about marriage may substitute notions of sexual passion, friendship, or simple exchange of companionship for ideals of "love" (see also Nardi 1999 on gay men's friendships). Or, they may equate love with intense passion rather than with permanence. In contrast, as I show below and in chapter 7, Americans oriented to the married ideal assume that a love that dies was not real love in the first place.

10. As Lenore Weitzman (1985) has pointed out, changes in divorce and divorce law actually redefine the institution of marriage. Traditional divorce law

assumed that spouses bound their fates together socially and economically (Prager 1982), while the modern no-fault divorce laws build in the assumption that spouses remain autonomous actors, with responsibility for maximizing their individual interests, despite the interdependencies of marriage. The substantial disadvantage divorced women suffer under the new laws may, however, indicate that women, at least, still organize their lives in some measure as if marriages were permanent and sacrificing for the relationship made sense.

11. This absence of a heroic myth of origins for individual marriages is particularly striking, since any relationship develops stories, memories, images that strengthen its solidarity. In addition, there is a certain social-structural truth to the love myth's insistence on the lovers' willingness to struggle against social obstacles. Young people do have to leave their families of origin and establish a new bond when they marry, a move often greeted with ambivalence by their families. Indeed, in his study of a small Midwestern town, Hervé Varenne (1977), sees just such a story of rebellious love as paradigmatic of the voluntarism of American culture. Such rebellion is central to American culture, both within and outside of the love story (Bellah et al. 1985). Nonetheless, for the people I studied, the heroic drama of love has shifted its focus away from a struggle with external obstacles and toward the struggle involved in maintaining the relationship itself. Those couples who had dramas of heroic rebellion to tell might have cast their stories differently on occasions that accented their mythic, rather than their prosaic, understandings of love.

12. Varenne (1977:163–87) describes a very different American love story—"tragic," fraught with conflict—but with a remarkably similar ending. Despite marrying a man her parents strongly disapproved of, "Sue" stood by her choice and ended up "happy" even with a husband who had a broken marriage, drug use, and a wild lifestyle in his background. If I had interviewed Sue during her marriage to "John," I might well have heard a story almost as prosaic as the others I was told. Varenne argues that the terms "love" and "happiness" reconcile the need of Americans to have a unique individuality on the basis of which to establish social commitments with the need to be or become members of a community.

13. Beck-Gernsheim (1998) nicely conveys participants' sense of the complex effort required to hold marriages and families together when families are a matter of individual choice, what she calls an "elective relationship," rather than of institutionalized obligation.

14. Illouz (1997:196–97) explains "the continuing coexistence of these two equally powerful repertoires of love, the 'organic' and the 'contractual,'" as a "result of a structural contradiction between marriage as an institution of social reproduction and marriage as a unit for the expression of the individual's emotions." But my interviews suggest that while the duality Illouz describes is real, she has the institutional anchors of the two understandings of love reversed. People emphasize the prosaic, "contractual" love that one has to work at when describing their

ongoing day-to-day relationships, while the "organic" metaphor of a once-and-for-all commitment is mobilized when describing decisions about "social reproduction"—whether to form or stay in a marriage.

15. The first quotation is from a Shakespeare sonnet; the second from an Everly Brothers song.

16. Simpson, Campbell, and Berscheid (1986:364, 366, 368) report that the largest shift has been among women. In 1967 just under 25 percent of college women reported that they would not marry a person who "had all the other qualities you desired . . . if you were not in love with him," while almost 65 percent of men answered no to the same question. In college-student surveys in 1976 and 1984, on the other hand, the gap between men and women had nearly closed with more than 80 percent of both women and men saying they would not marry without love.

17. In an interesting study of soap-opera romance, Harrington and Bielby (1991) point out that the ideal of lifelong commitment persists in American popular culture. They suggest that in the soap-opera world, as among my interviewees, the "modern" ideal of personal fulfillment is seen as compatible with enduring commitment, or indeed, that real commitment provides the challenges and satisfactions that lead to personal growth. While soap-opera plots recognize "modern" aspirations for individual fulfillment, they show the "traditional" solution of putting one's relationship first as the desirable outcome.

18. By the mid-1990s, M. Scott Peck's *The Road Less Traveled* (1978) had enjoyed more than 500 weeks on the *New York Times* bestseller list, a mind-boggling figure. It is heavy on terms like "discipline," "responsibility," and "commitment," as well as ideas of separateness, individual boundaries, and spiritual growth.

19. It is instructive to look at "stateless" societies—those without formal government. In such societies elaborate ritual continually reinforces marriage bonds and other kin obligations and alliance structures. Without constant cultural work, obligations and ties can unravel or fade away. In our society, on the other hand, a marriage continues to exist legally until positive steps are taken to dissolve it. See Jane Collier, *Marriage and Inequality in Classless Societies* (1988); and Karen Paige and Jeffrey Paige, *The Politics of Reproductive Ritual* (1981).

CHAPTER 7: TIES THAT DO NOT BIND

1. Because the assumption that cultures are unified, coherent, and deep has been so fundamental to thinking about culture (see chapter 1), few scholars have addressed the issue of what creates cultural unities as a *question*. Hervé Varenne in "Collective Representation in American Anthropological Conversations" (1984) has tried to show how a dominant discourse, while it may permit all sorts of things quite at variance with dominant assumptions to be thought and expressed, will alter them in the retelling—as they are taken up in public discourse—to conform to the dominant pattern. In "Talk and Real Talk" (1987) Varenne has pushed this

line of analysis further, arguing that what makes a particular "text" or piece of talk "American" is the "intertextual order" within which any particular utterance is heard and responded to. Thus "the original texts do not have to be internally individualized to be captured by America and made relevant to individualism" (p. 391). All they need is the intertextual "operator" that makes whatever is said a reflection of "the 'I' of the speaker" (p. 390).

Peter Stromberg (1981) has demonstrated through close textual analysis of interviews with members of a Swedish pentecostal church that different people can interpret the same symbol very differently, even within the same religious community, yet that symbol may play a common structural role in their experience (in this case, the symbol of Christ can provide a link between transcendent religious authority and individual action, even though the content of that authority and the kinds of demands it implies are understood very differently).

Finally, Michael Mann (1970) has argued that people are not persuaded by "dominant ideologies" when they think about day-to-day experience. But the dominant ideology, the one publicly promoted by mainstream cultural authorities, provides the primary resource people have available for thinking about the more abstract generalizations that might describe their society.

2. Steve Derné (1994) has made a complementary argument concerning the typical strategies of action of Hindu men in Banaras, India. Derné has argued that Indians talk as if being controlled by others were the only way to assure right and proper social action. In a sense, the guarantees of social solidarity, cooperation, loyalty, or mutual help that Indian men believe are assured only if people are controlled by others, Americans believe are guaranteed only if persons are autonomous individual actors.

3. See the extended discussion of moral action guided by utilitarian individualism in Steven Tipton, "The Moral Logic of Alternative Religions" (1983) and in Bellah et al. (1985:27–51).

4. The material and the thinking in this section draws heavily on Bellah et al., *Habits of the Heart* (1985), and on Steven Tipton, *Getting Saved from the Sixties* (1982), as well as on Hervé Varenne's *Americans Together* (1977).

5. This concern with being autonomous enough to remain "interesting" to one's spouse seems to be a particular preoccupation for women, while husbands are concerned with learning to communicate and share emotionally. Even Connie Newman, the Christian homemaker who believes with her husband that shared faith keeps their marriage strong, felt this way: "I would be a boring and noninteresting person if I don't read, if I don't have some other interests besides my husband. I wouldn't have anything to share with him if I don't do anything besides nothing."

6. Michael Mann (1970, 1973) has analyzed the sources of cultural dissensus and cohesion. He points out that while people may develop diverse perspectives based on their own experience, a coherent worldview articulated by public author-

ities clearly has an independent effect in shaping public discourse. Dominant ideologies are not "hegemonic" in the sense that they make other conceptions of reality unthinkable. But the dominant public discourse in Britain and the United States leads most Britons and Americans to agree with general statements about equality of opportunity even when they disagree with those ideas as descriptions of their concrete experience (Mann 1970). And French and Italian workers have an easier time thinking of their interests as fundamentally opposed to those of capitalists because Communist parties in France and Italy have kept an adversarial ideology alive (Mann 1973).

7. Catherine Riessman (1990) shows how, in the aftermath of divorce, men and women try to impose coherent meaning on their experience. Vered Vinitzky-Seroussi (1998:113–31) offers even more dramatic evidence (based on a study of participants in a high school reunion) that Americans will insist on continuity in their individual identities—"maintaining continuity based on the notion of a 'true self'" (p. 115)—even when they must account for striking discontinuities in their life experience.

8. While such optimism may sound like merely the fuzzy-headedness of the "Me Decade" of the 1970s, it has deep roots in American culture, from Emersonain mysticism through Dale Carnegie's advice on how to win by having the right attitude. See Lears (1981) and Bellah et al. (1985).

9. In a series of recent books, Robert Wuthnow has explored the paradoxes of American voluntarism as it affects both sacrificing for others and joining groups. In *Acts of Compassion* (1991) he shows that a very large proportion of Americans devote time to some form of voluntary community service, and in *Sharing the Journey* (1994) he illuminates Americans' passion for joining support groups. In both instances, however, these forms of collective involvement create "communities of limited liability." They engage people's energies and even their love, but without creating binding obligations or enduring commitments.

10. Naomi Quinn (1982) has done a careful linguistic analysis of the meanings of the word "commitment" in American marriage. Her work suggests that Americans use the term in a sense compatible with the analysis I offer here. Commitments are voluntary, and they are binding precisely because they are voluntary.

11. See the analysis by C. B. McPherson (1962) of *The Political Theory of Possessive Individualism,* in which the essence of the individual is its capacity to choose and to possess.

12. These two interviewees reflect what Alan Wolfe (1998) has emphasized is the extraordinary importance most Americans place on tolerating different values and ways of life (with the exception, Wolfe finds, of homosexuality).

13. Arditi (1998:8) defines "infrastructures of social relationships" as "The patterns of association and differentiation in a society and . . . the practices through which these patterns are produced and reproduced." He goes on to say

that "Each of the three infrastructures that I examine involves a different way of establishing similarity and difference among people, and each involves practices of relating to one another, a pragmatics, that is, of an entirely different order."

14. Michel Foucault argues similarly that institutional power constitutes knowledge and makes it real. The categories of the mentally ill versus the "sane" or the sexually deviant versus the "normal" are constituted by institutional practices that implement the categories and make them grounds for classifying, confining, and treating people. See Foucault, *Madness and Civilization* (1965), "Afterword: The Subject and Power" (1983), and *The History of Sexuality*, vol. 1 (1978). See also Mohr and Duquenne (1997) for a fascinating demonstration of how practices and categories mutually constitute each other. Of course, there are moments of cultural creativity when people imagine social possibilities that do not yet exist in practice, but even these are often modeled on and given plausibility by actual institutional arrangements. See, for example, William Sewell Jr.'s (1974:104–5) analysis of how the workers of nineteenth-century Marseille derived a vibrant understanding of socialism from their actual experience of the ways artisanal guilds organized labor.

15. The U.N. involvement in the effort to document crimes against humanity during civil wars in El Salvador, Bosnia, Kosovo, and Rwanda and attempts (at least sporadically) to discipline the perpetrators of those crimes give further institutional reality to the concept of a moral law higher than the laws of nation states. Of course, the abysmal failure of U.N. intervention in Bosnia, the very mixed "success" of NATO in Kosovo, and the abject failure to prevent human rights abuses in most of the world also indicate how limited is the actual institutional power behind the idea of human rights.

16. Will Wright (1975) makes a similar argument about the sources of the cowboy myth's compelling appeal. The myth describes how the unique, individual talents a market society requires can be reconciled with integration into a social community (the cowboy's special skill, which initially makes him an outsider, allows him to save the town and marry the schoolteacher). Cultural power comes from bridging the gaps that social institutions leave. There is a parallel in Bendix's discussion in *Work and Authority in Industry* (1974) of how the Czarist system kept re-creating the ultimate authoritativeness of the Czar—the notion that he was the appeal of last resort in all disputes—even though he almost never intervened. The system of antagonistic yet interdependent groups required an ultimate authority to resolve conflicts, so the cultural slot for a Czar who would be the father of his people and would adjudicate among them remained vital, despite the failures of the role's actual occupants.

17. Weber also saw the irresolvable contradictions in cultural systems as generating meaning. Of music Weber (1958b) writes that the dissonant seventh is the "stumbling block in the attempt to harmonize the simple major scale" (pp. 7–8), but these "rebels" which resist full rationalization are the source of music's aesthetic power. He points to "an elemental fact of music, that chordal rationaliza-

tion lives only in continuous tension with melodicism which it can never completely devour" (p. 10). In religion, it is the problem of "theodicy," the irresolvable contradiction between suffering and injustice and the idea that the world was created by an omnipotent and just God, that has stimulated the greatest religious creativity. Weber, however, thinks of the contradictions that generate religious meaningfulness as emerging within a rationalized world view (1946a:280–81), while I am arguing here that the powerful notion of a purely voluntary commitment to love is continually renewed by the contradiction between irreconcilable systems for organizing action. People become profoundly dependent on an enduring bond that they form and reproduce on the basis of personal choice.

18. This analysis of institutional incompleteness might be described in the language William Sewell Jr. (1992) offers for talking about "structure" as comprising cultural schemas and arrays of resources. The notion here would be that enacting the cultural schema for marriage no longer generates the reliable structure of resources the schema suggests. The interesting question is why this erosion in the actual structure of marriage has had so little effect on the basic schema—lifelong commitment, exclusivity, an all-or-nothing bond—that is "read" from the structure.

CHAPTER 8: CODES, CONTEXTS, AND INSTITUTIONS

1. As I discuss more fully in the conclusion, interviews reveal only traces of the codes, contexts, and institutions that structure culture's effects on action.

2. See the related arguments in Camerer 1988 and Zelizer 1994.

3. An earlier version of some of the ideas presented here is Swidler 1995.

4. The *Encyclopedia of American Social History* (Orsi 1993:1916) notes that Anna Jarvis, the holiday's founder,

> had wanted the day marked by church services, home-cooked meals, and small tokens of filial piety; by 1961, $875 million was being spent on the holiday, which had become a showcase for the powers of the advertising industry. Jarvis had disappeared from public awareness long before this; deeply disappointed by what had happened and defeated in her strenuous efforts to prevent it, she died alone and destitute.

5. Duncan (1979) offers an interesting empirical demonstration that gender-egalitarian ideologies have become more taken for granted than traditional views of gender, which increasingly show the extra structuredness that more egalitarian views had during an earlier period. Arlie Russell Hochschild (1989) and Goldscheider and Waite (1991) have traced the consequences for marriages of men's and women's shared acceptance of more egalitarian ideologies without corresponding changes in behavior.

6. The force of the Protestant ethic as Weber (1958a) portrayed it provides

one powerful example. While Weber described a system of internalized religious ethics that motivated individuals to lead disciplined, methodical lives, one might argue that what made the Protestant ethic so potent *socially* was that individual anxiety about salvation was allied with a powerful, public semiotic code. While Weber emphasized individuals' desire to know whether they were saved or damned, it was the visible social distinction between the elect and the reprobate that brought the issue of salvation home. The organization and ideology of Calvinist communities led people continually to ask themselves into which class they fell, the saints or the reprobates, and to ask the same question about their neighbors. The belief that the saints would manifest signs of their election gave powerful public sanction to Calvinism's recoding of the moral life. Weber (1946b) emphasizes this point in his essay on the Protestant sects when he asks why Protestant business ethics remained influential even after Protestant concern with salvation had weakened.

7. Dominant, pervasive semiotic codes may powerfully shape identity. Students of identity have pointed out that identity is in part a cognitive attribution to the self (Bem 1972; Schneider, Hastorf, and Ellsworth 1979:101–10; Fiske and Taylor 1984:154–67). A semiotic code that defines possible selves and their signs thus outlines the possibilities for identity. If people cannot control the ways they may be categorized, they must do elaborate internal monitoring to anticipate and shape others' attributions about them. Worrying about the category into which one falls may lead a person to internalize deeply both the category and the behaviors that locate her within it. It is not what one ought to do, or even one's strongest values, but rather preserving who one *is* that makes such cultural codes powerful.

Lawrence Kohlberg (1966) provides an example of such influence in his "Cognitive-Developmental Theory of Sex Role Socialization." There he argues that once boys and girls (at about age three) come to understand gender as a fundamental opposition and an unchangeable characteristic of the self, they actively seek out the behaviors that fit their gender identity. Kohlberg notes that rather than having to reward children for acting like the "correct" gender, adults find that gender affirming activity is itself a reward that can be used to obtain other sorts of compliance, as when an adult says, "brave boys don't cry," or "nice girls don't throw things," with the implication that misbehaving undermines being a real boy or girl. Kohlberg also notes that boys and girls who are still consolidating a gender identity often show much more rigid, exaggerated conceptions of properly gendered behavior (girls who insist on dresses, wear only pink; boys who play guns, pirates, cowboys, or superheroes) than they will at later ages when their gender identity is more firmly established.

8. John Meyer (1977) makes related arguments in his analysis of education as "status chartering." Meyer points out that what is important about schooling is less what it actually teaches children in classrooms than the powerful system of social categories it establishes: "first graders," "seventh graders," "high-school dropouts," "college graduates." In this sense education establishes an elaborate set of

coded social statuses, and then, Meyer argues, people attempt to learn whatever fits them for the status the educational system has assigned them.

9. Elisabeth Noelle-Neumann (1993), the German public-opinion researcher, has put this insight to powerful effect. She explains how a truly "public opinion" emerges as individuals seek to align themselves with what they conceive to be the dominant public view. She has developed ingenious survey questions that tap into people's fear of the isolation or hostility that might result from being seen as a holder of unpopular views or a member of the wrong party.

10. Similar processes of cultural systematization occur in situations of ethnic or religious conflict. Clifford Geertz (1973f) provides a wonderful example of the imposition of cultural consistencies in a situation of growing ethnic conflict. In a Javanese town where animist-Hindu syncretists had long relied on Moslem religious experts to dress corpses for funerals, a political split at the national level led local Moslems to deny their religious services to non-Moslems, leaving an animist-Hindu funeral in chaos and forcing a clearer differentiation between Moslem and syncretic cultural practices.

11. Similar dynamics have been observed in cults and other alternative religious movements. Harriet Whitehead (1987) notes that when L. Ron Hubbard's control over Dianetics was challenged, he moved to a much more extreme formulation of his views, involving past lives and arcane techniques of self-exploration. A cynic might say that straightforward ideas can be debated by competing factions; mystical revelations are known only to the leader and can be validated only by him (p. 69).

12. In an earlier paper (Swidler 1987), I discuss the fascinating debate between Sewell (1985) and Theda Skocpol (1985). Skocpol argues that culture could not have been a significant cause of the Revolution's dynamics since members of the revolutionary leadership frequently disagreed with one another; the leaders as individuals held contradictory views about both rights and privilege; and leaders' views before the Revolution did not predict their actions during it. My purpose here is to argue that culture did influence the Revolution, but not necessarily because particular individuals held coherent worldviews that directly governed their action. Rather the revolutionary context made ideas coherent and powerful that may well have been inconsistent and relatively ineffectual at the individual level.

13. Very similar mechanisms are, of course, at work in those tightly knit communities that have come to be called "cults." As Rosabeth Kanter (1972) noted in her research on nineteenth-century communes, such intentional communities attempt to cut off members' routes of escape from the collectivity. For the leader of such a group, continually pushing more and more extreme worldviews and making agreement with them the litmus test of loyalty to the group is a way of continually reasserting control. Thus the leaders themselves may be driven to increasingly radical views, not because they are psychologically unstable or driven by internal demons but because they are making drastic attempts to hold members by defining a code that increasingly cuts them off from the outside world.

14. William Sewell Jr. (1990) indirectly points to this phenomenon in his critique of Charles Tilly's argument that 1848 rather than 1789 was the critical turning point in repertoires of collective action in France. Sewell argues that the Revolution did create a fundamentally new "associational" form of public action, but that for a variety of political reasons, the older "communal" forms of collective action reasserted themselves after the Revolution and remained a frequent organizing principle for collective action until after 1848.

15. Madsen (1984) develops a very similar analysis of the ideological vicissitudes of a Chinese village after the Communist Revolution. Periods of intense social struggle, carried on in charged public meetings, made new ideologies powerful tools for reorganizing social action. But when the ideological campaigns faltered, much of the old repertoire—both of cultural understandings and sources of social power—was there to be reappropriated.

16. This may explain the paradox of increasing cultural homogenization noted by DiMaggio, Evans, and Bryson (1996) and by Bellah (1998): they point to the narrowing range of Americans' ideas and values despite the spectacular differentiation of information and entertainment media. An ever increasing variety of magazines, television channels, radio stations, and Internet chat rooms cater to every imaginable specialized taste. There is a growing insistence on multiculturalism and the diversity of identities. But the larger institutional environment has become increasingly homogenized, with the same educational credentials, the same labor and consumer markets, and the same family options as the basic determinants of individuals' life chances all across the society.

17. My use of the term "myth" and my understanding of how myths help people organize strategies of action have been influenced by Will Wright's *Sixguns and Society* (1975).

18. There has recently been a dramatic renewal of interest by sociologists in problems of differences across national societies (see Jepperson 1992; Lamont 1992, 2000; Soysal 1994; Dobbin 1994; Jepperson and Meyer 1991). Rather than assuming, as many earlier theorists seemed to do (Lipset 1963, 1990), that national cultural differences were due to enduring psychological differences, maintained perhaps by differences in family structure or childhood socialization transmitted from generation to generation, more recent arguments have sought more concrete, often institutional sources for what appear to be ineffable differences in national character or personality (see Corse 1997; Swidler 1992; Jepperson 1999; Meyer and Jepperson 2000).

19. The converse argument—that culture plays a fundamental, independent role in shaping institutions—is developed in the conclusion.

20. Erving Goffman (1974, 1981) and conversational analysts such as Schegloff (1992, 1996, 1999) focus directly on contexts and how contexts structure meanings. My interests differ from theirs because I am not seeking the universal principles that organize conversations or frame meanings. I am more inter-

ested in how particular symbolic meanings are or are not brought to bear on action. I do, however, believe that a great deal could be gained by uniting the rigor of the ethnomethodological and conversational analysis traditions with the more substantive concerns of the traditional sociology of culture.

CONCLUSION: HOW CULTURE MATTERS

1. Of course, other institutions with more fixed roles and obligations may generate cultural patterns with more stable, reified meanings. But this is a feature of the ways particular institutions order social action, not some necessary attribute of cultural "systems."

2. Renato Rosaldo (1989:92) describes this phenomenon experientially: "When in doubt, people find out about their worlds by living with ambiguity, uncertainty, or simple lack of knowledge until the day, if and when it arrives, that their life experiences clarify matters. In other words, we often improvise, learn by doing, and make things up as we go along."

3. The dominance of Chomskian structural linguistics has misled us even about how language works. Researchers willing to explore within—rather than simply replicate—the Chomskian paradigm report all sorts of innovative behavior as people attempt to give emphasis to the language they use by inventing "violations" of the linguistic rules. See Waugh (1980, 1993:78–82).

4. See Darlene Abiog's (1996) wonderful observations of the varying meanings different ethnic groups in a Northern California junior high school attributed to brands of footwear, precisely how one rolled one's jeans, how baggy pants should be and where they should hang, and so on. The point is not just that these youth created an intense subculture in which clothing styles communicated meanings—mostly about ethnic identity—but that the markers in this code were constantly being transformed by the effort of groups to distinguish themselves by their taste, coolness, ethnic pride, and so forth.

5. Geertz himself raises this issue of the multiplexity of actual cultural systems, not only when he traces the misunderstandings of people operating with different cultures (the trader Cohen, the French captain, and the Berber sheiks [Geertz 1973c] or Moslems and syncretic abangans in Modjokuto [Geertz 1973f]) but when he makes central to all culture the existence of multiple spheres of reality—the aesthetic, the religious, the commonsensical, and the scientific among others. According to Geertz (1973b), people shift from one of these orders of reality to another without apparent difficulty.

6. The need to explore contexts more fully is not limited to an interview study such as this one. Survey experiments by researchers such as Howard Schuman (Schuman and Presser 1981) have found that exact wording and placement in an interview greatly influence answers to survey questions. Those who study attitudes more generally (Reinarman 1987) have concluded that survey questions are more realistic if they provide the context. Researchers studying cultural activi-

ties now suggest that measures of arts participation or cultural knowledge make sense only if one specifies the context: attending a country music performance with middle-class suburban friends to get a kick out of the locals is very different from going alone to identify with the anguish of heroines and heroes of tragic love ballads (Richard A. Peterson, personal communication). And, finally, some psychologists (Mischel and Shoda 1995) have argued that what we normally interpret as individual "personality" is better understood as typical responses to types of situations. What has continuity is not an individual's global propensity to act in a certain way but a tendency to react in a specific way to specific contexts.

7. Weber (1968:5) notes that "The highest degree of rational understanding is attained in cases involving the meanings of logically or mathematically related propositions; their meaning may be immediately intelligible." He goes on to say, "In the same way we also understand what a person is doing when he tries to achieve certain ends by choosing appropriate means on the basis of the facts of the situation, as experience has accustomed us to interpret them. The interpretation of such rationally purposeful action possesses, for the understanding of the choice of means, the highest degree of verifiable certainty." Weber then argues that wide-ranging emotional empathy is also useful for understanding nonrational action. ("The more we ourselves are susceptible to such emotional reactions as anxiety, anger, ambition, envy, jealousy, love, enthusiasm, pride, vengefulness, loyalty, devotion, and appetites of all sorts, and to the 'irrational' conduct which grows out of them, the more readily can we empathize with them.") Yet rational action still serves as the baseline for analysis:

> For the purposes of a typological scientific analysis it is convenient to treat all irrational, affectually determined elements of behavior as factors of deviation from a conceptually pure type of rational action. . . . Only in this way is it possible to assess the causal significance of irrational factors as accounting for deviations from this type. The construction of a purely rational course of action in such cases serves the sociologist as a type (ideal type) which has the merit of clear understandability and lack of ambiguity. By comparison with this it is possible to understand the ways in which actual action is influenced by irrational factors of all sorts, such as affects and errors, in that they account for the deviation from the line of conduct which would be expected on the hypothesis that the action were purely rational. (p. 6)

8. Geertz (1973h) considers the problem of cultural reproduction as one of the compatibility or incompatibility of cultural experiences, but he never addresses the reproduction or change of such a culture in the more Bourdieuian sense of the relationship of social institutions to the strategic problem solving of individual actors. Since the self-reinforcing cycle of experience is his only way to analyze what reproduces the system he describes, he envisions change only as the disruption of that cycle:

Any development which would effectively attack Balinese person-perceptions, Balinese experiences of time, or Balinese notions of propriety would seem to be laden with potentialities for transforming the greater part of Balinese culture. These are not the only points at which such revolutionary developments might appear (anything which attacked Balinese notions of prestige and its bases would seem at least equally portentous), but surely they are among the most important. If the Balinese develop a less anonymized view of one another, or a more dynamic sense of time, or a more informal style of social interaction, a very great deal indeed—not everything, but a very great deal—would have to change in Balinese life, if only because any one of these changes would imply, immediately and directly, the others and all three of them play, in different ways and in different contexts, a crucial role in shaping that life. (Geertz 1973h:409)

9. Geertz (1973c) misleads when he claims that he seeks to understand only the "meaning" of social practices—the "code" or "context" within which "social events, behaviors, institutions or processes . . . can be intelligibly—that is thickly—described" (p. 14). In fact, the cultural logic he and many other theorists explicate is not a semiotic logic in the sense of relations among symbols and categories that take their meanings from their relations to the others. Rather, Geertz and many other anthropologists seek to understand the logic by which social practices, beliefs, and symbols fit together into a functional whole. It is true that such exploration can reveal the "meaning" of otherwise obscure practices, showing how they "make sense" for the people who live them, and even what meanings they convey. But their logic is not analogous to that of a language whose implicit rules help one to form and interpret utterances. Rather, the logic is what one might call pragmatic or problem-solving logic.

10. There is a parallel here to what Derné (1994) has described as the contrast between Hindu Indian and American ways of talking about motives and action. Derné notes that Indian vocabularies for understanding motives insist that people be controlled by the judgment of others, whatever their own feelings or wishes. Collier (1997) allows us to see the kind of institutional order within which such an understanding of motivation and such a display of subordination to others' wishes might make sense.

11. I write repeatedly here as if "institutional dilemmas" directly "generated" or structured cultural solutions. But this is shorthand for a more complicated idea. Institutions generate dilemmas only for those who act in relation to them. People develop strategies of action—often several alternative strategies, only some of which they may draw upon at any given time. One strategy of action in contemporary America would be marriage—or rather getting married and relying on marriage for some or all of one's social, economic, and emotional place in the world. Given a strategy of action oriented to a particular institution, actors are

motivated to develop cultural resources to solve the dilemmas of action that institution creates.

12. Jepperson (1991:150–51) has argued that it is not fruitful to identify institutions exclusively with normatively regulated systems. But Selznick's (1957) point that normative commitments tend to emerge within institutions might obtain even in institutional systems that were not primarily normatively regulated.

13. I have been struck, for example, by the way in which the coded meaning of sexual activity has shifted within the love story. In Samuel Richardson's *Pamela,* a woman's purity of soul was expressed through her sexual chastity. In many contemporary romances, a woman's purity of heart is signaled by the spontaneous, uncalculating way she offers sex. Some notion of virtue—even "virtue rewarded"—is still at the heart of the story, but what conveys that virtue has shifted radically.

14. David Laitin's *Hegemony and Culture* (1986) provides another provocative example of how the schemas that one might expect to be most influential do not always have such influence. Laitin analyzes the paradox that religious divisions in Yorubaland, which organize much of social life and reflect real social divisions, are largely excluded from Yoruba political life; while the ancestral village, which is primarily a holdover from the British pattern of "indirect" colonial rule, is a key organizer of political identities and alliances. It would be valuable theoretically to ascertain why the socially less consequential tie is more important politically, but Laitin doesn't provide quite enough information for this analysis. How it is that the British actually made the ancestral village an important organizer of Yoruba political life, and how ancestral village ties continue to operate, remains obscure.

METHODOLOGICAL APPENDIX

1. See Stromberg (1993). Stromberg, however, sees "style" not necessarily as an enduring aspect of individual personality, but as characteristic of the way a person performs a particular act—in this case recounting a conversion narrative—and thus as a key to the meaning of that narrative.

2. I am indebted to Steven Tipton for this advice about how to interview. See his *Getting Saved from the Sixties* (1982). For an argument that the process of going from example to generalization and back is how ordinary, common-sense thinking occurs, see Michael Billig, *Arguing and Thinking* (1987).

3. See C. Briggs (1986) for an extended discussion of the interview as a distinctive, culturally specific social context.

4. Here some professionals began talking about their own lives, their marriages, their families, as well as about their clients or parishioners. Where the professional seemed willing or eager to talk about both personal and professional matters, we used elements from the "Love and Relationships" and "General Values" parts of the basic interview, focusing on current understandings of love and personal relationships and less on personal history.

Bibliography

Abelson, R. P. 1981. "The Psychological Status of the Script Concept." *American Psychologist* 36:715–29.

Abercrombie, Nicholas, Steven Hill, and Bryan Turner. 1980. *The Dominant Ideology Thesis*. London: Allen and Unwin.

Abiog, Darlene, 1996. "Resisting Homogeneity: Hip-Hop Culture, Style Claiming, and the Social Construction of Ethnic Differences." Sociology Senior Honors Thesis, Department of Sociology, University of California, Berkeley.

Abrams, Dominic, and Michael A. Hogg, eds. 1990. *Social Identity Theory: Constructive and Critical Advances*. New York: Springer-Verlag, 1990.

———, eds. 1999. *Social Identity and Social Cognition*. Malden, Mass.: Blackwell.

Abu-Lughod, Lila. 1986. *Veiled Sentiments: Honor and Poetry in a Bedouin Society*. Berkeley: University of California Press.

Alexander, Jeffrey, and Philip Smith. 1993. "The Discourse of American Civil Society: A New Proposal for Cultural Studies." *Theory and Society* 22:151–207.

Alter, Robert. 1981. *The Art of Biblical Narrative*. New York: Basic Books.

Alwin, Duane F., Ronald L. Cohen, and Theodore M. Newcomb. 1991. *Political Attitudes Over the Life-Span: The Bennington Women After Fifty Years*. Madison: University of Wisconsin Press.

Ammerman, Nancy Tatom. 1987. *Bible Believers: Fundamentalists in the Modern World*. New Brunswick: Rutgers University Press.

Archer, Margaret S. 1988. *Culture and Agency: The Place of Culture in Social Theory*. Cambridge: Cambridge University Press.

Arditi, Jorge. 1998. *A Genealogy of Manners: Transformations of Social Relations in France and England from the Fourteenth to the Eighteenth Century*. Chicago: University of Chicago Press.

Armstrong, Elizabeth. Forthcoming. *Multiplying Identities: The Transformation of the Lesbian/Gay Community in San Francisco, 1960–1994*. Chicago: University of Chicago Press.

Asad, Talal. 1983. "Anthropological Conceptions of Religion: Reflections on Geertz." *Man* 18:237–59.

Bailey, Beth L. 1988. *From Front Porch to Back Seat: Courtship in Twentieth-Century America*. Baltimore: Johns Hopkins University Press.

———. 1999. *Sex in the Heartland*. Cambridge: Harvard University Press.

Barth, Fredrik. 1969. *Ethnic Groups and Boundaries*. Boston: Little, Brown.

Baudrillard, Jean. 1975. *The Mirror of Production,* trans. Mark Poster. St. Louis: Telos Press.

———. 1983. *Simulacra and Simulations.* New York: Semiotext(e).

Baxandall, Michael. 1972. *Painting and Experience in Fifteenth Century Italy.* Oxford: Oxford University Press.

———. 1980. *The Limewood Sculptors of Renaissance Germany.* New Haven: Yale University Press.

Beck, Ulrich, and Elisabeth Beck-Gernsheim. 1995. *The Normal Chaos of Love,* trans. Mark Ritter and Jane Wiebel. Cambridge, Mass.: Blackwell.

Beck-Gernsheim, Elisabeth. 1998. "On the Way to a Post-Familial Family: From a Community of Need to Elective Affinities." *Theory, Culture & Society* 15, nos. 3–4: 53–70.

Bell, Catherine. 1992. *Ritual Theory, Ritual Practice.* New York: Oxford University Press.

Bellah, Robert N. 1957. *Tokugawa Religion: The Values of Pre-Industrial Japan.* Glencoe, Ill.: Free Press.

———. 1964. "Religious Evolution." *American Sociological Review* 29:358–74.

———. 1970. "Religion and Belief: The Historical Background of 'Non-Belief.'" In *Beyond Belief: Essays on Religion in a Post-Traditional World,* pp. 216–29. New York: Harper and Row.

———. 1998. "Is There a Common American Culture?" *Journal of the American Academy of Religion* 66, no. 3 (fall): 613–25.

Bellah, Robert N., Richard Madsen, William M. Sullivan, Ann Swidler, and Steven M. Tipton. 1985. *Habits of the Heart: Individualism and Commitment in American Life.* Berkeley: University of California Press.

———. 1991. *The Good Society.* New York: Knopf.

Bem, Daryl J. 1972. "Self-Perception Theory." In *Advances in Experimental Social Psychology,* vol. 6, ed. Leonard Berkowitz. New York: Academic Press.

Bendix, Reinhard. 1974. *Work and Authority in Industry: Ideologies of Management in the Course of Industrialization.* Berkeley: University of California Press.

Benson, Rodney. 1996. "California Immigration as 'Social Problem': Explaining Its Shifting Magnitude and Discursive Boundaries, 1972–1994." Unpublished paper, Department of Sociology, University of California, Berkeley (files of the author).

Berger, Bennett M. 1981. *The Survival of a Counterculture: Ideological Work and Everyday Life Among Rural Communards.* Berkeley: University of California Press.

———. 1995. *An Essay on Culture: Symbolic Structure and Social Structure.* Berkeley: University of California Press.

Berger, Peter L., and Thomas Luckmann. 1967. *The Social Construction of Reality: A Treatise on the Sociology of Knowledge.* Garden City, N.Y.: Doubleday.

Bernstein, Basil. 1975. *Class, Codes and Control, III: Towards a Theory of Educational Transmissions.* London: Routledge and Kegan Paul.

Berscheid, Ellen, and Elaine Hatfield Walster. 1978. *Interpersonal Attraction.* 2nd ed. Reading, Mass.: Addison Wesley.

Biernacki, Richard. 1995. *The Fabrication of Labor: Germany and Britain, 1640–1914.* Berkeley: University of California Press.

———. 1999. "Method and Metaphor after the New Cultural History." In *Beyond the Cultural Turn: New Directions in the Study of Society and Culture,* ed. Victoria E. Bonnell and Lynn Hunt, pp. 62–92. Berkeley: University of California Press.

Billig, Michael. 1987. *Arguing and Thinking: A Rhetorical Approach to Social Psychology.* Cambridge: Cambridge University Press.

———. 1992. *Talking of the Royal Family.* London: Routledge.

Binder, Amy. 1993. "Constructing Racial Rhetoric: Media Depictions of Harm in Heavy Metal and Rap Music." *American Sociological Review* 58 (December): 753–67.

Bloch, Marc. 1961 [1940]. *Feudal Society,* trans. L. A. Manyon. Chicago: University of Chicago Press; London: Routledge & Kegan Paul.

Bloch, R. Howard. 1977. *Medieval French Literature and Law.* Berkeley: University of California Press.

Boli, John, and George M. Thomas. 1997. "World Culture in the World Polity: A Century of International Non-Governmental Organization." *American Sociological Review* 62 (April): 171–90.

Boli-Bennett, John. 1979. "The Ideology of Expanding State Authority in National Constitutions, 1870–1970." In *National Development and the World System,* ed. John Meyer and Michael Hannan. Chicago: University of Chicago Press.

Boltanski, Luc, and Laurent Thévenot. 1991. *De la justification: Les économies de la grandeur.* Paris: Gallimard.

Bonfenbrenner, Urie. 1966. "Socialization and Social Class Through Time and Space." In *Class, Status, and Power: Social Stratification in Comparative Perspective,* 2nd ed., ed. Reinhard Bendix and Seymour Martin Lipset, pp. 362–77. New York: Free Press.

Bosco, Antoinette. 1972. *Marriage Encounter: The Rediscovery of Love.* St. Meinrad, Ind.: Abbey Press.

Bourdieu, Pierre. 1977. *Outline of a Theory of Practice.* Cambridge: Cambridge University Press.

———. 1984. *Distinction: A Social Critique of the Judgement of Taste,* trans. Richard Nice. Cambridge: Harvard University Press.

———. 1990. *The Logic of Practice.* Stanford: Stanford University Press.

Bourdieu, Pierre, and Loic Wacquant. 1992. *An Invitation to Reflexive Sociology.* Chicago: University of Chicago Press.

Briggs, Charles L. 1986. *Learning How to Ask: A Sociolinguistic Appraisal of the Role of the Interview in Social Science Research.* Cambridge: Cambridge University Press.

Briggs, Jean L. 1991. "Mazes of Meaning: The Exploration of Individuality in Culture and of Culture Through Individual Constructs." In *The Psychoanalytic Study of the Child,* vol. 16, ed. L. Bryce Boyer and Ruth M. Boyer, pp. 111–53. Hillsdale, N.J.: Analytic Press.

Brint, Steven G., and Jerome Karabel. 1989. *The Diverted Dream: Community Colleges and the Promise of Educational Opportunity in America, 1900–1985.* New York: Oxford University Press.

Burke, Kenneth. 1970. *The Rhetoric of Religion: Studies in Logology.* Berkeley: University of California Press.

———. 1973. "Literature as Equipment for Living." In *The Philosophy of Literary Form,* pp. 293–304. Berkeley: University of California Press.

Butler, Judith P. 1990. *Gender Trouble: Feminism and the Subversion of Identity.* New York: Routledge.

———. 1993. *Bodies That Matter: On the Discursive Limits of "Sex."* New York: Routledge.

Camerer, Colin. 1988. "Gifts as Economic Signals and Social Symbols." In *Organizations and Institutions: Sociological and Economic Approaches to the Analysis of Social Structure,* ed. Christopher Winship and Sherwin Rosen. Special supplement to the *American Journal of Sociology* 94.

Camic, Charles. 1986. "The Matter of Habit." *American Journal of Sociology* 91:1039–87.

Cancian, Francesca M. 1975. *What Are Norms? A Study of Beliefs and Action in a Maya Community.* London: Cambridge University Press.

———. 1987. *Love in America: Gender and Self Development.* Cambridge: Cambridge University Press.

Capellanus, Andreas. 1957. *The Art of Courtly Love* (edited and abridged by Frederick W. Locke). New York: Frederick Unger. Selections, pp. 39–46 in Stephens 1968.

Caplow, Theodore. 1982. "Christmas Gifts and Kin Networks." *American Sociological Review* 47:383–92.

———. 1984. "Rule Enforcement without Visible Means: Christmas Gift Giving in Middletown." *American Journal of Sociology* 89:1306–23.

Chatman, Seymour B. 1978. *Story and Discourse: Narrative Structure in Fiction and Film.* Ithaca: Cornell University Press.

Cherlin, Andrew J. 1992. *Marriage, Divorce, Remarriage.* Revised edition. Cambridge: Harvard University Press.

Chodorow, Nancy J. 1999. *The Power of Feelings: Personal Meaning in Psychoanalysis, Gender, and Culture.* New Haven: Yale University Press.

Clark, Burton R. 1960. *The Open Door College.* New York: McGraw-Hill.

Clifford, James, and George E. Marcus, eds. 1986. *Writing Culture: The Poetics and Politics of Ethnography.* Berkeley: University of California Press.

Cohen, Abner. 1974. *Two Dimensional Man: An Essay on the Anthropology of Power and Symbolism in Complex Society.* Berkeley: University of California Press.

Collier, Jane Fishburne. 1988. *Marriage and Inequality in Classless Societies.* Stanford: Stanford University Press.

———. 1997. *From Duty to Desire: Remaking Families in a Spanish Village.* Princeton: Princeton University Press.

Collins, Randall. 1977. *Conflict Sociology.* New York: Academic Press.

———. 1981. "On the Microfoundations of Macrosociology." *American Journal of Sociology* 86 (March): 984–1014.

———. 1988. "The Micro Contribution to Macro Sociology." *Sociological Theory* 6 (fall): 242–53.

Colson, Elizabeth. 1974. *Tradition and Contract: The Problem of Order.* Chicago: Aldine.

Comaroff, Jean, and John Comaroff. 1991. *Of Revelation and Revolution: Christianity, Colonialism, and Consciousness in South Africa.* Vol. 1. Chicago: University of Chicago Press.

Condit, Celeste Michelle. 1990. *Decoding Abortion Rhetoric: Communicating Social Change.* Urbana: University of Illinois Press.

Corse, Sarah M. 1997. *Nationalism and Literature: The Politics of Culture in Canada and the United States.* Cambridge: Cambridge University Press.

Crozier, Michel, and Erhard Friedberg. 1980. *Actors and Systems: The Politics of Collective Action,* trans. Arthur Goldhammer. Chicago: University of Chicago Press.

D'Andrade, Roy G. 1984. "Cultural Meaning Systems." In *Culture Theory: Essays on Mind, Self, and Emotion,* ed. Richard A. Shweder and Robert A. LeVine, pp. 88–119. Cambridge: Cambridge University Press.

———. 1995. *The Development of Cognitive Anthropology.* Cambridge: Cambridge University Press.

D'Andrade, Roy, and Claudia Strauss. 1992. *Human Motives and Cultural Models.* Cambridge: Cambridge University Press.

Davis, Natalie Z. 1975. "The Rites of Violence." In *Society and Culture in Early Modern France,* pp. 158–87. Stanford: Stanford University Press.

———. 1986. "Boundaries and the Sense of Self in Sixteenth-Century France." In *Reconstructing Individualism: Autonomy, Individuality, and the Self in Western Thought,* ed. Thomas C. Heller, Morton Sosna, and David E. Wellbery, pp. 53–63. Stanford: Stanford University Press.

Demarest, Donald, Marilyn Sexton, and Jerry Sexton. 1977. *Marriage Encounter: A Guide to Sharing.* St. Paul, Minn.: Carillon Books.

Derné, Steve. 1992. "Beyond Institutional and Impulsive Conceptions of Self: Family Structure and the Socially Anchored Real Self." *Ethos* 20:259–88.

―――. 1994. "Cultural Conceptions of Human Motivation and Their Significance for Culture Theory." In *The Sociology of Culture*, ed. Diana Crane, pp. 267–87. Cambridge: Blackwell, 1994.

―――. 1995. *Culture in Action: Family Life, Emotion, and Male Dominance in Benares, India.* Albany: State University of New York Press.

Dillon, Michele. 1993. "Argumentative Complexity of Abortion Discourse." *Public Opinion Quarterly* 57:305–14.

DiMaggio, Paul. 1982. "Cultural Entrepreneurship in Nineteenth-Century Boston." Parts 1 and 2. *Media, Culture and Society* 4:33–50, 303–22.

―――. 1987. "Classification in Art." *American Sociological Review* 52 (August): 440–55.

―――. 1997. "Culture and Cognition." *Annual Review of Sociology* 23: 263–87.

DiMaggio, Paul, John Evans, and Bethany Bryson. 1996. "Have Americans' Social Attitudes Become More Polarized?" *American Journal of Sociology* 102 (November): 690–755.

DiMaggio, Paul J., and Walter W. Powell. 1991. Introduction to *The New Institutionalism in Organizational Analysis.* Chicago: University of Chicago Press.

Dobbin, Frank. 1994. *Forging Industrial Policy: The United States, Britain and France in the Railway Age.* Cambridge: Cambridge University Press.

Douglas, Mary. 1982. "The Effects of Modernization on Religious Change." *Daedalus* (winter): 1–19.

Dreyfus, Hubert L. 1979. *What Computers Can't Do: The Limits of Artificial Intelligence.* New York: Harper & Row.

Dreyfus, Hubert L., and Paul Rabinow. 1983. *Michel Foucault: Beyond Structuralism and Hermeneutics.* 2nd ed. Chicago: University of Chicago Press.

Duncan, Otis Dudley. 1979. "Indicators of Sex Typing: Traditional and Egalitarian, Situational and Ideological Responses." *American Journal of Sociology* 85 (September): 251–60.

Eisenstadt, S. N., ed. 1970a. *The Protestant Ethic and Modernization.* New York: Basic Books.

―――. 1970b. "The Protestant Ethic Thesis in an Analytical and Comparative Framework." In *The Protestant Ethic and Modernization*, ed. S. N. Eisenstadt, pp. 3–45. New York: Basic Books.

Eisenstein, Elizabeth L. 1969. "The Advent of Printing and the Problem of the Renaissance." *Past and Present* 45:19–89.

Elias, Norbert. 1983 [1969]. *The Court Society,* trans. Edmund Jephcott. New York: Pantheon.

————. 1994 [1939]. *The Civilizing Process: The History of Manners, and State Formation and Civilization.* Oxford: Basil Blackwell.

Eliasoph, Nina. 1990. "Political Culture and the Presentation of a Political Self." *Theory and Society* 19:465–94.

————. 1998. *Avoiding Politics: How Americans Produce Apathy in Everyday Life.* Cambridge: Cambridge University Press.

Ellison, Christopher G., John P. Bartkowski, and Michelle L. Segal. 1996. "Conservative Protestantism and the Parental Use of Corporal Punishment." *Social Forces* 74, no. 3 (March): 1003–28.

Ellison, Christopher G., and Darren E. Sherkat. 1993. "Conservative Protestantism and Support for Corporal Punishment." *American Sociological Review* 58: 131–44.

Fallers, Lloyd A. 1966. "A Note on the 'Trickle Effect.'" In *Class, Status, and Power: Social Stratification in Comparative Perspective,* 2nd ed., ed. Reinhard Bendix and Seymour Martin Lipset, pp. 402–5. New York: Free Press.

Fernandez, James W. 1965. "Symbolic Consensus in a Fang Reformative Cult." *American Anthropologist* 67:902–29.

Fingarette, Herbert. 1963. *The Self in Transformation: Psychoanalysis, Philosophy and the Life of the Spirit.* New York: Harper & Row.

Fiske, Susan T., and Shelley E. Taylor. 1984. *Social Cognition.* Reading, Mass.: Addison-Wesley.

Fligstein, Neil. 1990. *The Transformation of Corporate Control.* Cambridge: Harvard University Press.

————. 1996. "Markets as Politics: A Political-Cultural Approach to Market Institutions." *American Sociological Review* 61, no. 4: 656–73.

Foucault, Michel. 1965. *Madness and Civilization: A History of Insanity in the Age of Reason,* trans. R. Howard. New York: Random House.

————. 1970. *The Order of Things: An Archaeology of the Human Sciences,* trans. A. Sheridan-Smith. New York: Random House.

————. 1972. *The Archaeology of Knowledge.* New York: Pantheon.

————. 1977. *Discipline and Punish: The Birth of the Prison,* trans. Alan Sheridan. New York: Random House.

————. 1978. *The History of Sexuality,* . vol. 1, trans. Robert Hurley. New York: Pantheon.

————. 1983. "Afterword: The Subject and Power." In *Michel Foucault: Beyond Structuralism and Hermeneutics,* 2nd ed., ed. Hubert Dreyfus and Paul Rabinow, pp. 208–26. Chicago: University of Chicago Press.

Friedland, Roger, and Robert R. Alford. 1991. "Bringing Society Back In: Symbols, Practices and Institutional Centralizations." In *The New Institutionalism in Organizational Analysis,* pp. 223–62. Chicago: University of Chicago Press.

Friedland, Roger, and Richard D. Hecht. 1996. *To Rule Jerusalem*. New York: Cambridge University Press.

Frith, Simon. 1981. *Sound Effects: Youth, Leisure, and the Politics of Rock'n'Roll*. New York: Pantheon.

Fulbrook, Mary. 1983. *Piety and Politics: Religion and the Rise of Absolutism in England, Wurttemberg, and Prussia*. Cambridge: Cambridge University Press.

Furet, François. 1981. *Interpreting the French Revolution*, trans. Elborg Forster. Cambridge: Cambridge University Press.

Gaines, Donna. 1991. *Teenage Wasteland: Suburbia's Dead End Kids*. New York: Pantheon Books.

Gallagher, Chuck. 1975. *The Marriage Encounter: As I Have Loved You*. Garden City, N.Y.: Doubleday.

Gamson, William A. 1992. *Talking Politics*. Cambridge: Cambridge University Press.

Geertz, Clifford. 1968. *Islam Observed: Religious Development in Morocco and Indonesia*. New Haven: Yale University Press.

———. 1973a. *The Interpretation of Cultures*. New York: Basic Books.

———. 1973b. "Religion as a Cultural System." In *Interpretation of Cultures*, pp. 87–125. New York: Basic Books.

———. 1973c. "Thick Description: Toward An Interpretive Theory of Culture." In *Interpretation of Cultures*, pp. 3–30. New York: Basic Books.

———. 1973d. "Ethos, World View, and the Analysis of Sacred Symbols." In *Interpretation of Cultures*, pp. 126–41. New York: Basic Books.

———. 1973e. "Deep Play: Notes on the Balinese Cockfight." In *Interpretation of Cultures*, pp. 412–53. New York: Basic Books.

———. 1973f. "Ritual and Social Change: A Javanese Example." In *Interpretation of Cultures*, pp. 142–69. New York: Basic Books.

———. 1973g. "The Impact of the Concept of Culture on the Concept of Man." In *Interpretation of Cultures*, pp. 33–54. New York: Basic Books.

———. 1973h. "Person, Time, and Conduct in Bali." In *Interpretation of Cultures*, pp. 360–411. New York: Basic Books.

———. 1973i. "Ideology as a Cultural System." In *Interpretation of Cultures*, pp. 193–233. New York: Basic Books.

———. 1973j. "The Integrative Revolution: Primordial Sentiments and Civil Politics in the New States." In *Interpretation of Cultures*, pp. 255–310. New York: Basic Books.

———. 1976. "Art as a Cultural System." *Modern Language Notes* 91:1473–99.

———. 1980. *Negara: The Theatre State in Nineteenth-Century Bali*. Princeton: Princeton University Press.

———. 1983a. "Common Sense as a Cultural System." In *Local Knowledge:*

Further Essays in Interpretive Anthropology, pp. 73–93. New York: Basic Books.

———. 1983b. "'From the Native's Point of View': On the Nature of Anthropological Understanding." In *Local Knowledge: Further Essays in Interpretive Anthropology*, pp. 55–70. New York: Basic Books.

Geertz, Clifford, Hildred Geertz, and Lawrence Rosen. 1979. *Meaning and Order in Moroccan Society: Three Essays in Cultural Analysis*. Chicago: University of Chicago Press.

Gerschenkron, Alexander. 1966. "Economic Backwardness in Historical Perspective." In *Economic Backwardness in Historical Perspective*, pp. 5–30. Cambridge: Harvard University Press.

Gerson, Kathleen. 1985. *Hard Choices: How Women Decide About Work, Career, and Motherhood*. Berkeley: University of California Press.

Giddens, Anthony. 1981. *A Contemporary Critique of Historical Materialism*. Volume 1: *Power, Property and the State*. London: Macmillan.

———. 1984. *The Constitution of Society: Outline of the Theory of Structuration*. Berkeley and Los Angeles: University of California Press.

———. 1992. *The Transformation of Intimacy*. Stanford: Stanford University Press.

Ginsburg, Faye D. 1998. *Contested Lives: The Abortion Debate in an American Community*, updated edition. Berkeley: University of California Press.

Ginzburg, Carlo. 1980. *The Cheese and the Worms: The Cosmos of a Sixteenth-Century Miller*, trans. John and Anne Tedeschi. New York: Penguin.

Gitlin, Todd. 1983. *Inside Prime Time*. New York: Pantheon.

Goffman, Erving. 1959. *The Presentation of Self in Everyday Life*. Garden City, N.Y.: Doubleday.

———. 1961. *Asylums: Essays on the Social Situation of Mental Patients and other Inmates*. Garden City, N.Y.: Anchor Books.

———. 1963. *Behavior in Public Places: Notes on the Social Organization of Gatherings*. New York: Free Press.

———. 1967. *Interaction Ritual: Essays on Face-to-Face Behavior*. Garden City, N.Y.: Anchor Books.

———. 1974. *Frame Analysis. An Essay on the Organization of Experience*. New York: Harper & Row.

———. 1981. *Forms of Talk*. Philadelphia: University of Pennsylvania Press.

Goldscheider, Frances K., and Linda J. Waite. 1991. *New Families, No Families? The Transformation of the American Home*. Berkeley: University of California Press.

Goode, William J. 1959. "The Theoretical Importance of Love." *American Sociological Review* 24:38–47.

Gorski, Philip. 1993. "The Protestant Ethic Revisited: Disciplinary Revolution and

State Formation in Holland and Prussia." *American Journal of Sociology* 99 (September): 265–316.

———. Forthcoming. *The Disciplinary Revolution: Calvinism, Confessionalism and the Growth of State Power in Early Modern Europe, 1517–1750.* Chicago: University of Chicago Press.

Gourevitch, Peter Alexis. 1979. "The Reemergence of 'Peripheral Nationalisms': Some Comparative Speculations on the Spatial Distribution of Political Leadership and Economic Growth." *Comparative Studies in Society and History* 31:303–322.

Greely, Andrew M. 1989. *Religious Change in America.* Cambridge: Harvard University Press.

Greenblatt, Stephen. 1980. *Renaissance Self-Fashioning: From More to Shakespeare.* Chicago: University of Chicago Press.

———. 1999. "The Touch of the Real." In *The Fate of "Culture": Geertz and Beyond,* ed. Sherry B. Ortner, pp. 14–29. Berkeley: University of California Press.

Griswold, Wendy. 1987. "The Fabrication of Meaning: Literary Interpretation in the United States, Great Britain, and the West Indies," *American Journal of Sociology* 92 (March): 1077–1117.

Hamabata, Matthews Masayuki. 1990. *Crested Kimono: Power and Love in the Japanese Business Family.* Ithaca: Cornell University Press.

Hannan, Michael T. 1979. "The Dynamics of Ethnic Boundaries in Modern States." In *National Development and the World System: Educational, Economic, and Political Change, 1950–1970,* ed. John Meyer and Michael T. Hannan, pp. 253–75. Chicago: University of Chicago Press.

Hannerz, Ulf. 1969. *Soulside: Inquiries into Ghetto Culture and Community.* New York: Columbia University Press.

Haraway, Donna. 1983. "Teddy Bear Patriarchy: Taxidermy in the Garden of Eden, New York City, 1908–1936." *Social Text:*20–64.

———. 1991. *Simians, Cyborgs, and Women: The Reinvention of Nature.* New York: Routledge.

Harrington, C. Lee, and Denise D. Bielby. 1991. "The Mythology of Modern Love: Representations of Romance in the 1980s." *Journal of Popular Culture* 24 (spring): 129–44.

Hazan, Cindy, and Phillip R. Shaver. 1987. "Romantic Love Conceptualized as an Attachment Process." *Journal of Personality and Social Psychology* 52: 511–24.

Heath, Shirley Brice. 1983. *Ways With Words.* Cambridge: Cambridge University Press.

Hebdige, Dick. 1979. *Subculture: The Meaning of Style.* London: Routledge.

Heirich, Max. 1977. "Change of Heart: A Test of Some Widely Held Theories about Religious Conversion," *American Journal of Sociology* 83:653–80.

Hewitt, John P. 1989. *Dilemmas of the American Self.* Philadelphia: Temple University Press.

Hill, Christopher. 1961. *The Century of Revolution, 1603–1714.* London: Thomas Nelson and Sons, Ltd.

Hill, Richard J. 1981. "Attitudes and Behavior." In *Social Psychology: Sociological Perspectives,* ed. Morris Rosenberg and Ralph Turner, pp. 347–77. New York: Basic Books.

Hinton, William. 1966. *Fanshen: A Documentary of Revolution in a Chinese Village.* New York: Vintage Books.

Hobsbawm, Eric, and Terence Ranger, eds. 1983. *The Invention of Tradition.* Cambridge: Cambridge University Press.

Hochschild, Arlie Russell. 1983. *The Managed Heart: Commercialization of Human Feeling.* Berkeley: University of California Press.

———. 1989. *The Second Shift: Working Parents and the Revolution at Home.* New York: Viking.

Hochschild, Jennifer L. 1981. *What's Fair: American Beliefs about Distributive Justice.* Cambridge: Harvard University Press.

Hoge, Dean R. 1974. *Commitment on Campus: Changes in Religion and Values Over Five Decades.* Philadelphia: Westminster Press.

Hogg, Michael A., and Dominic Abrams. 1988. *Social Identifications: A Social Psychology of Intergroup Relations and Group Processes.* New York: Routledge.

Honess, Terry, and Krystia Yardley, eds. 1987. *Self and Identity: Perspectives across the Lifespan.* London: Routledge & Kegan Paul.

Hopper, Joseph. 1993. "The Rhetoric of Motives in Divorce." *Journal of Marriage and the Family* 55 (November): 801–13.

Huber, Joan, and William H. Form. 1973. *Income and Ideology.* New York: Free Press.

Huizinga, Johan. 1954 [1924]. *The Waning of the Middle Ages.* Garden City, N.Y.: Doubleday.

———. 1956. *Homo Ludens: A Study of the Play Element in Culture.* Boston: Beacon Press.

Hummon, David. 1990. *Commonplaces: Community Ideology and Identity in American Culture.* Albany: State University of New York Press.

Hunt, Lynn. 1984. *Politics, Culture, and Class in the French Revolution.* Berkeley: University of California Press.

———. 1992. *The Family Romance of the French Revolution.* Berkeley: University of California Press.

Hunt, Morton M. 1994. *The Natural History of Love,* revised edition. New York: Anchor Books.

Hunt, William. 1983. *The Puritan Moment: The Coming of Revolution in an English County.* Cambridge: Harvard University Press.

Hunter, James Davison. 1983. *American Evangelicalism: Conservative Religion and the Quandary of Modernity.* New Brunswick, N.J.: Rutgers University Press.

Ikegami, Eiko. 1995. *The Taming of the Samurai: Honorific Individualism and the Making of Modern Japan.* Cambridge: Harvard University Press.

Illouz, Eva. 1997. *Consuming the Romantic Utopia: Love and the Cultural Contradictions of Capitalism.* Berkeley: University of California Press.

Jepperson, Ronald L. 1991. "Institutions, Institutional Effects, and Institutionalism." In *The New Institutionalism in Organizational Analysis,* ed. Walter W. Powell and Paul J. DiMaggio, pp. 143–63. Chicago: University of Chicago Press.

————. 1992. "National Scripts: The Varying Construction of Individualism and Opinion across the Modern Nation-States." Unpublished doctoral dissertation, Department of Political Science, Yale University.

————. 1999. "Institutional Logics: Two Fundamental Dimensions of Structuration Distinguishing Variants of the Modern Nation-State." Annual Meetings of the American Sociological Association, Chicago.

Jepperson, Ronald L., and John W. Meyer. 1991. "The Public Order and the Construction of Formal Organizations." In *The New Institutionalism in Organizational Analysis,* ed. Powell and DiMaggio, pp. 204–31. Chicago: University of Chicago Press.

Jepperson, Ronald L., and Ann Swidler. 1994. "What Properties of Culture Should We Measure?" *Poetics* 22:359–371.

Joas, Hans. 1996. *The Creativity of Action,* trans. J. Gaines and P. Keast. Chicago: University of Chicago Press.

Johnston, Hank, and Bert Klandermans, eds. 1995. *Social Movements and Culture.* Minneapolis: University of Minnesota Press.

Jonsen, Albert R., and Stephen Toulmin. 1988. *The Abuse of Casuistry: A History of Moral Reasoning.* Berkeley: University of California Press.

Kanter, Rosabeth Moss. 1972. *Commitment and Community: Communes and Utopias in Sociological Perspective.* Cambridge: Harvard University Press.

Katriel, Tamar, and Gerry Philipsen. 1981. "What We Need Is Communication: 'Communication' as a Cultural Category in Some American Speech." *Communication Monographs* 48:301–17.

Katz, Elihu, and Tamar Liebes. 1987. "Decoding *Dallas:* Notes from a Cross-Cultural Study." In *Television: The Critical View,* fourth edition, ed. Horace Newcomb, pp. 419–32. New York: Oxford University Press.

Kaufman, Debra R. 1991. *Rachel's Daughters: Newly Orthodox Jewish Women.* New Brunswick, N.J.: Rutgers University Press.

Keesing, Roger M. 1974. "Theories of Culture." In *Annual Review of Anthropology* 3, pp. 73–97. Palo Alto: Annual Reviews, Inc.

Kelley, Harold H. 1983. "Love and Commitment." In *Close Relationships,* ed. Harold H. Kelley et al., pp. 265–314. New York: W. H. Freeman.

Kelman, Mark. 1981. "Interpretive Construction in the Substantive Criminal Law." *Stanford Law Review* 33 (April): 591–673.

Kern, Stephen. 1992. *The Culture of Love: Victorians to Moderns.* Cambridge: Harvard University Press.

Kertzer, David I. 1988. *Ritual, Politics, and Power.* New Haven: Yale University Press.

Kluegel, James R., and Eliot R. Smith. 1986. *Beliefs About Inequality: Americans' Views of What Is and What Ought to Be.* New York: Aldine de Gruyter.

Kohlberg, Lawrence. 1966. "A Cognitive-Developmental Theory of Sex Role Socialization." In *The Development of Sex Differences,* ed. Eleanor E. Maccoby, pp. 82–173. Stanford: Stanford University Press.

———. 1981. *Essays on Moral Development.* San Francisco: Harper & Row.

———. 1984. *The Psychology of Moral Development: The Nature and Validity of Moral Stages.* San Francisco: Harper & Row.

Komarovsky, Mirra. 1964. *Blue-Collar Marriage.* New York: Random House.

Kondo, Dorinne. 1990. *Crafting Selves: Power, Gender, and Discourses of Identity in a Japanese Workplace.* Chicago: University of Chicago Press.

Kuhn, Thomas S. 1970. *The Structure of Scientific Revolutions,* 2nd ed. Chicago: University of Chicago Press.

Laitin, David D. 1986. *Hegemony and Culture: Politics and Religious Change among the Yoruba.* Chicago: University of Chicago Press.

Lamont, Michèle. 1992. *Money, Morals, and Manners: The Culture of the French and American Upper-Middle Class.* Chicago: University of Chicago Press.

———. 2000. *The Dignity of Working Men: Morality and the Boundaries of Race, Class, and Immigration.* Cambridge: Harvard University Press.

Lamont, Michèle, and Marcel Fournier, eds. 1992. *Cultivating Differences: Symbolic Boundaries and the Making of Inequality.* Chicago: University of Chicago Press.

Lancaster, Roger N. 1988. *Thanks to God and the Revolution: Popular Religion and Class Consciousness in the New Nicaragua.* New York: Columbia University Press.

Lane, Robert E. 1962. *Political Ideology: Why the American Common Man Believes What He Does.* New York: Free Press.

Laqueur, Thomas. 1990. *Making Sex: Body and Gender from the Greeks to Freud.* Cambridge: Harvard University Press.

Leach, Edmund. 1976. *Culture and Communication: The Logic by Which Symbols Are Connected.* Cambridge: Cambridge University Press.

Lears, T. J. Jackson. 1981. *No Place of Grace: Antimodernism and Its Transformation of American Culture, 1880–1920.* New York: Pantheon Books.

Leifer, Eric. 1991. *Actors as Observers: A Theory of Skill in Social Relationships.* New York: Garland.

Lerner, Daniel. 1958. *The Passing of Traditional Society: Modernizing the Middle East.* Glencoe, Ill.: Free Press.

Le Roy Ladurie, Emmanuel. 1978. *Montaillou: Cathars and Catholics in a French Village, 1294–1324.* London: Scolar.

Lévi-Strauss, Claude. 1963. *Structural Anthropology,* trans. Clair Jacobson and Brooke Grundfest Schoepf. New York: Basic Books.

LeVine, Robert A. 1984. "Properties of Culture: An Ethnographic View." In *Culture Theory: Essays on Mind, Self, and Emotion,* ed. Richard A. Shweder and Robert A. LeVine, pp. 67–87. Cambridge: Cambridge University Press.

Lewis, C. S. 1959. *The Allegory of Love: A Study in Medieval Tradition.* London: Oxford University Press.

Lichterman, Paul. 1992. "Self-Help Reading as a Thin Culture." *Media, Culture and Society* 14(3): 421–47.

Liebes, Tamar, and Elihu Katz. 1990. *The Export of Meaning: Cross-Cultural Readings of Dallas.* New York: Oxford University Press.

Lifton, Robert Jay. 1989. *Thought Reform and the Psychology of Totalism: The Study of "Brainwashing" in China.* Chapel Hill: University of North Carolina Press.

Linde, Charlotte. 1993. *Life Stories: The Creation of Coherence.* New York: Oxford University Press.

Lindholm, Charles. 1998. "Love and Structure." *Theory, Culture & Society* 15, nos. 3–4: 243–63.

Lipset, Seymour Martin. 1963. *The First New Nation: The United States in Historical and Comparative Perspective.* New York: Basic Books.

Lipset, Seymour Martin. 1990. *Continental Divide: The Values and Institutions of the United States and Canada.* New York: Routledge.

Luhmann, Niklas. 1986. *Love as Passion: The Codification of Intimacy,* trans. J. Gaines and D. L. Jones. Cambridge: Harvard University Press.

Luker, Kristin. 1984. *Abortion and the Politics of Motherhood.* Berkeley: University of California Press.

Lutz, Catherine. 1988. *Unnatural Emotions: Everyday Sentiments on a Micronesian Atoll and Their Challenge to Western Theory.* Chicago: University of Chicago Press.

Lystra, Karen. 1989. *Searching the Heart: Women, Men, and Romantic Love in Nineteenth-Century America.* New York: Oxford University Press.

MacPherson, C. B. 1962. *The Political Theory of Possessive Individualism: Hobbes to Locke.* Oxford: Clarendon Press.

Maddox, Richard. 1993. *El Castillo: The Politics of Tradition in an Andalusian Town.* Urbana: University of Illinois Press.

Madsen, Richard. 1984. *Morality and Power in A Chinese Village.* Berkeley: University of California Press.

Madsen, Richard, Anita Chen, and Jonathan Unger. 1984. *Chen Village: the Recent History of a Peasant Community in Mao's China.* Berkeley: University of California Press.

Mancini, Janet K. 1980. *Strategic Styles: Coping in the Inner City.* Hanover, N.H.: University Press of New England.

Mann, Michael. 1970. "The Social Cohesion of Liberal Democracy." *American Sociological Review* (June): 423–39.

———. 1973. *Consciousness and Action among the Western Working Class.* London: Macmillan.

Mannheim, Karl. 1936. *Ideology and Utopia: An Introduction to the Sociology of Knowledge,* trans. L. Wirth, E. Shils. New York: Harcourt, Brace.

Marshall, Gordon. 1982. *In Search of the Spirit of Capitalism: An Essay on Max Weber's Protestant Ethic Thesis.* New York: Columbia University Press.

Markus, Hazel. 1977. "Self-Schemata and Processing Information about the Self." *Journal of Personality and Social Psychology* 35:63–78.

Marx, Karl, and Frederick Engels. 1970. *The German Ideology.* New York: International Publishers.

Massey, Douglas S., and Nancy A. Denton. 1993. *American Apartheid: Segregation and the Making of the Underclass.* Cambridge: Harvard University Press.

McKeon, Michael. 1987. *The Origins of the English Novel, 1600–1740.* Baltimore: Johns Hopkins University Press.

McNeely, Connie L. 1995. *Constructing the Nation State: International Organization and Prescriptive Action.* Westport, Conn.: Garland Press.

Mead, George Herbert. 1967 [1934]. *Mind, Self and Society.* Chicago: University of Chicago Press.

Meyer, John W. 1977. "The Effects of Education as an Institution." *American Journal of Sociology* 83 (July): 55–77.

———. 1983. "Conclusion: Institutionalization and the Rationality of Formal Organizational Structure." In *Organizational Environments: Ritual and Rationality,* by Meyer and Scott, pp. 261–82. Beverly Hills: Sage.

———. 1987. "The World Polity and the Authority of the Nation State," In *Constituting State, Society, and the Individual,* ed. George M. Thomas, John W. Meyer, Francisco O. Ramirez, and John Boli, pp. 41–70. Beverly Hills: Sage.

Meyer, John W., John Boli, George M. Thomas, and Francisco O. Ramirez. 1997. "World Society and the Nation-State." *American Journal of Sociology* 103 (July): 144–81.

Meyer, John W., and Ronald L. Jepperson. 2000. "The 'Actors' of Modern Society: The Cultural Construction of Social Agency." *Sociological Theory* 18, no. 1: 100–20.

Meyer, Leonard B. 1956. *Emotion and Meaning in Music.* Chicago: University of Chicago Press.

Meyers, Jerome K., and Bertram H. Roberts. 1959. *Family and Class Dynamics in Mental Illness.* New York: Wiley.

Miller, Perry. 1956. *Errand into the Wilderness.* Cambridge: Harvard University Press.

Miller, Richard B. 1996. *Casuistry and Modern Ethics: A Poetics of Practical Reasoning.* Chicago: University of Chicago Press.

Mischel, Walter, and Yuichi Shoda. 1995. "A Cognitive-Affective System Theory of Personality: Reconceptualizing Situations, Dispositions, Dynamics, and Invariance in Personality Structure." *Psychological Review* 102(2): 246–68.

Modleski, Tania. 1984. *Loving with a Vengeance: Mass Produced Fantasies for Women.* New York: Methuen.

Mohr, John, and Vincent Duquenne. 1997. "The Duality of Culture and Practice: Poverty Relief in New York City, 1888–1917." *Theory and Society* 26: 305–356.

Nardi, Peter M. 1999. *Gay Men's Friendships: Invincible Communities.* Chicago: University of Chicago Press.

Newcomb, Theodore M. 1943. *Personality and Social Change: Attitude Formation in a Student Community.* New York: Henry Holt & Co.

Nicolopoulu, Ageliki, and Jeff Weintraub. Forthcoming. "Individual and Collective Representations in Social Context: A Modest Contribution to Resuming the Interrupted Project of a Sociocultural Developmental Psychology." *Human Development.*

Nie, Norman H., Sidney Verba, and John Petrocik. 1976. *The Changing American Voter.* Cambridge: Harvard University Press.

Noelle-Neumann, Elisabeth. 1993. *The Spiral of Silence: Public Opinion—Our Social Skin,* 2nd edition. Chicago: University of Chicago Press.

Omi, Michael, and Howard Winant. 1986. *Racial Formation in the United States: From the 1960s to the 1980s.* New York: Routledge & Kegan Paul.

Orsi, Robert A. 1993. "Parades, Holidays, and Public Rituals." In *Encyclopedia of American Social History,* vol. 3, ed. Mary Kupiec Cayton, Elliott J. Gorn, and Peter W. Williams, pp. 1913–22. New York: Charles Scribner's Sons.

Ortner, Sherry. 1984. "Theory in Anthropology since the Sixties." *Comparative Studies in Society and History* 26:126–66.

———. 1989. *High Religion: A Cultural and Political History of Sherpa Buddhism.* Princeton: Princeton University Press.

———. 1993. Ethnography among the Newark: The Class of '58 of Weequahic High School. *Michigan Quarterly Review* 32 (summer): 410–29.

———. 1998. "Identities: The Hidden Life of Class." *Journal of Anthropological Research* 54 (spring): 1–17.

———, ed. 1999. *The Fate of "Culture": Geertz and Beyond.* Berkeley: University of California Press.

Ozouf, Mona. 1988. *Festivals and the French Revolution,* trans. Alan Sheridan. Cambridge: Harvard University Press.

Padgett, John F., and Christopher K. Ansell. 1993. "Robust Action and the Rise of the Medici, 1400–1434." *American Journal of Sociology* 98 (May): 1259– 1319.

Paige, Karen Ericksen, and Jeffrey M. Paige. 1981. *The Politics of Reproductive Ritual.* Berkeley: University of California Press.

Palmer, R. R. 1989 [1941]. *Twelve Who Ruled: The Year of the Terror in the French Revolution.* Princeton: Princeton University Press.

Parsons, Talcott. 1951. *The Social System.* Glencoe, Ill.: Free Press.

———. 1961. "An Outline of The Social System." In *Theories of Society,* ed. Parsons, Edward Shils, Kaspar Naegele, and Jesse Pitts, pp. 30–79. New York: Free Press.

Peck, M. Scott. 1978. *The Road Less Traveled: A New Psychology of Love, Traditional Values, and Spiritual Growth.* New York: Simon and Schuster.

Perin, Constance. 1977. *Everything in Its Place: Social Order and Land Use in America.* Princeton: Princeton University Press.

Petersen, Larry R., and Gregory V. Donnenwerth. 1997. "Secularization and the Influence of Religion on Beliefs about Premarital Sex." *Social Forces* 75:3 (March): 1071–89.

Popovich, Nicholas J. 1989. "A Comparative Examination of Homosexual and Heterosexual Men's Friendships." Senior Honors Thesis, Department of Sociology, University of California, Berkeley.

Prager, Susan Westerberg. 1982. "Shifting Perspectives on Marital Property Law." In *Rethinking the Family: Some Feminist Questions,* ed. Barrie Thorne with Marilyn Yalom, pp. 111–30. New York: Longman.

Press, Andrea L. 1991. *Women Watching Television: Gender, Class, and Generation in the American Television Experience.* Philadelphia: University of Pennsylvania Press.

Propp, Vladimir. 1968. *Morphology of the Folktale.* Austin: University of Texas Press.

Quinn, Naomi. 1982. "'Commitment' in American Marriage: A Cultural Analysis." *American Ethnologist* 9:775–798.

———. 1987. "Convergent Evidence for a Cultural Model of American Marriage." In *Cultural Models in Language and Thought,* ed. Dorothy Holland and Naomi Quinn. Cambridge: Cambridge University Press, pp. 173–92.

———. 1996. "Culture and Contradiction: The Case of Americans Reasoning about Marriage." *Ethos* 24(3): 391–425.

Radcliffe-Brown, A. R. 1964. *The Andaman Islanders.* New York: Free Press.

Radway, Janice. 1991. *Reading the Romance: Women, Patriarchy, and Popular Literature,* 2nd ed. Chapel Hill: University of North Carolina Press.

Rainwater, Lee, Richard P. Coleman, Gerald Handel. 1962. *Workingman's Wife: Her Personality, World and Life Style.* New York: MacFadden-Bartell.

Rainwater, Lee. 1974. *What Money Buys: Inequality and the Social Meanings of Income.* New York: Basic Books.

Reddy, William, Jr. 1984. *The Rise of Market Culture: The Textile Trade and French Society, 1750–1900.* Cambridge: Cambridge University Press.

Reinarman, Craig. 1987. *American States of Mind: Political Beliefs and Behavior Among Private and Public Workers.* New Haven: Yale University Press.

Riesebrot, Martin. 1993. *Pious Passion: The Emergence of Modern Fundamentalism in the United States and Iran,* trans. Don Reneau. Berkeley: University of California Press.

Riessman, Catherine Kohler. 1990. *Divorce Talk: Woman and Men Make Sense of Personal Relationships.* New Brunswick, N.J.: Rutgers University Press.

Rokeach, Milton. 1973. *The Nature of Human Values.* New York: Free Press.

Roof, Wade Clark. 1978. *Community and Commitment: Religious Possibility in a Liberal Protestant Church.* New York: Elsevier.

Rosaldo, Michelle Zimbalist. 1980. *Knowledge and Passion: Ilongot Notions of Self and Social Life.* Cambridge: Cambridge University Press.

Rosaldo, Renato. 1989. *Culture and Truth: The Remaking of Social Analysis.* Boston: Beacon Press.

Rosen, Lawrence. 1984. *Bargaining For Reality: The Construction of Social Relations in a Muslim Community.* Chicago: University of Chicago Press.

Rothman, Ellen. 1987. *Hands and Hearts: A History of Courtship in America.* Cambridge: Harvard University Press.

Rougemont, Denis de. 1956. *Love in the Western World.* New York: Pantheon.

Rubin, Lillian B. 1973. *Worlds of Pain: Life in the Working Class Family.* New York: Basic Books.

Rubin, Zick. 1973. *Liking and Loving: An Invitation to Social Psychology.* New York: Holt, Rinehart and Winston.

Rubin, Zick, Letitia Anne Peplau, and C. Hill. 1981. "Loving and Leaving: Sex Differences in Romantic Attachments." *Sex Roles* 7:821–835.

Sabini, John, and Maury Silver. 1982. *Moralities of Everyday Life.* New York: Oxford University Press.

Sahlins, Marshall. 1981. *Historical Metaphors and Mythical Realities: Structure in the Early History of the Sandwich Islands Kingdom.* Ann Arbor: University of Michigan Press.

Scarf, Maggie. 1987. *Intimate Partners: Patterns in Love and Marriage.* New York: Random House.

Schama, Simon. 1989. *Citizens: A Chronicle of the French Revolution.* New York: Knopf.

Schegloff, Emmanuel A. 1992. "Repair after Next Turn: The Last Structurally Provided Defense of Intersubjectivity in Conversation." *American Journal of Sociology* 97 (March): 1295–1345.

———. 1996. "Confirming Allusions: Toward an Empirical Account of Action. *American Journal of Sociology* 102 (July): 161–216.

———. 1999. "What Next?: Language and Social Interaction Study at the Century's Turn." *Research on Language and Social Interaction* 32 (1–2): 141–48.

Schlozman, Kay Lehman, and Sidney Verba. 1979. *Injury to Insult: Unemployment, Class, and Political Response.* Cambridge: Harvard University Press.

Schluchter, Wolfgang. 1981. *The Rise of Western Rationalism: Max Weber's Developmental History.* Berkeley: University of California Press.

Schneider, David J., Albert H. Hastorf, and Phoebe C. Ellsworth. 1979. *Person Perception,* 2nd edition. Reading, Mass.: Addison-Wesley.

Schneider, David M. 1976. "Notes Toward a Theory of Culture." In *Meaning in Anthropology,* ed. Keith H. Basso and Henry A. Selby, pp. 197–220. Albuquerque: University of New Mexico Press.

Schneider, Mark A. 1993. *Culture and Enchantment.* Chicago: University of Chicago Press.

Schonrock, Gisela. 1984. "Changes in Courtship and Conceptions of Love." Unpublished dissertation, Department of Sociology, University of Pennsylvania.

Schudson, Michael. 1989. "How Culture Works: Perspectives from Media Studies on the Efficacy of Symbols." *Theory and Society* 18:153–80.

Schuman, Howard, and Amy D. Corning. 2000. "Collective Knowledge of Public Events: The Soviet Era from the Great Purge to Glastnost." *American Journal of Sociology* 105:4 (January): 913–956.

Schuman, Howard, and Michael P. Johnson. 1976. "Attitudes and Behavior." *Annual Review of Sociology* 2:161–207.

Schuman, Howard, and Stanley Presser. 1981. *Questions and Answers in Attitude Surveys: Experiments on Question Form, Wording, and Context.* New York: Academic Press.

Schuman, Howard, and Cheryl Rieger. 1992. "Historical Analogies, Generational Effects, and Attitudes toward War." *American Sociological Review* 5 (June): 315–26.

Schuman, Howard, and Jacqueline Scott. 1989. "Generations and Collective Memories." *American Sociolological Review* 54 (June): 359–81.

Schurmann, Franz. 1970. *Ideology and Organization in Communist China,* 2nd edition. Berkeley: University of California Press.

Scott, W. Richard. 1994. "Institutions and Organizations: Toward a Theoretical Synthesis." In W. Richard Scott, John Meyer, and associates, *Institutional Environments and Organizations: Structural Complexity and Individualism,* pp. 55–80. Thousand Oaks, Calif.: Sage.

Searle, John R. 1969. *Speech Acts: An Essay in the Philosophy of Language.* Cambridge: Cambridge University Press.

Seidman, Steven. 1991. *Romantic Longings: Love in America, 1830–1980.* New York: Routledge.

Selznick, Philip. 1957. *Leadership in Administration.* New York: Harper & Row.

———. 1992. *The Moral Commonwealth: Social Theory and the Promise of Community.* Berkeley: University of California Press.

Sewell, William H., Jr. 1974. "Social Change and the Rise of Working-Class Politics in Nineteenth-Century Marseille." *Past and Present* 65 (November): 75–109.

———. 1980. *Work and Revolution in France: the Language of Labor from the Old Regime to 1848.* Cambridge: Cambridge University Press.

———. 1985. "Ideologies and Social Revolutions: Reflections on the French Case." *Journal of Modern History* 57(March): 57–85.

———. 1990. "Collective Violence and Collective Loyalties in France: Why the French Revolution Made a Difference." *Politics and Society* 18 (4): 527–52.

———. 1992. "A Theory of Structure: Duality, Agency, and Transformation." *American Journal of Sociology* 98 (July): 1–29.

———. 1996. "Historical Events as Transformations of Structures: Inventing Revolution at the Bastille." *Theory and Society* 25: 841–81.

———. 1999. "The Concept(s) of Culture." In *Beyond the Cultural Turn: New Directions in the Study of Society and Culture,* ed. Victoria E. Bonnell and Lynn Hunt, pp. 35–61. Berkeley: University of California Press.

Shankman, Paul. 1984. "The Thick and the Thin: On the Interpretive Theoretical Program of Clifford Geertz." *Current Anthropology* 25(3): 261–79.

Sherkat, Darren E., and Christopher G. Ellison. 1997. "The Cognitive Structure of a Moral Crusade: Conservative Protestantism and Opposition to Pornography." *Social Forces* 75(3): 957–82.

Shively, JoEllen. 1992. "Perceptions of Western Film Among American Indians and Anglos." *American Sociological Review* 57 (December): 725–34.

Shore, Bradd. 1996. *Culture in Mind: Cognition, Culture, and the Problem of Meaning.* New York: Oxford University Press.

Shweder, Richard A. 1991. *Thinking Through Cultures: Expeditions in Cultural Psychology.* Cambridge: Harvard University Press.

Shweder, Richard A., and Edmund J. Bourne. 1984. "Does the Concept of the Person Vary Cross-Culturally?" In *Culture Theory: Essays on Mind, Self, and Emotion,* ed. Richard A. Shweder and Robert LeVine, pp. 158–99. Cambridge: Cambridge University Press.

Shweder, Richard A., and Robert LeVine, eds. 1984. *Culture Theory: Essays on Mind, Self, and Emotion.* Cambridge: Cambridge University Press.

Sikkink, David. 1998. "I Just Say I'm a Christian: Symbolic Boundaries and Identity Formation Among Churchgoing Protestants." In *Re-Forming the Center: American Protestantism, 1900 to the Present,* ed. Douglas Jacobsen and Vance Trollinger Jr., pp. 49–69. Grand Rapids: Eerdmans.

Simpson, Jeffrey A., Bruce Campbell, and Ellen Berscheid. 1986. "The Association Between Romantic Love and Marriage: Kephart (1967) Twice Revisited." *Personality and Social Psychology Bulletin* 12 (September): 363–72.

Skocpol, Theda. 1985. "Cultural Idioms and Political Ideologies in the Revolutionary Reconstruction of State Power: A Rejoinder to Sewell." *Journal of Modern History* 57 (March): 86–96.

Skolnick, Arlene S. 1987. *The Intimate Environment: Exploring Marriage and the Family,* 4th ed. Boston: Little, Brown.

———. 1991. *Embattled Paradise: The American Family in an Age of Uncertainty.* New York, Basic.

Slater, Philip E. 1963. "On Social Regression." *American Sociological Review* 28 (June): 339–364.

Smith, Christian. 1998. *American Evangelicalism: Embattled and Thriving.* Chicago: University of Chicago Press.

Soysal, Yasemin Nuhoglu. 1994. *Limits of Citizenship: Migrants and Postnational Membership in Europe.* Chicago: University of Chicago Press.

———. 1997. "Changing Parameters of Citizenship and Claims-Making: Organized Islam in European Public Spheres." *Theory and Society* 26(4): 509–27.

Sprecher, Susan, Arthur Aron, Elaine Hatfield, Anthony Cortese, Elena Potapova, and Anna Levitskaya. 1994. "Love: American Style, Russian Style, and Japanese Style." *Personal Relationships* 1 (December): 349–69.

Stacey, Judith. 1990. *Brave New Families: Stories of Domestic Upheaval in Late Twentieth Century America.* New York: Basic Books.

Stark, Rodney, and William Sims Bainbridge. 1980. "Networks of Faith: Interpersonal Bonds and Recruitment to Cults and Sects." *American Journal of Sociology* 85:1376–95.

Stephens, William, ed. 1968. *Reflections on Marriage.* New York: Thomas Y. Crowell.

Sternberg, Robert J. 1998. *Cupid's Arrow: The Course of Love through Time.* Cambridge: Cambridge University Press.

Stout, Jeffrey. 1986. "Liberal Society and the Language of Morals." *Soundings* 69, nos. 1–2 (spring/summer): 32–59.

Strauss, Claudia, and Naomi Quinn. 1997. *A Cognitive Theory of Cultural Meaning.* Cambridge: Cambridge University Press.

Stromberg, Peter G. 1981. "Consensus and Variation in the Interpretation of Religious Symbolism: A Swedish Example." *American Ethnologist* 8:544–59.

———. 1985. "Ideology and Culture: A Critique of Semiotic Approaches in Anthropology." Unpublished paper, Department of Anthropology, University of Arizona.

———. 1986. *Symbols of Community: The Cultural System of a Swedish Church.* Tucson: University of Arizona Press.

———. 1993. *Language and Self-Transformation: A Study of the Christian Conversion Narrative.* Cambridge: Cambridge University Press.

Sudnow, David. 1978. *Ways of the Hand: The Organization of Improvised Conduct.* Cambridge: Harvard University Press.

Swanson, Guy E. 1971. "An Organizational Analysis of Collectivities." *American Sociological Review* 36 (August): 607–23.

———. 1978. "Travels through Inner Space: Family Structure and Openness to Absorbing Experiences." *American Journal of Sociology* 83 (4): 890–919.

Swidler, Ann. 1973. "The Concept of Rationality in the Work of Max Weber." *Sociological Inquiry* 43 (winter): 35–42.

———. 1979. *Organization without Authority: Dilemmas of Social Control in Free Schools.* Cambridge: Harvard University Press.

———. 1980. "Love and Adulthood in American Culture." In *Themes of Work and Love in Adulthood,* ed. Neil Smelser and Erik Erikson, pp. 120–47. Cambridge: Harvard University Press.

———. 1986. "Culture in Action: Symbols and Strategies." *American Sociological Review* 51 (April): 273–86.

———. 1987. "The Uses of Culture in Historical Explanation." Paper presented at the Annual Meeting of the American Sociological Association, Chicago Illinois, August 17–21.

———. 1992. "Inequality in American Culture: The Persistence of Voluntarism." *American Behavioral Scientist* 35 (March/June): 606–29.

———. 1995. "Cultural Power and Social Movements." In *Social Movements and Culture,* ed. Hank Johnston and Bert Klandermans, pp. 25–40. Minneapolis, University of Minnesota Press.

———. 1998. "Geertz's Ambiguous Legacy." In *Required Reading: Sociology's Most Influential Books,* ed. Dan Clawson, pp. 79–84. Amherst: University of Massachusetts Press.

Tarrow, Sidney G. 1998. *Power in Movement: Social Movements and Contentious Politics,* 2nd ed. Cambridge: Cambridge University Press.

Taylor, Charles. 1989. *Sources of the Self: The Making of the Modern Identity.* Cambridge: Harvard University Press.

Taylor, Gabrielle. 1994. "Gossip as Moral Talk." In *Good Gossip,* ed. Robert F. Goodman and Aaron Ben Ze'ev. Lawrence: University Press of Kansas.

Thomas, Keith V. 1971. *Religion and the Decline of Magic.* New York: Scribner.

Thomas, George M., John W. Meyer, Francisco O. Ramirez, and John Boli. 1987. *Institutional Structure: Constituting State, Society, and the Individual.* Newbury Park, Calif.: Sage.

Thompson, E. P. 1963. *The Making of the English Working Class.* New York: Random House.

Thompson, John B. 1990. *Ideology and Modern Culture: Critical Social Theory in the Era of Mass Communication.* Stanford: Stanford University Press.

Tipton, Steven M. 1982. *Getting Saved from the Sixties: Moral Meaning in Conversion and Cultural Change.* Berkeley: University of California Press.

———. 1983. "The Moral Logic of Alternative Religions." In *Religion and America: Spirituality in a Secular Age,* ed. Tipton and Mary Douglas, pp. 79–107. Boston: Beacon Press.

Tobin, Joseph J., David Y. H. Wu, and Dana H. Davidson. 1989. *Preschool in Three Cultures: Japan, China, and the United States.* New Haven: Yale University Press.

Todorov, Tzvetan. 1969. "Structural Analysis of Narrative." *Novel* 3(fall): 70–76.

———. 1977. *The Poetics of Prose,* trans. Richard Howard. Ithaca: Cornell University Press.

Toulmin, Stephen. 1981. "The Tyranny of Principles—Regaining the Ethics of Discretion." *The Hastings Center Report* 11 (December): 31–39.

Turner, Stephen P. 1994. *The Social Theory of Practices: Tradition, Tacit Knowledge, and Presuppositions.* Chicago: University of Chicago Press.

Turner, Victor. 1969. *The Ritual Process: Structure and Anti-Structure.* Chicago: Aldine Publishing Co.

———. 1974. *Dramas, Fields and Metaphors: Symbolic Action in Human Society.* Ithaca: Cornell University Press.

Ullman, Sharon R. 1997. *Sex Seen: The Emergence of Modern Sexuality in America.* Berkeley: University of California Press.

Varenne, Hervé. 1977. *Americans Together: Structured Diversity in a Midwestern Town.* New York: Teacher's College Press.

———. 1984. "Collective Representation in American Anthropological Conversations: Individual and Culture." *Current Anthropology* 25 (June): 281–99.

———. 1987. "Talk and Real Talk: The Voices of Silence and the Voices of Power in American Family Life." *Cultural Anthropology* 2:369–94.

Veroff, Joseph, Elizabeth Douvan, and Richard Kulka. 1981. *Mental Health in America: Patterns of Help Seeking.* New York: Basic Books.

Vinitzky-Seroussi, Vered. 1998. *After Pomp and Circumstance: High School Reunion as an Autobiographical Occasion.* Chicago: University of Chicago Press.

Walder, Andrew G. 1986. *Communist Neo-Traditionalism: Work and Authority in Chinese Industry.* Berkeley: University of California Press.

Wallace, Anthony F. C. 1956. "Revitalization Movements." *American Anthropologist* 58:264–81.

Waller, Willard, and Reuben Hill. 1951. *The Family: A Dynamic Interpretation,* revised edition. New York: Dryden Press.

Walster, Elaine, and G. William Walster. 1978. *A New Look at Love.* Reading, Mass.: Addison-Wesley.

Walzer, Michael. 1973. *The Revolution of the Saints.* Cambridge: Harvard University Press.

Warner, R. Stephen. 1978. "Toward a Redefinition of Action Theory: Paying the Cognitive Element Its Due." *American Journal of Sociology* 83:1317–49.

Waters, Mary. 1990. *Ethnic Options.* Berkeley: University of California Press.

Watt, Ian. 1957. *The Rise of the Novel.* Berkeley: University of California Press.

Waugh, Linda R. 1980. "The Poetic Function and the Nature of Language." *Poetics Today* 2.1a:25–39.

———. 1993. "Against Arbitrariness: Imitation and Motivation Revived, with Consequences for Textual Meaning." *Diacritics: A Review of Contemporary Criticism* 23 (summer): 71–87.

Weber, Max. 1946a [1922–23]. "The Social Psychology of the World Religions." In *From Max Weber,* ed. H. H. Gerth and C. Wright Mills, pp. 267–301. New York: Oxford University Press.

———. 1946b [1922–23]. "The Protestant Sects and the Spirit of Capitalism." In *From Max Weber,* ed. H. H. Gerth and C. Wright Mills, pp. 302–22. New York: Oxford University Press.

———. 1958a [1904–5]. *The Protestant Ethic and the Spirit of Capitalism,* trans. Talcott Parsons. New York: Charles Scribner's Sons.

———. 1958b [1921]. *The Rational and Social Foundations of Music,* trans. Don Martindale, Johannes Riedel, and Gertrude Neuwirth. Carbondale: Southern Illinois University Press.

———. 1968 [1920–22]. *Economy and Society: An Outline of Interpretive Sociology,* ed. Guenther Roth and Claus Wittich. Berkeley: University of California Press.

———. 1993 [1922]. *The Sociology of Religion.* Boston: Beacon Press.

Weick, Karl E. 1976. "Educational Organizations as Loosely Coupled Systems." *Administrative Science Quarterly* 21:1–19.

Weitzman, Lenore. 1985. *The Divorce Revolution: The Unexpected Social and Economic Consequences for Women and Children in America.* New York: Free Press.

White, Hayden V. 1973. *Metahistory: The Historical Imagination in Nineteenth-Century Europe.* Baltimore: Johns Hopkins University Press.

Whitehead, Harriet. 1987. *Renunciation and Reformulation: A Study of Conversion in an American Sect.* Ithaca: Cornell University Press.

Whyte, William Foote. 1943. *Street Corner Society: The Social Structure of an Italian Slum.* Chicago: University of Chicago Press.

Wikan, Unni. 1992. "Beyond the Words: The Power of Resonance." *American Ethnologist* 19 (August): 460–82.

Williams, Raymond. 1973. "Base and Superstructure in Marxist Cultural Theory." *New Left Review* 82 (Nov.–Dec.): 3–16.

———. 1977. *Marxism and Literature.* Oxford: Oxford University Press.

Willis, Paul. 1977. *Learning to Labor: How Working Class Kids Get Working Class Jobs.* New York: Columbia University Press.

Wolfe, Alan. 1998. *One Nation, After All: What Middle-Class Americans Really Think About: God, Country, Family, Racism, Welfare, Immigration, Homosexuality, Work, the Right, the Left, and Each Other.* New York: Viking.

Worsely, Peter. 1957. *The Trumpet Shall Sound: A Study of Cargo Cults in Melanesia.* London: McGibbon and Kee.

Wright, Will. 1975. *Sixguns and Society: A Structural Analysis of the Western.* Berkeley: University of California Press.

Wuthnow, Robert. 1976. *The Consciousness Reformation.* Berkeley: University of California Press.

———. 1980. "World Order and Religious Movements." In *Studies of the Modern World System,* ed. Albert Bergesen, pp. 57–75. New York: Academic.

———. 1987. *Meaning and Moral Order: Explorations in Cultural Analysis.* Berkeley: University of California Press.

———. 1989. *Communities of Discourse: Ideology and Social Structure in the Reformation, the Enlightenment, and European Socialism.* Cambridge: Harvard University Press.

———. 1991. *Acts of Compassion: Caring for Others and Helping Ourselves.* Princeton: Princeton University Press.

———. 1994. *Sharing the Journey: Support Groups and America's New Quest for Community.* New York: Free Press.

Wuthnow, Robert, James Davison Hunter, Albert Bergessen, and Edith Kurzweil. 1984. *Cultural Analysis: The Work of Peter L. Berger, Mary Douglas, Michel Foucault, and Jurgen Habermas.* London: Routledge and Kegan Paul.

Zablocki, Benjamin. 1971. *The Joyful Community: An Account of the Bruderhof, a Communal Movement Now in Its Third Generation.* Baltimore: Penguin. Books.

Zaret, David. 1985. *The Heavenly Contract: Ideology and Organization in Pre-Revolutionary Puritanism.* Chicago: University of Chicago Press.

Zelizer, Viviana A. 1994. *The Social Meaning of Money.* New York: Basic Books.

Zerubavel, Eviatar. 1992. *Terra Cognita: The Mental Discovery of America.* New Brunswick, N.J.: Rutgers University Press.

———. 1997. *Social Mindscapes: An Invitation to Cognitive Sociology.* Cambridge: Harvard University Press.

Ziegler, Nicholas J. 1997. *Governing Ideas: Strategies for Innovation in France and Germany.* Ithaca: Cornell University Press.

Index

Names in quotation marks are pseudonyms of interviewees.

Abiog, Darlene, 261*n*4
Alexander, Jeffrey, 182
Archer, Margaret, 74
Arditi, Jorge, 156, 255*n*13
Armstrong, Elizabeth, 211
art in cultural systems, 21
attitudes
    definition of, 36
    formulation of, 37
Austen, Jane, 11, 113

Balinese cockfight interpretation, 20
Balinese cultural logic, 194–95
Baptists' view of relationships, 140–41. *See also* religion
"Beckett, Larry," 141
Beck-Gernsheim, Elisabeth, 252*n*13
Bellah, Robert N., 238*n*4, 260*n*16
Bendix, Reinhard, 213, 256*n*16
Berger, Bennett, 45
Berger, Peter, 16
Bernstein, Basil, 52
Berscheid, Ellen, 253*n*16
Bielby, Denise D., 253*n*17
Biernacki, Richard
    on cultural coherence, 182
    on cultural schemas, 208, 211
    on cultural texts, 238*n*8
    on influence of cultural style, 245*n*4
Billig, Michael, 44, 182
Bloch, R. Howard, 156
Bourdieu, Pierre
    definition of culture, 12
    fields, 186
    habitus, 245*n*3, 247*n*11
    logic of practice, 192
    rules of behavior versus games, 204
    skills, styles, and habits, 245*n*3
bourgeois love, 113–14, 250–51*nn* 4, 5

Briggs, Charles, 242*n*1
British and German wage structure, 208–9
Bryson, Bethany, 260*n*16
Burke, Kenneth, 74, 189
Buscaglia, Leo, 132

Calvinism, 69, 78, 102–3, 188. *See also* Protestantism; religion
Campbell, Bruce, 253*n*16
Cancian, Francesca, 2
"Carpenter, Ben," 66–68
Catholicism. *See also* religion
    belief in, 46, 48, 51, 243*n*7
    contraception and, 51, 104, 243*n*7
Chinese Communists, 174, 260*n*15
chivalry, 112
Chomskian linguistics, 261*n*3
Christianity. *See also* religion
    commitment as foundation, 140–41
    discipline and, 141–43
    obligation to love, 60–61, 65–66
    view of self in, 146
    worldly activities vs., 165–66
codes
    cultural meaning and, 184–85
    expressive variation in, 184–85
    local context of, 185, 261*n*4
    movement among different, 185, 261*n*5
    semiotic
        binding nature of public codes, 162–63
        constraints on action, 162–63
        influence on action, 165–66, 258*n*7
        institutions and, 204, 205
        personal identity and, 166, 258*n*7
        political struggle over, 164
        power of, 168–69
        public interpretation of individual action, 166–67, 259*n*9

culture
capacities from. *See* cultured capacities
coherence of. *See* cultural coherence
constitutive role, 24
definitions of, 12–13
depth and power as dimensions of
influence, 207–11
influence of everyday practices, 208–9,
264*n*14
influence on action. *See* common sense;
ideology; tradition
institutions and
basis for shared culture, 176–77,
260*n*16
coherence given to individual
strategies, 176
cultural repertoires linked to,
178–79
disjointedness between societies,
177, 260*n*18
market society influences, 177
issue of diversity and variable use,
22–23
people's distance from
change in impact over time, 13–14
diversity of available viewpoints, 15
historical examples of skepticism, 16
process of appropriation, 17–18
selective adoption of viewpoints, 17,
19, 238*n*5
skepticism about ideal love, 14–15
skepticism about viewpoints, 15–16
public practices, power of, 211–12
quality of outside forces, 161
range of embeddedness, 94, 248*n*3
as a repertoire. *See* cultural repertoires
semiotic codes. *See* codes
social contexts
ideologies adopted to organize action, 170–72, 259*nn* 11, 13
impact of, 169, 179–80, 260–61*n*20
interviews influenced by, 174–75
needed to inspire action, 173
people's roles in divorce, 172
polarizations during revolutions,
169–70, 259*n*10
revolutions' effects on cultural
meanings, 170–71, 259*n*10
sanctions' support of, 173–74

study's approach to, 5–6
understanding of workings of, 71–72,
245*n*1
what it is used for. *See* strategies of action
cultured capacities
action and. *See* strategies of action
becoming a certain kind of self, 72–74,
245*n*2, 246*n*7
exercise of cultural skills, 74, 246*n*6
to mark group membership, 74–75
skills, styles, and habits, 73–74, 77,
245*nn* 3, 4, 5
view of self and choices, 75–77
worldview management through, 75, 78,
246*n*8
culture of love
influence on action, 133
love myths
choices about marriage and, 119
courtly love tradition, 112
heroic themes in marriage, 122
nature of love for bourgeois, 113–14,
250*nn* 4, 5
notion of one right person, 127–28
origins of, 112
in romantic novels, 112–13
romantic love
nature of, 201, 202
reasons for loving, 240*n*4
romantic-love complex, 111, 250*n*1
stories and symbols about, 11
tradition of, 2

D'Andrade, Roy, 182, 203–4, 210
Dallas, 45, 237*n*2
DaSilva, Melinda
on knowing your authentic self, 143–44,
254*n*5
on value of shared experiences, 145
DaSilva, Thomas
on infatuation vs. love, 124
search for true love, 125–28
on value of shared experiences, 145
Davis, Natalie Z., 87
"Davis, Cindy," 150–51, 152, 154
Derné, Steve, 166–67, 254*n*1, 263*n*10
Dewey, John, 81
Dianetics, 259*n*11
DiMaggio, Paul, 205, 260*n*16